brussels

a. pocket guide

First published in 2002
Virgin Books Ltd, London w6 9ha
Copyright 2002 © Virgin Books Ltd, London

contents

Written by 20 local contributors in-the-know, this guide gives the inside take on Brussels and the surrounding area. The focus is on having fun, where to hang out, shop, eat, relax, enjoy and spoil yourself – and there's also a selection of the top cultural hotspots.

area lowdown

Brussels is divided into 20 key areas, each with its own distinct character. For those who are exploring beyond Brussels itself, information about four of Belgium's other main cities is also contained in this book: Antwerpen, Gent, Brugge and Leuven.

Anderlecht   *off map*

This run-down former industrial district, with a large Northwest African community, is famed for its football team and blamed for most of Brussels' crime problems. The glass-and-steel former abattoir now houses an excellent meat market, while the little-visited western parts of Anderlecht are refreshingly rural.

Central   *maps 2, 3, 6 & 7*

It's no accident that Brussels' most famous spire belongs not to a cathedral but to the main town hall: commerce and bureaucracy come first here, and nowhere is this more apparent than in the glorious Grand' Place with the soaring Gothic Hôtel de Ville and gleaming guildhouses. The square, which lies at the heart of a medieval medley of cobbled streets and narrow passageways, is surrounded by cutesy houses crammed with bars and restaurants; some fabulous, some tourist traps, while tacky stores flog frilly lace and star-spangled Eurotat. Few people live here, but buyers and boozers find plenty of entertainment. Amid some of Europe's finest architecture are crumbling husks of buildings, left to rot by unscrupulous developers. Above the centre, the Royal Quarter is a touch sterile. But none of this can kill the centre's deliriously authentic atmosphere. Leave the tourists to their doilies and Manneken Pis and you'll find some of the best (and cheapest) restaurants, a host of earthy taverns and refreshingly unpretentious nightlife.

Evere   *off map*

Few visitors traipse out here unless they know someone who works for NATO, which hurriedly moved its HQ here when France briefly pulled out of the alliance in the 1960s. It's a dismal compound resembling a prison-cum-barracks.

Jette
off map

Northwest Brussels is mainly residential, but Jette is worth a visit for the Musée René Magritte, the surprisingly bourgeois home of the arch surrealist from 1930–1954, and for its lighthouse-style cultural centre.

Heysel (Heizel)
off map

Home of the Atomium, the notorious, once-eponymous football stadium (now renamed *Stade Roi Boudouin*), and Bruparck Village, a sublimely tacky leisure complex with fast-food joints housed in mock-baroque houses, a water park, the Kinepolis multiplex and the itsch-tastic model monuments of Mini-Europe.

Ixelles (East)
maps 11 & 12

The Bruxellois love to describe themselves as *zinneke* (meaning mongrel' or 'bastard'), and eastern Ixelles is as *zinneke* as it gets. You can taste the difference as you leave the dreary Toison d'Or and plunge into the Matongé, a vibrant jumble of cafés, restaurants and fabric shops that's home to the city's Central African community (a by-product of colonialism the colonisers didn't expect). A short walk, and a world away, place St-Boniface is a fast-developing trendster hangout favoured by the city's young international set. To the west lies chaussée d'Ixelles, the area's main artery; a workaday high street at the northern end, it gains character as it rolls south. The Art Nouveau residences around the willow-lined Ixelles ponds are the exclusive domain of the local bourgeoisie, while further south, chaussée de Boondael's lively taverns and myriad ethnic eateries attract a never-ending stream of students from the nearby uni.

Ixelles (West)
map 10 and off map

Coming from central Brussels, western Ixelles can be disappointing at first sight. The lashings of concrete house such international names as Gucci, Hermès et al, who attract a fur-clad clientele of local ladies and Eurocrats. Beyond the hustle and bustle, however, lies one of the city's most elegant neighbourhoods, with heaps of intimate restos and chic one-off boutiques; even the Irish bars have a touch of class. The main public spaces have a laid-back, villagey feel with bistros, cafés, and bookshops dotting place Brugmann, cosy parvis de la Trinité, and leafy place Châtelain. Traditionally the haunt of artists and intellectuals – Victor Horta and sculptor Constantin Meunier both lived here – western Ixelles is now a magnet for media types, while its 19th-century town houses, with wrought-iron balconies and large front doors, have been snapped up by the seriously rich.

Laeken (Laken)
♪ off map

Even though their castle is off-limits for the proles, you can't escape the influence of the Belgian royals in this verdant northern suburb: the Église Notre-Dame de Laeken houses the royal crypt, while the public Laeken Park contains a Chinese pavilion and Japanese tower, both built for Léopold II.

Les Marolles
♪ map 6

Downhill from the swanky Sablon, Les Marolles couldn't be more different. Where the former is all snoot and show, this area is poor and gritty – and proud of it. It's a rowdy place of working-class heroes and politically active priests who have triumphed in the face of adversity; like when King Léopold kicked out thousands of locals to build his preposterous Palais de Justice in 1883 or during the Nazi oppression in WWII, when Marolliens sheltered hundreds of Jews. These days cheap rents and cute-but-chichi restaurants are luring the trendy, and techno temple The Fuse is helping to turn the area into Brussels' clubbing epicentre. Early-rising bargain-hunters find rummaging heaven at the flea market on place du Jeu Balle and in the bric-a-brac shops of rues Haute and Blaes. Gentrification has made the area more fun for visitors, but those who inhabit its (still) rough edges – the dwindling population of Marolliens, the post-war Spanish migrants, and the more recent arrivals from North Africa – haven't seen much benefit.

Midi (Zuid)
♪ maps 8 & 9

Gare du Midi is the Eurostar terminus, its surroundings might make you wonder why you came. The office developments can't quite hide the district's down-at-heel nature, although the large migrant communities have led to cheap Greek, Spanish, and Portuguese restaurants. On Sundays, the drab streets are brought to life by a massive, souk-like market.

Molenbeek
*map 1

Like Anderlecht, this canalside district has seen better days, but cheap rents and unused industrial spaces are drawing venues and cultural spaces into the area. The bizarre Art Deco Eglise de St-Jean Baptiste has a looping concrete ribcage that's part dinosaur, part underpass.

Quartier Européen
*maps 4 & 8

On weekends, when the offices lie empty and most restaurants are closed, this concrete embodiment of a European superstate could induce Europhobia. On weekdays, however, the streets buzz with a Babelesque linguistic hubbub. This is the daytime hangout of lobbyists, translators, and all who feed off the Commission. Gossip hums through the air in the pubs, snack bars, and expense-account restaurants. National-themed shops mean homesick Eurocrats can pay over the odds for Nordic furniture and baked beans, while at night, the Irish bars are packed until the early hours with gregarious young professionals and stagiaires. For a less-manufactured scene, head for the fantastical Art Nouveau buildings of squares Marie Louise and Ambiorix, unwind in pretty Parc Léopold, the former playground of the city's bourgeoisie, or check out the latest international hangouts on revitalized place du Luxembourg.

Ste-Catherine
*maps 1 & 2

It's a familiar story: bustling trading area, work dries up, jobs dry up, properties get run-down, prices plummet, broke bohos move in and trendiness breaks out. Place Ste-Catherine was once the heart of the port district, with a spectacular glass-and-steel fish market (all that's left now is a fountain). As the canal's importance declined, the area went to seed. Nobody 'respectable' wanted to live there, until, in the 1980s, the low rents, belle époque architecture and central location proved irresistible for avant-garde designers, Flemish media types, and the gay community. Hip boutiques, bars, and restaurants came in their wake, and now the area's only problem is that it's too popular for its own good. Though the overcrowded place St-Géry and über-trendy rue Dansaert, with cutting-edge clothes and chichi cafés, feel almost too commercial, the Beursschouwburg and De Markten cultural centres draw an artsy crowd. Amid all the aching fashionability, you'll still find a few local hangouts.

St-Josse and Schaerbeek ♫ map 4

These once-rich areas, now home to the city's Turkish community, are too often tarred with the 'crime and grime' brush. True, both have seen better days, but their streets are still boisterous and bustling, especially the main thoroughfares, chaussée de Louvain and chaussée de Haecht. More than half the population of tiny St-Josse is non-Belgian, including a sizeable expat crowd drawn by comfy town-house conversions and proximity to Euroland. Halles de Schaerbeek and Le Botanique provide top-class evening entertainment in this area that has been home to Puccini and chanson legend Jacques Brel. Schaerbeek, the larger of the communes, has emerged from the grip of a right-wing mayor who whipped up tension between long-time residents and the migrant population; its elegant 19th-century houses and Art Nouveau gems rub shoulders with Moroccan spice shops and Turkish bakeries.

St-Gilles ♫ map 9

It's got a reputation for being run-down, and tourists tend to pretty much keep their noses out, but St-Gilles' most loyal inhabitants wouldn't dream of living anywhere else. Once one of the city's richest communes, as proved by the extravagant Hôtel de Ville, it has an unbelievable number of glorious belle époque, Art Deco, and Art Nouveau houses, the city's best-stocked beer bar (Moeder Lambic), a thriving gallery culture, and plenty of ethnic eateries, from rough-diamond couscous joints to top-end Portuguese establishments. In the richer east, the swish restaurants of chaussée de Charleroi offer a more sophisticated take on international cuisine; in the poorer west, which has a large North African population, Brussels' largest market sprawls around the Gare du Midi on Sundays; in between, there's a cosy bohemian scene that's long been acting as a magnet for aesthetes and artists alike.

Le Sablon ♫ map 6

The terraces of the cobbled place du Grand Sablon are the spot to observe the fur-clad and well-heeled in their natural habitat. Big-shot lawyers blow their salaries on penthouse pads in the 17th- and 18th-century houses lining the square, while those confined to ground level find designer boutiques, classy interiors stores, upscale antiques shops, and elegant restaurants and bars. If all the posing makes you paranoid, head to the Petit Sablon, an elegant garden

dged with statues depicting the medieval guilds, or to the museums
of the Mont des Arts. The Sunday antiques market, in front of the
recently scrubbed Gothic Eglise Notre-Dame du Sablon, is the opposite
of the Marolles flea market – ordered, expensive, and predictable –
although Jeu de Balle regulars may find some of the stock, if not the
prices, eerily familiar. You're more likely to find bargains in the hidden
passageways off the main square, or in the streets leading down to
the heart of town.

Tervuren $\mathring{P}$ off map

Beloved of British expats because it's near the British School,
this Dutch-speaking suburb has a pleasant wooded park and a cobbled central square. The Musée Royal de l'Afrique Centrale is the main
attraction, although the local sausage shop has hordes of admirers.

Uccle (Ukkel) $\mathring{P}$ off map

A green and pleasant land bordering on the Forêt de Soignes.
Well-heeled residents live in the villas (detached houses) and the
elegant Art Nouveau and fake neoclassical town houses on and
around avenue Molière. The locals' discerning palates demand fine
dining, while those oppressed by the not-so-discreet charm of
the bourgeoisie can escape to tranquil Dieweg Cemetery,
rambling Wolvendael Park, or the more humble Quartier du Chat
('cat quarter').

Watermael-Boitsfort (Watermaal-Bosvoorde) $\mathring{P}$ off map

Low-key, laid-back and bohemian, this is an artsy district with plenty
of green spaces, a few galleries, and several charming council cot-
tages. Great for an early-evening stroll, with options galore if you've
worked up an appetite.

Woluwe St-Pierre & Woluwe St-Lambert (St Pieters-Woluwe & St-Lambrechts-Woluwe) $\mathring{P}$ off map

The eastern suburbs of Brussels are favoured by Eurocrat families,
more because they're handy for the office than because of any
thrill factor. WSP is the cosier, with rolling Parc Woluwe and the
whitewashed proto-Art Deco Palais Stocklet (now closed to the
public because visitors kept stealing the exhibits).

Antwerpen

off map

Antwerpen (Antwerp) is at the forefront of everything it turns its hand to: the world's largest uncut-diamond market, the second-biggest port in Western Europe, a business hub, a fashion mecca, and a magnet for culture. It's progressive, cosmopolitan, and crammed with bars, clubs, shops, and eateries, yet has a weirdly conservative undertow. In Belgium's most radical city, support for the far-right Vlaams Blok reaches 25%. For a town of 500,000 souls, it's a complicated place.

Gent

off map

No less charming than Brugge, tourist-free Gent (Gand) has canals and cobbles aplenty, yet it's anything but a museum town. Sedition has been the style in this forward-thinking city since 1540, when Charles V quashed a revolt by forcing burghers to parade with nooses round their necks. There are great bars and mucho culture, and the proud locals love a party, especially during July's Gentse Feesten.

Brugge

off map

Known as the Venice of the north, Brugge (Bruges) certainly lives up to its reputation. Cynics point out that much of the 'medieval' stuff was built in the 19th century, and in summer it's a citywide game of sardines, but who cares? Brugge is somewhere you'll never forget.

Leuven

off map

Home to the world's oldest Catholic university (1425), this historic Flemish town comes alive during term-time, when its cafés fill with students and its cobbled streets rattle with chatter and bicycles.

area index

Tels Quels (drinking dens/gay scene) 98/114
Wilde (hip hangouts) 101

CLUBS
Le Sparrow 112
Studio Live 112
Le Sud 112

RESTAURANTS & CAFÉS
Aux Armes de Bruxelles (seafood) 91
Café Métropole (cafés) 68
Le Cirio (cafés) 69
Comme Chez Soi (French) 75
Le Falstaff (cafés) 69
't Kelderke (Belgian) 61
Ricotta & Parmesan (French) 77
Le Roy d'Espagne (cafés) 72
Samourai (Japanese) 84
Sea Grill (seafood) 92
Taverne du Passage (brasseries & bistros/seafood) 66 & 93
El Metekko (cafés) 69

SHOPS
Anticyclone des Açores (books) 26
Au Grand Rasoir (kitchenware) 50
Balthazar (menswear) 53
Biodrome (food) 39
Elvis Pompilio (hats) 45
FNAC (CDs, records & tapes) 28
Gillis (hats) 46
Kaat Tilley (designer clothes) 33
Lauffer (kitchenware) 50
Léonidas (chocolates) 29

Maison Dandoy (food) 41
Marjolaine (gifts) 44
Mary's (chocolates) 30
Musicmania (CDs, records & tapes) 28
Neuhaus (chocolates) 30
Noire d'Ivoire (interiors) 48
Het Plaizier (art) 24
Shoe's victim.com (shoes) 55
Sterling (books) 27
Tast (designer clothes) 36
Tintin (bandes dessinées) 26
Virgin Megastore (CDs, records & tapes) 28
Waterstone's (books) 27

SIGHTS, MUSEUMS & GALLERIES
ARAU (tours) 159
Artesia Center for the Arts (exhibition spaces) 151
L'Autre Musée (exhibition spaces) 151
La Bourse (landmarks) 128
Cathédrale St-Michel-&-St-Gudule (landmarks/religious buildings) 128
Centre Belge de la Bande Dessinée (the big six/art nouveau) 133 & 149
Chapelle de la Madeleine (religious buildings) 145
Chatterbus (tours) 159
Colonne du Congrès (landmarks) 128
De Boeck's Sightseeing Tours (tours) 159
Eglise St-Nicolas (religious buildings) 147
FNAC (exhibition spaces) 151
Grand' Place (landmarks) 128

vere

Gent

Heysel

Ixelles (East)

Ixelles (West)

Molenbeek

Quartier Européen

Le Sablon

SHOPS

Godiva (chocolates) 29
Isabelle Baines (designer clothes) 33
Kenzo (designer clothes) 33
Linen House (linen) 50
Ma Maison de Papier (books) 27
Natan (designer clothes) 34
L'Objet du Désir (interiors) 48
Pierre Marcolini (chocolates) 30
Senses Art Nouveau (gifts) 45
Yannick David (antiques) 25
Wittamer (chocolates) 30
La Vaisselle à Kilo (interiors) 49

SIGHTS, MUSEUMS & GALLERIES

Eglise Notre Dame du Sablon (religious buildings) 146
Eglise Protestante (religious buildings) 146
Eglise St-Jacques-sur-Coudenberg (religious buildings) 147
Jardin d'Egmont (the green scene) 156
Palais de Justice (landmarks) 129
Palais des Beaux-Arts (exhibition spaces) 152
Palais Royal (landmarks) 129
Place Poelaert (viewpoints) 132
Place Royal (landmarks) 130
Magasin Old England (viewpoints/art nouveau) 132 & 150
Mont des Arts (viewpoints) 132
Musée D'Art Ancien (the big six) 133
Musée D'Art Moderne (the big six) 134
Musée des Instruments de Musique (one-offs) 144
Synagogue Communauté Israélite de Bruxelles (religious buildings) 149

Ste-Catherine

BARS

L'Acrobat (club/bars) 96
Beursschouwburg (hip hangouts) 99
Coaster (drinking dens) 97
Le Greenwich (traditional bars) 107
Le Java (hip hangouts) 100
Kafka (weird & wild) 109
Mappa Mundo (hip hangouts) 100
O'Reilly's (Irish bars) 103
Le Roi des Belges (hip hangouts) 101
La Tentation (weird & wild) 109
Zebra (hip hangouts) 72

RESTAURANTS & CAFÉS

L'Archiduc (cafés) 67
La Belle Maraichère (seafood) 91
Bij den Boer (seafood) 91
Bonsoir Clara (Mediterranean) 73
Den Teepot (vegetarian) 94
La Fin de Siècle (Mediterranean) 83
Le Greenwich (cafés) 70
Kasbah (North African) 88
Mappa Mundo (cafés) 71

shops

Brussels and the surrounding area may not have the cachet or choice of London or New York, but it's sure got the style. First-timers imagine row upon row of chocolate and comic shops; while the more experienced know that Belgian designer gear and accessories, trendy vintage togs, and fine antiques are the real draw. And though much of it is centred in the inner ring, each of Brussels' communes retains neighbourhood shopping at its best, with specialities the name of the game.

accessories

Au Bon Marché   *♪off map*
Handbags, trinkets, slippers, and jewellery.
Hoornstraat, Gent ☎ 09.269.02.60

Lorenzo Lebon   *♪B11*
Notable one-off boutique selling a variety of sleek, hand-crafted, trendy leather handbags.
200 chaussée d'Ixelles, Ixelles (East) ☎ 02.646.35.01

Pakjeshuis   *♪off map*
If you're after anything – from furry handbags to stylish Italian coffee machines – plunge into Pakjeshuis' eclectic world.
30 Mechelsestr, Leuven ☎ 016.29.09.11

☆ LES PRÉCIEUSES   *♪D1*
The beaded handbags, fringed scarves and other colourful accessories at Les Précieuses are extravagent. Designer Pili Collado's style at this store is flirty mixed with gypsy.
83 rue Antoine Dansaert, Ste-Catherine ☎ 02.503.28.98

☆ THÉO DÉPÔT   *♪D1*
Théo Dépôt helps the look with stylish eyewear that ranges from nervy-pervy to bug-eyed sexy – the signature model being specs minus the arms. How do they stay on? An antenna shoots out from between the eyeframes, curves up over your forehead and keeps going until it's wrapped around the back of your neck.
81 rue Antoine Dansaert, Ste-Catherine ☎ 02.511.04.07

BLEUE COMME...UNE ORANGE
off map

argains are commonplace at Bleue comme...une orange, which
eddles mirrors, dinner and tea services, vases, and anything else for
e home that takes the owner's fancy.

9 rue Alphonse Renard, Ixelles (West) ☎ 02.344.92.23

atherine Ghadimi
D6

you prefer to splash out on your abode rather than yourself, there's
e Catherine Ghadimi gallery, where Art Nouveau glass and
rvings from the Orient are sold.

rue Bodenbroeck, Le Sablon ☎ 02.511.74.49

ento Anni
D6

e Cento Anni gallery has florid Art Nouveau vases and figurines.

place du Grand Sablon, Le Sablon ☎ 02.514.56.33

ollector's Gallery
D6

ollectors with a sense of humour and limited dosh can slink
wards the city centre to the Collector's Gallery. Totally kitsch, and
oud of it, the shop has a section dedicated to Barbie memorabilia,
 well as vintage perfume bottles, classic toys, and other high-class
nk from the early 1900s to the 1970s.

rue Lebeau, Le Sablon ☎ 02.511.46.13

ominique
D6

t Deco furniture, lamps and knick-knacks.

rue Ernest Allard, Le Sablon V 02.514.25.41

ESPACE 161
E6

eed a lion statue for your grounds? Try Espace 161. This mini-mall of
ntiques and brocante dealers has Limoges dishware, carousel
onies, baby grand pianos, Murano glass, and other amazing curiosities.
ock changes constantly.

1 rue Haute, Les Marolles ☎ 02.502.31.64

sences de Siècle
off map

t Nouveau and Art Deco furniture.

3 rue Franz Merjay, Ixelles (West) ☎ 02.345.37.39

Faisons un Rêve *♀off map*
Good for Bakelite (a Belgian invention) jewellery, ceramics, and more portable Art Deco objets such as candlesticks and mirrors.
avenue Louis Lepoutre, Ixelles (West) ☎ 02.347.34.29

☆ **FIN DES SIÈCLES ET PLUS** *♀E6*
Art Deco specialists selling portable items – toys, lamps, shaving kits – from the early 1900s.
157 rue Haute, Les Marolles ☎ 02.502.66.35

Galerie des Minimes *♀E6*
Make way, and time, for megastore Galerie des Minimes, with over 500m/sq of floor space devoted to bric-a-brac, art, and antiques.
23 rue des Minimes, Le Sablon ☎ 02.511.28.25

Ghadmimi Gallery *♀E6*
The Ghadmimi Gallery does vintage Persian carpets just south of the square.
1 rue des Minimes, Le Sablon ☎ 02.512.98.41

Hôtel des Ventes Horta *♀off map*
Holds evening viewings and auctions to try to attract private buyers.
70–74 avenue de Rodebeek, St-Gilles ☎ 02.741.60.60

Hôtel des Ventes St-Georges *♀E10*
A diverse line-up of antiques.
199 ave Louise, Ixelles (West) ☎ 02.640.76.12

Hôtel des Ventes Vanderkindere *♀off map*
On a smaller scale, but well worth a look.
685–687 chaussée d'Alsemberg, St-Gilles ☎ 02.344.54.46

Oude Spiegels & Bureau's *♀off map*
Hunt for old mirrors and desks here.
68–79 Kloosterstraat, Antwerpen ☎ 03.238.73.62

Philippe Dufrasne *♀E6*
Louis XV paintings and *belle époque* furniture and paintings are available at Philippe Dufrasne.
15 rue des Minimes, Le Sablon ☎ 02.503.36.01

RAMBAGH ASIAN HOMESTYLE
C6

Balances old and new, with antique furniture and homewares from India and Korea. For those on a tight budget, this spacious two-floor shop also does knock-offs. A new branch has recently opened just across the road.

4 rue Haute, Les Marolles ☎ 02.514.58.27

Sablon Antiques Market
D6

Even if you're not in the market for original Audubon prints or Fabergé eggs, the Marché place du Grand Sablon is worth a look. Going strong every weekend for the past 40 years, it's where stamps, coins, art, and other collectors' faves are sold in red-and-green tents. Aristocrats and regular civilians mingle, and it's as good for people-watching as it is for dealing.

Place du Grand Sablon, Le Sablon

Salle de Ventes au Palais des Beaux-Arts
A7

Those on a mission should check out the city's auction houses (salles de ventes in French or veilinghuizen in Flemish). Most prestigious is the Salle de Ventes au Palais des Beaux-Arts.

o rue Royale, Central ☎ 02.513.60.80

SCÈNES DE MÉNAGE
off map

An eclectic mix of old and new bed quilts, new and antique linen (including pyjamas), cutlery, and glassware.

place Brugmann, Ixelles (West) ☎ 02.344.32.95

TABLE D'HÔTES
F9

Table d'Hôtes is reminiscent of past glory days with its antiques from the 1920s – a stash of crockery, objets d'art, Art Deco scent bottles, and lamps. Also a reliable bet for Val St-Lambert crystal vases and ash-trays, and dinner services.

5 avenue Demeur, St-Gilles ☎ 02.534.70.25

Tony Boogaert Antiques
off map

The façade of Tony Boogaert Antiques is as weird as its interior.

Kloosterstraat, Antwerpen ☎ 03.237.89.55

Les Vieux Sablons
D6

The antique maps, religious icons, books, and prints within this mini maze of shops are of consistently high quality.

place du Grand Sablon, Le Sablon ☎ 02.502.14.32

Zen Gallery
♯D6

Zen Gallery specializes in Asiatica: buddhas, vishnus, and other god-like figures.

23 rue Ernest Allard, Le Sablon ☎ 02.511.95.10

art

Baltazar
♯E7

For lining the walls of minimalist interiors go to Baltazar, where signed lithographs and original artworks by living Belgian artists like Benoît Jacques are for sale.

100 rue de Stassart, Ixelles (West) ☎ 02.512.85.13

Boon Gallery
♯E6

Boon Gallery is home to realistic portraits.

24 rue des Minimes, Le Sablon ☎ 02.503.24.94

L'Instant Présent
♯E6

Photographer Nicolas Springael brings images of his travels to the framed prints and postcards sold here.

136 rue Blaes, Les Marolles ☎ 02.513.28.91

M Koenig Ethnography
♯E6

This rue des Minimes establishment sells museum-quality tribal art and archaeological pieces.

27 rue des Minimes, Le Sablon ☎ 02.511.75.07

☆ HET PLAIZIER
♯B6

Shows the joys of the world, but mostly Brussels, in postcard form. Some kitsch classics, others trad and tasteful, this navel-sized shop is a real find.

50 rue des Eperonniers, Central ☎ 02.513.47.30

Rabier Art Nègre
♯E6

Totems and statues in wood from Central Africa, some resembling penises, giving a whole new phallic meaning to 'showing wood'.

8–10 rue des Minimes, Le Sablon ☎ 02.512.86.74/02.514.51.50

Rue Haute
♯E6

The archives of photographs here are worth a look – from classic European scenes in the mode of Cartier-Bresson to nudes by Avedon.

203 rue Haute, Les Marolles ☎ 02.513.96.09

Schleiper *♭D10*
A German artists' supplies shop, you can buy portfolios, top-notch
stationery, and expensive prints and brushes; a must for amateurs
and pros alike.
■49–151 chaussée de Charleroi, St-Gilles ☎ 02.541.05.41

☆ **YANNICK DAVID** *♭D6*
Specializing in architectural drawings, miniatures, and 19th-century
furniture.
■27 rue Watteeu, Le Sablon ☎ 02.513.37.48

bandes dessinées (comic strip)

La Bande des Six Nez *♭off map*
Serious collectors of vintage comic albums, pre-or-post war, should
hotfoot it here to leaders of the comic strip pack.
■79 chaussée de Wavre, Ixelles (East) ☎ 02.513.72.58

Bédémania *♭F9*
Bédémania can't fail to please Hergé fans. It's a smallish store, but
there's plenty of vintage greats – including albums and figurines.
■69 chaussée de Waterloo, St-Gilles ☎ 02.537.96.20

Het Besloten Land *♭off map*
If you've been bitten by the Bande Dessinée bug, Het Besloten Land
has stacks of comics in Dutch, English, and French.
■6 Parijsstraat, Leuven ☎ 016.22.58.40

☆ **LE DEUXIÈME SOUFFLE** *♭C4*
Bande dessinée central; a comic-book shop for lovers of the so-called
eighth art. All the stock is in French. It has been on the scene for two
decades.
■5 rue Braemt, St-Josse ☎ 02.219.17.70

Multi BD *♭off map*
For a more central address for buying comics, try Multi BD.
■26 boulevard Anspach, Central ☎ 02.513.01.86

Schlirf Book *♭off map*
Unbeatable for new albums and objects.
■752 chaussée de Waterloo, Uccle ☎ 02.648.04.40

☆ **TINTIN** *F2*

Brussels wouldn't be Brussels without comic-strip hero Tintin. The namesake store has T-shirts, stationery, collectors' models, and other memorabilia of the intrepid reporter.

13 rue de la Colline, Central ☎ 02.514.51.52

☆ **ZIGGOURAT** *B10*

Bande dessinée fans should make a beeline for Ziggourat, whose monthly exhibitions make shopping there all the more enticing.

34 rue Dejoncker, St-Gilles ☎ 02.538.40.37

beauty supplies

Housewives on Fire *off map*

Walk up the stairs of this one-time warehouse, grab a snack, and get your hair done up in a beehive at Housewives on Fire.

36-38 Kammenstraat, Antwerpen ☎ 03.232.93.02

Maison Chevalier *C8*

Luxurious all-natural bath products and other scented goodies.

7 rue Marie de Bourgogne, Quartier Européen ☎ 02.513.03.14

books

☆ **ANTICYCLONE DES AÇORES** *F2*

The best bet for guidebooks. This store counts NATO as one of its biggest customers. It carries vintage maps of the Eastern bloc, guides to the world's worst places to visit, and books on destinations you may never have heard of.

34 rue du Fossé aux Loups, Central ☎ 02.217.52.46

Antiquariaat Erik Toonen *off map*

Take in the smell of old books here.

48 Kloosterstraat, Antwerpen ☎ 03.237.94.66

Copyright *off map*

For a cultural refill, Copyright has what seems like every book on art and architecture in a cool black-and-white setting.

22 Haarstraat, Antwerpen ☎ 03.232.94.16

☆ LIBRAIRIE CANDIDE & LIBRAIRIE DE ROME ⚜off map
Glossy interiors mags and multilingual newspapers are sold at Librairie Candide and Librairie de Rome.
Librairie Candide 1–2 place Brugmann, Ixelles (West) ☎ 02.344.81.94
Librairie de Rome 50b avenue Louise, Ixelles (West) ☎ 02.511.79.37

☆ MA MAISON DE PAPIER ⚜B6
With old books, vintage posters, and advertisements going back to the 1800s, it's like rummaging through an attic.
6 Galerie de Ruysbroek, Le Sablon ☎ 02.512.22.49

☆ NIJINSKI ⚜off map
Nijinski is where Brussels' international crowd sell their books. This is the place for bargain English-language lit.
15–17 rue du Page, Ixelles (West) ☎ 02.539.20.28

☆ PEINTURE FRAÎCHE ⚜off map
An international selection of coffee-table tomes on architecture, art, and design.
10 rue du Tabellion, Ixelles (West) ☎ 02.537.11.05

☆ PÊLE MÊLE ⚜B5
Two shops that prove one man's trash is another man's trashy reading, with old issues of Elle, Marie-Claire, and Photo as well as comics and bona fide literature. The shop also has a good used-CD section.
55 blvd Lemmonnier, Les Marolles ☎ 02.548.78.00

☆ STERLING ⚜F2
A new arrival on the scene, selling rags and mags, but also a good selection of novels, reference books, and travel books. Sterling is browser-friendly. It even boasts a kids' and baby area with heaps of sofas.
38 rue du Fossé aux Loups, Central ☎ 02.223.62.23

☆ WATERSTONE'S ⚜D2
For the biggest variety of English-language publications, it's best to head to the Brussels branch of Waterstone's.
71–75 boulevard Adolphe Max, Central ☎ 02.219.27.08

cds, records & tapes

Arlequin ♪F7
For a leisurely browse, go to one of two Arlequin shops, which have been peddling used CDs and vinyl for years. One sells rock, funk, African and reggae imports; the other classical, videos, jazz, and good old chanson.
7 & 8 rue de l'Athenée, Ixelles (East) ☎ 02.512.15.86

☆ FNAC ♪A3
French chain-store FNAC is arguably the biggest book and CD shop in Brussels, but if your taste runs beyond Madonna, Céline, or Mariah, the selection in sounds is lacking.
City 2, 123 rue Neuve, Central ☎ 02.275.11.11

Lowlands & Stereophonic Records ♪off map
Come here to get the latest elektro, drum 'n' bass, hip-hop, techno, hard-core, acid jazz, or tempo. You can even get that classic wild dragon tattoo.
70 Kammenstraat, Antwerpen ☎ 03.232.98.70

Metrophone ♪off map
Dive into Metrophone for the most contemporary sounds in clubland.
47 Kammenstraat, Antwerpen ☎ 03.231.18.65

☆ MUSICMANIA ♪F2
The best range of vinyl in the city with fierce hip-hop, trance, trip-hop, and other new flavas. The graffiti decor and skateboard-kid patrons make it alternative heaven.
4 rue de la Fourche, Central ☎ 02.217.53.69

☆ VIRGIN MEGASTORE ♪E/F2
A wider choice than most of the others.
30 Anspach Centre, Central ☎ 02.218.55.46

children's wear

Basile et Boniface ♪E11
The city's smartest parents go to Basile et Boniface to buy top-of-the-range Belgian and French clothes and baby equipment at prices to match.
77 rue Washington, Ixelles (West) ☎ 02.534.81.18

laude Hontoir *♭off map*
aul Smith for babes to teens is on offer at this friendly one-off boutique.
place Brugmann, Ixelles (West) ☎ **02.346.59.47**

e Groene Wolk *♭off map*
keep the under 10's in high fashion, head here.
Korte Gasthuisstraat, Antwerpen ☎ **03.234.18.47**

ardin des Fleurs *♭off map*
his is the place for doting relatives of the under 18-months, special-
ing in Italian knitwear and shawls.
rue Darwin, Ixelles (West) ☎ **02.344.18.89**

at & Muis *♭E2*
heck out this trendy store for cutting-edge designer labels.
rue Antoine Dansaert, Ste-Catherine ☎ **02.514.32.34**

icard *♭A6*
on't miss out on a trip to one of rue du Lombard's joke and costume
hops: Picard has been here since the turn of the century.
rue du Lombard, Central ☎ **02.513.07.90**

hocolates

GODIVA *♭D6*
odiva has the name, but has it got the quality to live up to its rep?
ell, having invented the truffle, and with customers able to choose
e type of cocoa bean in their chocolates, it certainly seems so,
though they are expensive.
place du Grand Sablon, Le Sablon ☎ **02.502.99.06**

LÉONIDAS *♭D2*
r some of the best chocs in town, go to Léonidas. They might have
ranches worldwide and are a household name in connoisseur
rcles, but you'll find plenty of pralines they don't export. Léonidas'
re the cheapest and sweetest.
boulevard Anspach, Central ☎ **02.218.03.63**

MANON *♭F3*
r a sugar rush Belgian-style, with over 80 different varieties of pralines,
e tiny Manon ranks as one of the best chocolate shops in Brussels.
a chaussée de Louvain, St-Josse ☎ **02.217.45.00**

☆ MARY'S   ♪A7
The official chocolate supplier to the royal family.
15 rue Royale, Central ☎ 02.217.45.00

☆ NEUHAUS   ♪F2
The oldest kid on the block. Swissman Jean Neuhaus opened a pharmacy in 1857 in Galerie de la Reine – now the flagship – selling marshmallows, liquorice, and the odd piece of chocolate. When his son Frédéric got involved, they started Confiserie et Chocolaterie Neuhaus-Perrin. Since the day Neuhaus senior's grandson came up with the first bite-sized praline and a protective box, there's been no looking back.
Galerie de la Reine, Central ☎ 02.512.63.59

☆ PIERRE MARCOLINI   ♪D6
A recent winner of the Chocolatier of the World award, new-wave fave thirty-something Marcolini is a relative newcomer on the chocolate scene (with only four shops in Belgium). His semi-sculptural creations have a sinfully high cocoa content. He focuses on bittersweet chocolate sculptures for sophisticates. Subtle flavours like jasmine and bergamot are used to flavour his pralines, among the most expensive in Belgium.
39 place du Grand Sablon, Le Sablon ☎ 02.514.12.06

Planète Chocolat   ♪A6
Planète Chocolat is run by Frank Duval, who commissions local sculptors to design the chocolate moulds into which he pours his delicately flavoured, high cocoa-content chocolate. For a potted history of chocolate-making, there's a tiny museum at the back.
24 rue du Lombard, Central ☎ 02.511.07.55

☆ WITTAMER   ♪D6
Family-run Wittamer, doing freshly made chocs since 1910, is a favourite of many expat Belgians when visiting home. The shop puts as much into its packaging as it does into its pricey pralines: gold-leaf boxes, baskets, and lots of ribbons. Its namesake café serves wickedly divine pastries that are also wickedly expensive. It takes a more elitist approach by keeping small and to trad methods.
6 & 12–13 place du Grand Sablon, Le Sablon ☎ 02.512.37.42

☆ AMANDINE   *F10*

Glitzy old dress and jewellery hire store Amandine hires out stunning ballgowns, chic cocktail dresses and wedding robes at a moment's notice; good for posh functions.

50 rue Defacqz, Ixelles (West) ☎ 02.539.17.93

Ann Demeulemeester   *off map*

Ann Demeulemeester focuses on the intimate relationship between clothes and the individual. Her cool corner shop – opposite the Fine Arts Museum – sells the perfect clothes for women taking a stand in a man's world – she was one of the first designers to create city-style pinstripe suits for women. The Antwerpen store is the only one in the world to stock both her men's and women's ranges.

Leopold de Waelstraat, Antwerpen ☎ 03.216.01.33

☆ ANNÉMIE VERBEKE   *E2*

The clothes are practical but her knitwear, made from butter-soft wools and tasty alpacas have delightful twists.

64 rue Antoine Dansaert, Ste-Catherine ☎ 02.511.21.71

☆ AZNIV AFSAR   *D1*

A Belgo-Iranian designer and a hot new name. Her ultra-fem clothes are well sought after.

33 rue Léon Lepage, Ste-Catherine ☎ 02.512.30.96

☆ CACHEMIRE   *off map*

Gorgeous contemporary space Cachemire is a homage to Italian design, where the rails are filled with classic separates with a twist. Shoes by Carshoe and the equally expensive Heschung are downstairs.

rue Franz Merjay, Ixelles (West) ☎ 02.647.09.88

☆ CAMELOT   *E11*

Bombay and Goan store Camelot chose Brussels as its first out-of-India branch, with work by the cream of India's avant-garde, such as Alpana, Bawa and Abraham & Thakore.

47–48 rue Châtelain, Ixelles (West) ☎ 02.647.22.27

César et Rosalie   *D6*

Belgian label César et Rosalie does womenswear that's a bit more fun: think Esprit-like comfort filtered through Paul Smith style.

50 rue de Rollebeek, Le Sablon ☎ 02.514.58.64

Charlotte aux Pommes
‡D6

High-style labels like Jil Sander, Jean Paul Gaultier, Issey Miyake and Prada are available here, an intimate little boutique that draws well-turned-out women.

29 rue de Rollebeek, Le Sablon ☎ 02.512.34.59

Chine
‡E2

Adds zest to a woman's quest for a great wardrobe; colours and styles are more trendy than avant-garde – think Sarah Jessica Parker.

2 rue Van Artevelde, Ste-Catherine ☎ 02.503.14.99

Cocoon
‡F7

Unmissable for recent end-of-line bargains by Belgian designer Olivier Strelli, as well as quirky accessories by local designers.

41 rue de la Paix, Ixelles (East) ☎ 02.512.64.86

☆ DA ZIA
‡off map

Multi-coloured jumpers and scarves by Belgian Valérie Barkowski created for her Mia Zia label, made by Marrakesh artisans and sold at her shop here.

61 rue Darwin, Ixelles (West)

Dod
‡E11 & E4

Last season's designer gear for men and women and lingerie at bargain prices. Upmarket designer fashion at fell-off-the-back-of-a-lorry prices is their speciality. Most clothes at its five branches are end-of-the-line collections or recent stock bought from stores gone bankrupt. Among the goodies on sale here are Dolce & Gabbana's sexy, feminine dresses, DKNY's classic T's, as well as designs by Calvin Klein and Tommy Hilfiger. Complete the look with top-notch footwear by the likes of Airwalk, JP Tod's, and others.

89-91 rue du Bailli, Ixelles (West) ☎ 02.219.43.52
44 chaussée de Louvain, St-Josse ☎ 02.218.24.68

Emporio Armani
‡D6

The Sablon is the hotspot of Brussels swank. That's why Giorgio Armani chose the cobblestoned place du Grand Sablon as the location for Brussels' Emporio Armani. It has the usual mix of suits that mean business, plus street and casualwear with an upmarket twist.

37 place du Grand Sablon, Le Sablon ☎ 02.551.04.04

Gaya and Momento ♫C7

Womenswear that is preppy-meets-career-gal-meets-art-student chic: Paul Smith, JP Tod's, and French label Victoire are just some of the lines carried at these sister stores.

48 & 47 rue du Namur, Le Sablon ☎ 02.512.23.76/02.511.23.71

☆ **GERALD WATELET** ♫F11

Justice is done to Belgium by haute couturier Gerald Watelet's ready-to-wear line Simply Couture, with lots of hand-finished details.

268 avenue Louise, Ixelles (West) ☎ 02.647.35.50

☆ **HARMONY** ♫off map

Cutting-edge Irish fashion can be had here, with natty separates by John Rocha and Paul Costelloe alongside hand-crocheted numbers in luxury yarns by Lainey Keogh.

405/415 ave Louise, Ixelles (West) ☎ 02.648.84.32

☆ **ISABELLE BAINES** ♫C7

Look here for her classic cardigans, schoolgirl-sweet twinsets and other knits that look like traditional wardrobe staples, until you look at the fine detailing.

18 rue du Pépin, Le Sablon ☎ 02.502.13.73

Johanne Riss ♫D1

Although not on rue Dansaert, Johanne Riss was also one of the pioneers in putting Ste-Catherine on the fashion map – the French designer opened her flagship shop just a little after Stijl. Raw and refined is her modus operandi: rough leathers and denim, as well as silk and chiffon, figure in her womenswear, and she does brutal but sleek jewellery, too.

35 pl du Nouveau Marché aux Grains, Ste-Catherine ☎ 02.513.09.00

☆ **KAAT TILLEY** ♫F4

Think Stevie Nicks meets Tolkien on the way to a funeral and you've got her style down to a T. Intricately woven capes, web-like corsets and fairy-goddess styles are mixed with vampire sexiness.

4 Galerie du Roi, Central ☎ 02.514.07.63

☆ **KENZO** ♫C7

Japanese designer Kenzo creates suits that mix classic with up-to-the-minute casual styles, as well as exotic holiday gear fit for your island getaway (upstairs for women, downstairs for men).

14 rue de Namur, Le Sablon ☎ 02.514.04.48

Lieve van Gorp ♮*off map*
She's the one who favours the black leather goth look.
1 Hopland, Antwerpen ☎ 03.231.19.17

Louis ♮*off map*
New wave Antwerpen designers – including Raf Simons, Jurgi Persoons, Véronique Branquinho, Martin Margiela, and AF Vandervorst to name a few – can be found here. Owned by Geert Bruloot, this was one of the first shops to stock collections by the Antwerp Six, and remains Antwerp's champion of new Belgian talent.
2 Lombardenstraat, Antwerpen ☎ 03.232.98.72

Mariella Burani ♮*C7*
Any woman bigger than a teenager is well-served by Burani's flouncy skirts, la Parisienne blouses and ultra-feminine flowery dresses that whisper femme fatale.
29 rue de Namur, Le Sablon ☎ 02.514.08.85

Marien Perez ♮*A2*
Perez is taking Brussels by storm with her latest collections that just ooze style.
99 rue de Canal, Ste-Catherine ☎ 02.223.68.27

☆ MING TSY ♮*E11*
At this one-off shop, there are slinky embroidered cocktail numbers, simple shifts, and a cool line in accessories and stationery – handmade papers from Tsy's native Taiwan.
rue du Page, Ixelles (West) ☎ 02.424.29.68

Modepaleis ♮*off map*
The realm of Dries Van Noten. Even if you're not after a super-feminine dress or a shirt from Van Noten's menswear collection, the shop, a beauty from 1881, warrants a visit on architectural merits alone.
16 Nationalestraat, Antwerpen ☎ 03.233.94.37

☆ NATAN ♮*E2 & C7*
None of the madness of McQueen or Margiela for Belgium's pre-eminent couture house. The shop sells womens and menswear that is clearly inspired by the best of US sportswear. If you're after something a bit more sleek, Edouard Vermeulen is your man. The local answer to Armani, his Natan label serves up ready-to-wear womens-and menswear at two different shops on rue du Namur. A top couturier, Vermeulen dresses Mathilde, Belgium's very own Princess Di.

Think Gucci meets Marc Jacobs meets Yves Saint Laurent and you've got a handle on his style, and price range.
* **rue Antoine Dansaert, Ste-Catherine** ☎ 02.514.15.17
* 58 **rue de Namur, Le Sablon** ☎ 02.503.53.56 (men's)
* 8 **rue de Namur, Le Sablon** ☎ 02.512.75.00 (women's)

☆ NINA MEERT $F7

Chic evening clothes, bridalwear, and accessories reflects the upbeat tone of rue St-Boniface.
* **rue St-Boniface, Ixelles (East)** ☎ 02.514.22.63

Obius $off map

If you're a dedicated follower of Belgian fashion, head here for men's shoes and clothes by the likes of Dirk Bikkembergs and Ann Demeulemeester.
2 **Meersenierstraat, Gent** ☎ 09.233.82.69

Pax $F7

Clothes by Carhartt and Dickies and 1970s props are worth checking out here.
8 **rue de la Paix, Ixelles (East)** ☎ 02.502.52.31

Profiel $off map

A vibrantly decorated boutique selling clothes by all the Flemish fashion gurus.
17 **Mechelsestr, Leuven** ☎ 016.23.72.62

Santi's $F9

Hair guru Frédéric Blondel's flamboyant salon Santi's is a shrine to the area's Art Nouveau heritage. He attracts a gay clubland scene and women after tea, sympathy, a cool cut, or the clubby labels displayed at the front of the shop.
22 **ave Paul Dejaer, St-Gilles** ☎ 02.534.64.22

☆ SMADJA FEMME $off map

Britpack women's fashion is brought to Ixelles by Smadja Femme: Whistles, Ghost, Paul Smith, Joseph, and then some.
16 **place Brugmann, Ixelles (West)** ☎ 02.347.66.70

☆ STIJL $E2

The first place to champion Belgian designers before the rest of the fashion world jumped on the bandwagon, this mega-shop still sells mens and womenswear by the 'old guard' – Ann Demeulemeester, Dries Van Noten, and Martin Margiela – as well newcomers Veronique Branquinho and AF Vandervorst. Sonia Noël has been in the fashion biz for yonks, and was one of the first people to have faith in the Dansaert area of Ste-Catherine, 16 years ago, by opening this ultra-trendy clothes store. Noël has also done much to boost Brussels' general fashion profile. She was one of the original pioneers of Parcours de Stylistes – an annual celebration of fashion that consumes the city centre for a weekend. Collections by the so-called third-wave avant-garde set are also here. Brussels-born Xavier Delcour made a beeline for Stijl, as did (Italian-born, but Antwerpen Academy graduate) Angelo Figus.
74 rue Antoine Dansaert, Ste-Catherine ☎ 02.512.03.13

☆ STUDIO PITSCHON $D1

Allows women to pick from its brochure. Several basic styles are available, and clients choose the fabric they want from exotic wools and silks. Designer Patrick Pitschon's creations feature a lot of wrapping, a lot of tunics, frayed seams and unfinished hems – very earthmother on skid row.
90 rue Antoine Dansaert, Ste-Catherine ☎ 02.502.54.08

☆ TAST $E2

An earthbound selection: womenswear by Joseph, Atsuro Tayama, and others whose clothes have sleek twists.
118 boulevard Anspach, Central ☎ 02.502.10.99

☆ VAN V $D1

Fashion for femmes who think high style more than hot trends: Comme des Garçons with a Belgian flavour. The back of the shop features their pricey couture section, while the front stocks the more affordable ready-to-wear collection.
10 rue Léon Lepage, Ste-Catherine ☎ 02.513.01.80

☆ VIA DELLA SPIGA $E2

For label choice, Via della Spiga is Stijl's only real competition. Smaller, it shares the minimal cool-decor aesthetic that lets the clothes take centre stage. Vivienne Westwood and Alexander McQueen are some of the fashionable labels on show.
42 rue Antoine Dansaert, Ste-Catherine ☎ 02.502.20.97

Walter
off map

Owned by two Antwerp Six members – Walter van Beirendonck and Dirk van Saene. Clothes are displayed here like gallery installations in a converted garage. It is a perfect backdrop for labels like Bad Baby Boys, Wild and Lethal Trash, and the newer Aesthetic Terrorists.
12 St-Antoniusstraat, Antwerpen ☎ 03.213.26.44

fashion

Double Face
off map

Avant-garde fashion for both sexes can be yours at Ann Huybens' store.
2 Trommelstraat, Gent ☎ 09.371.56.37

Fish & Chips
off map

Buy into the lifestyle of the raver, skater, and clubber.
36–38 Kammenstraat, Antwerpen ☎ 03.227.08.24

Inno
D2

The country's only true department store is better after a revamp, but doesn't rank well against its European peers.
111 rue Neuve, Central ☎ 02.211.21.11

Jonathan Bernard
A6

Clubwear for fashion victims (men and women) with a sense of humour: 70s disco, 80s new romantic, 90s glamazon and beyond. Disposable chic is Bernard's modus operandi.
53 rue du Lombard, Central ☎ 02.537.90.91

☆ KENLIS
E8

If you're after something not designed by a Euro committee, try the comfy wool sweaters from Ireland available here.
48 rue Archimède, Quartier Européen ☎ 02.230.69.11

Kirane
A11

Cashmere collectables woven in Mauritius are piled high. Timeless staples like twin-sets, scarves, and jerseys come in tens of colours.
67b avenue Louise, Ixelles (West) ☎ 02.539.16.02

☆ RUE BLANCHE
E2

Sensibly stylish womenswear (think job interview at an advertising agency) as well as a range of items for the home.
37–41 rue Antoine Dansaert, Ste-Catherine ☎ 02.512.00.33

flowers & plants

Catleya
off map

Treat yourself to a bouquet of flowers at Catleya, where florist Brigitte Fux is in the same league as Britain's Packer & Prycke.
118 avenue Lepoutre, Ixelles (West) ☎ **02.344.63.64**

Grani-Flora
C13

Head here for a colourful selection of flowers.
30 square Marguerite, Quartier Européen ☎ **02.734.49.90**

food

African Asian Foods
E7

The place for fresh fruit.
25 chaussée de Wavre, Ixelles (East) ☎ **02.514.03.86**

Agadir II
E8

For a blast from the Med, be prepared to queue at this family-run Moroccan store, where fresh fish is piled high.
213 chaussée de Wavre, Ixelles (East) ☎ **02.648.57.51**

☆ À LA PETITE VACHE
E4

For cheeses, head down to place St-Josse, where small À la Petite Vache keeps fromage lovers happy. A Brussels institution, it has one of the very best selections in the city.
69 chaussée de Louvain, St-Josse ☎ **02.217.39.69**

☆ L'ATELIER GOURMAND
off map

If cooking is out, there's a master chef at this classy traiteur. This deli's cordon-bleu takeaways can't be faulted, but expect to pay through the nose.
470 rue Vanderkindere, Ixelles (West) ☎ **02.344.51.90**

☆ L'ATELIER DE LA TRUFFE NOIR
F11

If truffles make you tick, don't miss L'Atelier de la Truffe Noire, which sells truffle-seeped, new-laid eggs, truffles by the 100 g, and cutters and storage containers for this highly prized fungi; the café does an excellent (if expensive) line in lux sarnies and cooked breakfasts. It shares the same owner as Michelin-star resto La Truffe Noire.
300 avenue Louise, Ixelles (West) ☎ **02.640.54.55**

Au Suisse *⌖E2*
Arguably the best sandwiches in town are on offer here, a magnet for downtown's hungry at lunchtime.
73–75 boulevard Anspach, Central ☎ 02.512.95.89

☆ **BIODROME** *⌖A6*
Biodrome is at the healthier end of the spectrum, a health supermarket-resto-massage centre great for loading up on herbal teas, tofu, and snacks.
76–78 rue du Marché au Charbon, Central ☎ 02.502.12.10

Brûlerie Française *⌖E10*
Connoisseurs of the coffee kind find their fix here, where they blend, grind, and sell a wicked choice of whole coffee beans.
280 chaussée de Waterloo, St-Gilles ☎ 02.537.48.06

Claire Fontaine *⌖D6*
Herbal teas for whatever ails you. The country village-styled deli also has classy nibbles such as foie gras and artily-packaged marmalades and olive oils that make great hamper gifts.
3 rue Ernest Allard, Le Sablon ☎ 02.512.24.10

La Crémerie de la Vache *⌖B10*
This style-conscious café-cum-brunch place sells patisseries, bottled olive oils, and Mariage Frères teas.
6 rue Jean Stas, St-Gilles ☎ 02.538.28.18

☆ **DEGROOF** *⌖off map*
Coffee doesn't come much better. Whole or ground arabica beans can be bought by the kilo, as can fine teas.
427 rue Vanderkindere, Ixelles (West) ☎ 02.343.54.36

☆ **LE DÉJEUNER SUR L'HERBE** *⌖off map*
This up-market convenience store has a great selection of wines, gourmet tins, organic veg, and takeaways.
6 ave Louis Lepoutre, Ixelles (West) ☎ 02.346.17.59

☆ **THE ENGLISH SHOP** *⌖E13*
Sells a vast selection of teas.
186 rue Stévin, Quartier Européen ☎ 02.735.11.38

Exotic Foods *♭E7*
Good for Congolese dried river fish, frozen greens from Burundi, and moambé (a peanut chicken stew).
27 chaussée de Wavre, Ixelles (East) ☎ 02.512.94.50

☆ LA FERME LANDAISE *♭E2*
La Ferme Landaise's forte is foie gras. Fresh game, fine wines, smoked salmon and other delicious treats to take out are on offer.
43 rue Melsens, Ste-Catherine ☎ 02.512.95.39

Fromageon *♭off map*
For the cheese course, regional specialities are in tip-top condition here.
309 rue Vanderkindere, Ixelles (West) ☎ 02.344.26.12

Fromagerie Maison Baguette-Gaspard *♭F7*
Cheese-lovers shouldn't miss the array of delights here, complete with fab marble-top shop fittings. It's tiny, has been here forever, and the owner, a master cheese-seller, knows all there is to know about Belgium's specialities, including the delish medium-hard Maredsous. She also sells fantastic goat's milk cheeses made by Trappist monks in Orval and Chimay.
28 rue de la Longue Vie, Ixelles (East) ☎ 02.511.70.95

Fromagerie Vinothèque *♭E11*
Regional speciality cheeses.
106 rue du Bailli, Ixelles (West) ☎ 02.537.66.53

Goossens *♭off map*
Queue up with the rest of Antwerpen for the finest rye raisin bread and sweet delicacies you've ever tasted.
31 Korte Gasthuisstraat, Antwerpen ☎ 03.226.07.91

Le Grande Cerf *♭F6*
Le Grand Cerf sells old-style, decadent dishes and food gifts.
22 rue du Grand Cerf, Le Sablon ☎ 02.511.44.83

☆ HIMI *♭F8*
Sells pre-marinated halal lamb brochettes and fillets.
269 chaussée de Wavre, Ixelles (East) ☎ 02.640.30.98.

ack O'Shea
C13

his Irish butcher does a brisk trade with organic pork and hams, specially on high days and holidays.

o rue Le Titien, Quartier Européen ☎ 02.732.53.51

☆ MAISON DANDOY
E2

Maison Dandoy has been satisfying those with a discriminating weet tooth since 1825. The old-style spot does wicked biscuits, sinful marzipan, and the best version of speculoos, the brown-sugar and innamon biscuit that is a national fave.

1 rue au Beurre, Central ☎ 02.513.10.57

☆ MARY'S
D11

eady-to-eat take away food couldn't be better at Mary's, run by Irish ook Mary Fehily, the sideline to her high-society catering business. ry her seafood lasagnes, traditional moussakas, or salads with a twist.

20 rue Lesbroussart, Ixelles (East) ☎ 02.648.56.58.

☆ MATTHYS VAN GAEVER
E2

ver so decadent, and very delicious.

8 rue Melsens, Ste-Catherine ☎ 02.512.09.47

☆ MC NÉGOCES
off map

ells dried fruits, tea, and spices, as well as couscous pots, velvet aintings, silk flowers, and other assorted kitsch. Best buy: the nosque alarm clock.

30 rue de Brabant, St-Josse ☎ 02.219.22.46

☆ MERCI-CASH
off map

ike MC Négoces Merci-Cash sells dried fruits, tea, and spices, as well s other assorted kitsch.

3 rue de Brabant, St-Josse ☎ 02.223.49.03

a Miche de Pain
off map

he finest bakers in an area of many: fab baked-sugar pies, custard artlets, and wholemeal loaves.

a avenue Brugmann, St-Gilles ☎ 02.345.87.60

Mosterdwinkel Tierenteyn
off map

ine vinegars, rare herbs, and spicy mustards in a wonderfully pre-erved interior.

Groentemarkt, Gent ☎ 09.225.83.36

Le Petit Forcado ♭F10
For the best Portuguese pastries.
2 rue Américaine, St-Gilles ☎ 02.537.92.20

☆ ST-AULAYE ♭off map
For dessert, try this top-notch patisserie's yummy fruit tarts and pastries.
4 rue Jean Chapelié, Ixelles (West) ☎ 02.345.77.85

☆ TAGAWA SUPERSTORE ♭F11
Sushi to go is on offer here, and it also does a great line in rice, fresh fish, and exotic tinned and packet foods.
119 chaussée de Vleurgat, Ixelles (East) ☎ 02.648.59.11

☆ DEN TEEPOT ♭F1
If you're more health-conscious hungry, head for Den Teepot, a deli with a cheap and cheerful restaurant attached. Yoghurts, dried fruit, nuts and sugar-free cakes and biscuits are sold here, as well as prepared meals.
66 rue des Chartreux, Ste-Catherine ☎ 02.511.94.02

☆ LA TSAMPA ♭E11
Healthfood shop La Tsampa keeps the same hours as its restaurant out back. Pulses, beansprouts, wholemeal bread, organic fruit, and essentials for healthy living are sold here.
109 rue de Livourne, Ixelles (West) ☎ 02.647.03.67

galeries

Galeries de L'Agora ♭B6
One-off shops selling leatherwear and watches. Weekend stalls sell tacky jewellery as well as leather bags and jackets, tie-dyed and secondhand togs, goth jewellery and henna. It's completely alternative, with a faint whiff of hemp about it.
Central

Galeries Bortier ♭B6
Shares the same architect as Galeries Royales St-Hubert. It's small, charming, and lined with antiquarian book and map shops.
Central

Galeries Louise ♭A11
This is where avenue Louise's window shoppers pile in at the first sign of rain or cold weather. It's lined with international chain stores.
Ixelles (East)

Galeries Royales St-Hubert *♯F2*

The jewel in the crown of Brussels' galeries. Beautifully restored mid-19th-century arcade with up-market one-off clothes and jewellery shops, Neuhaus' flagship store, and a branch of Delvaux, the up-market Belgian designer shop.
Central

Galeries de la Toison D'Or *♯E7*

Mall shopping is a national pastime, and this modern warren of mid-range boutiques is one of the most popular in town.
Ixelles (East)

gifts

Bali-Africa *♯E6*

Wooden and leather masks, drums, and other trinkets and totems from Angola to Zanzibar pack every inch of its three storeys. It has a helpful yellow line painted on the floor to guide you through, otherwise you'd never get out alive – almost too much of a good thing.
154–156 rue Blaes, Les Marolles ☎ 02.514.47.92

La Caravane Passe *♯E10*

For today's ethnic decor at knock-down prices, head to this shop in the heart of the North African community. It sells tagines, silver teapots for mint tea, and colourful scatter cushions to bring Morocco to you.
2 rue du Tamines, St-Gilles ☎ 02.538.05.90

Côté Provence *♯C6*

If you want to treat yourself to something, Côté Provence has the goods: aromatic candles, knick-knacks, and incense from Provence.
69 rue Haute, Les Marolles ☎ 02.502.30.92

Davidoff *♯D6*

Fancy a Cuban cigar? Davidoff is the best place in Brussels to get them. Humidors, gold lighters, cigar boxes in materials like leather and crocodile, and other smoking accessories are sold in this upscale boutique – as well as all brands of cigarettes.
1 place du Grand Sablon, Le Sablon ☎ 02.512.94.22

Dune *♭E6*
French artist Muriel Bardinet draws from her years in Africa and the
south of France in her shop-cum-studio. The result: sleek objets in
teak, seashells and other exotic materials.
234 rue Haute, Les Marolles ☎ 02.511.17.21

Eurotempo *♭E13*
You can pick up Euro-souvenirs at virtually any newsstand in the
Rond Point/Schuman area but, for the best variety, head to
Eurotempo, where the familiar 12 gold stars are on everything from
pens to gold watches.
14 rue Archimède, Quartier Européen ☎ 02.230.04.11

Fallen Angel Gallery *♭off map*
The shop for retro freaks – old tin cans, kitsch postcards, and model cars.
29–31 Jan Breydelstraat, Gent ☎ 09.233.39.04

☆ MAGICLAND *♭E11*
If kitsch clutter pleases this is the place to go, where, alongside wacky
clubwear, there are lots of trinkets, pink faux-fur, and novelty items
for the home.
41 rue du Bailli, Ixelles (West) ☎ 050.62.88.06

☆ MARJOLAINE *♭B6*
Collectors' dolls and knick-knacks that are great for giving.
7 rue de la Madeleine, Central ☎ 02.513.20.54

☆ MONT-DE-PIÉTÉ *♭C6*
You might luck into something *typiquement Belge* at Mont-de-Piété,
where one man's debt is another man's deal. This auction has been
selling objects pawned for quick cash since 1618. If it can be hocked, it
can be bought here.
19 rue St-Ghislain, Les Marolles ☎ 02.512.13.85

Nordica *♭A14*
Handmade ornaments and dainty household decorations from
Scandinavia.
220 rue Belliard, Quartier Européen ☎ 02.230.13.05

Nuhr Nebi
♮C6

Gifts from afar are Nuhr Nebi's speciality. Dreadlocked Belgian Fabienne Goris hand-selects the oils, incense, kilims, and other exotica on sale at her two shops from regular trips to Africa and Asia.
23 rue Blaes & 55 rue Haute, Les Marolles
☎ 02.514.04.29/02.411.45.44

Rosalie Pompon
♮B6

Whimsical things that make wonderful gifts: heart-shaped clocks, rhinestone genie bottles, and hand-crafted beaded jewellery.
1 rue de l'Hôpital, Central ☎ 02.512 35 93

★SENSES ART NOUVEAU
♮D6

A good compromise for the fiscally challenged collector. Reproductions of Art Nouveau trinkets and Klimt-inspired candelabras are done mostly in cost-conscious pewter.
31 rue Lebeau, Le Sablon ☎ 02.502.15.30

hats

☆ CHRISTOPHE COPPENS
♮D1

For headgear, clue into twenty-something Christophe Coppens, Belgium's answer to Philip Treacy and Stephen Jones. His hats, some coming close to gallery-worthy works of art, are displayed elegantly in his oval-shaped shop, also home to an exquisite collection of Art Deco objets. Coppens was less talked about than mad hatter Elvis Pompilio until he opened a first shop. He's been garnering attention ever since, and his handmade hats have graced many a Paris fashion show.
2 rue Léon Lepage, Ste-Catherine ☎ 02.512.77.97

☆ ELVIS POMPILIO
♮A6

Pompilio brought the hat back to the Belgians. He is renowned for his kooky sombreros, fedoras, double-brims, and bonnets, and his candy-coloured shop features chapeaux for dudes and babes.
18 rue du Lombard, Central ☎ 02.511.11.88

☆ **GILLIS** ♫A6

A traditional hatmaker since the turn of the century (19th to 20th, that is), who does made-to-measure hats for every society occasion. The hat shop for men and women with classic tastes. It's been here since the 1940s and the milliners still use authentic wooden casts from bygone days.
17 rue du Lombard, Central ☎ 02.512.09.26

Sjapoo ♫off map

For something a little less obvious, try Ria Dewilde's Sjapoo. Dewilde designs her own hats and, if you're after an interesting dress or the perfect accessory, you've come to the right spot.
29 Sluizeken, Gent ☎ 09.225.75.35

Tarlatane ♫F7

Bang up-to-date, Valérie Janssens' natty hats and bead jewellery are for sale in this eye-catching shop.
22 rue Ernest Solvay, Ixelles (East) ☎ 02.502.79.29

interiors

Annick Goutal ♫A11

Essential finishing touches can be snapped up here, a Parisian perfumier with sublime floral home fragrances and scented candles.
52 avenue Louise, Ixelles (West) ☎ 02.514.56.64

☆ **ANTITHÈSE** ♫off map

Wonderful furniture and smaller homeware items designed by Christophe Delcourt, Marie-Claude Bérard, and Xavier Lust.
17 rue du Mail, Ixelles (West) ☎ 02.539.03.93

☆ **LE CHIEN DU CHIEN** ♫B1

Exquisite fabrics, buttons, and other sewing needs that are a cut above the chains and department stores: the shop's atmosphere, with a billiard table on which to cut the fabric and a boat for holding the rolls of material, is quirky and worth a good look.
50a quai des Charbonnages, Ste-Catherine ☎ 02.414.84.00

☆ **CINABRE** ♫off map

A minimalist approach is taken here, with Japanese-style ceramics, lacquered dishes, and glassware by Belgium's Harry Dean.
5 rue Washington, Ixelles (West) ☎ 02.345.26.95

☆ COMPAGNIE DE L'ORIENT ET DE LA CHINE $B10

Lend an Oriental touch to the home at Compagnie de l'Orient et de la Chine, which sells crockery and soft furnishings.

1a place Stephanie, Ixelles (West) ☎ 01.511.43.82

Curiosa $off map

Superb handmade lamps and other design goodies.

9 Onderbergen, Gent ☎ 09.233.02.41

Edouard Vermeulen $C11

Of the Natan ready-to-wear stores, Vermeulen has his haute couture nerve centre here. Upstairs is a lifestyle emporium of furniture and objects for the home, hand-picked by trendsetter Sophie Campion.

Natan, 158 avenue Louise, Ixelles (West) ☎ 02.647.10.01

Space Bizarre $E2

Completely multi-national – a German company with a French name selling Oriental-styled ceramics, futons and furniture – Espace Bizarre is a real find. It also does cool Italian shelf units, Danish lamps and other modern furniture with minimalist (but by no means minimal) appeal.

19 rue des Chartreux, Ste-Catherine ☎ 02.514.52.56

The Gallery $F7

European style is on offer at The Gallery, where German collector Konrad Kern sells contemporary furniture and objects by the Milanese Memphis group, Bakelite necklaces from the 1950s, and pieces by Italian contemporary furniture designer Andrea Branzini.

39 rue de la Paix, Ixelles (East) ☎ 02.513.27.97

☆ GRAPHIE SUD $off map

Sells women's clothes, accessories, and an enlightened choice of homeware for modern living.

15 avenue Georges Brugmann, Ixelles (West) ☎ 02.344.31.92

Home Store $C7

Works home style from a different angle: goat-skin rubbish bins, wooden vases, sleek dishware, and contemporary tables. The shop has a *Wallpaper* magazine-style chill to match the sleek stock.

65 rue de Namur, Le Sablon ☎ 02.502.39.09

Imanza   *♭F1*

Fans of Middle Eastern and North African style should stop here, where Algerian Nabijla Belkacem and Moroccan Karima Benmansour sell the bounty from their travels throughout their homelands, as well as Pakistan, India and many other Asian countries. Most pieces are craftsman-made, and some are antiques. The delectable objects come as big as armoires and as small as brass ashtrays.

50 rue Van Artevelde, Ste-Catherine ☎ 02.512.06.36

Marie-Rêve   *♭D6*

Rustic furniture and homewares are given a refined finish. It's the sole outlet of home furnishings by Belgian artist Isabelle de Borchgrave, who specializes in tapestries, fabrics and brocades that reek of luxe abandon. Luxuriously decadent bath oils, candles and other items to pamper yourself are also on sale.

27 rue de Rollebeek, Le Sablon ☎ 02.514.36.39

☆ NEW DE WOLF   *♭C6*

Martha Stewart meets IKEA at this one-stop shop for the home. Almost every genre of decor is available. The main shop spans a whole block, with a smaller store selling kitschier knick-knacks across the street. New De Wolf does current, cost-conscious copies of older styles.

91 rue Haute & 46 rue Blaes, Les Marolles ☎ 02.511.10.18/ 02.503.38.36

☆ NOIRE D'IVOIRE   *♭B6*

Agnès Emery designs furniture, ceramics and tiles that range from rustic to rococo chic here. Everything is made in Morocco, finished with a craftsman's flourish and sold in her deceptively small-looking boutique.

25–27 rue de l'Hôpital, Central ☎ 02.534.47.70

☆ L'OBJET DU DÉSIR   *♭D6*

Fans of modern Italian and Scandinavian design shouldn't miss out on a visit here. Retro futuristic furniture and home furnishings by Alessi and others have Barbarella/Space Odyssey/Jetsons vibe.

21 place du Grand Sablon, Le Sablon ☎ 02.512.42.43

De Prinses op de Erwt   *♭off map*

The Princess on the Pea – for decking out children's bedrooms or for natty accessories like jewellery and scarves.

65 Volkstraat, Antwerpen ☎ 03.216.41.18

☆ LA VAISSELLE À KILO $D6

Meaning 'dishes by the kilo'. Warehouse sale is the atmosphere, with a mix of Limoges, Royal Boch, and tableware for everyday use. Upstairs there's a better than average selection of authentic Belgian beer glasses.

8a rue Bodenbroek, Le Sablon ☎ 02.513.49.84

ewellery

☆ ANNICK TAPERNOUX $E2

Her penchant is beaten silver objets d'art and austere jewellery. And she made the spoons at superchef Alain Ducasse's eaterie Spoon, Food & Wine in Paris.

28 rue du Vieux Marché aux Grains, Ste-Catherine ☎ 02.512.43.79

☆ CHRISTA RENIERS $E2

Reniers takes the sea and stars as prototypes: starburst earrings, coral-like pendants and shell-like bracelets done mostly in silver for high-sheen appeal. She is a fave with style queens. Silver flower cluster rings and pendants are among her top signatures, but diversity is the key to her success. Happily her prices won't break the bank – earrings and rings without semi-precious rocks start at 1500BF.

29 rue Antoine Dansaert, Ste-Catherine ☎ 02.514.17.73

Claude Noëlle $D6

The pick of vintage jewellery from the likes of Cartier and Boucheron.

20 place du Grand Sablon, Le Sablon ☎ 02.511.41.72

☆ FAISONS UNE REVE $off map

Art Deco jewellery, lots of Bakelite objets, and choice ceramics.

avenue Lepoutre, Ixelles (West) ☎ 02.347.34.29

☆ LES PRÉCIEUSES $D1

A softer approach is taken by fashion designer Pili Collado. This is a sideline to her day job so the opening hours are erratic. Collado makes gorgeous costume jewellery for the modern twinset brigade – glass-bead chokers, bracelets, and earrings threaded onto silver wire. Jamin Puech's collectable beaded bags are also on sale here. But nothing comes cheap – expect to pay 3500BF for a necklace.

83 rue Antoine Dansaert, Ste-Catherine ☎ 02.503.28.98

kitchenware

☆ AU GRAND RASOIR
♭B6
Supplier to the Royal Court. This small shop stocks not only knives and cutlery, but also elegant straight razors with handles in bone or jade, Swiss Army knives of all sizes, hair clippers, and manicure sets.
7 rue de l'Hôpital, Central ☎ 02.512.49.62

☆ LA COUTELLERIE
♭A10
Recommended cutlery and penknife specialist, selling the type of utensils that the Conran Shop would charge double the price for, such as grooming kits and herb cutters.
187 rue de l'Hôtel des Monnaies, St-Gilles ☎ 02.538.86.39

☆ DILLE EN KAMILLE
♭B10
This hip kitchenware store also does scrumptious organic food.
16 rue Jean Stas, St-Gilles ☎ 02.538.81.25

☆ FAHRENHEIT
♭C11
Aficionados of stainless-steel kitchen utensils will be sorted here – at a price.
130b avenue Louise, Ixelles (West) ☎ 02.644.28.00

☆ LAUFFER
♭F2
For 125 years, this shop has sold kitchen equipment to professionals and has a selection of knives for carving, butchering and everyday use.
59 rue des Bouchers, Central ☎ 02.511.15.92

linen

Cinabre
♭E11
A mecca for trendy ceramics and glassware, Cinabre also sells household linen supplies for committed lifestylers. The designers' names are obscure, but the quality of pieces is unbeatable.
5 rue Washington, Ixelles (West) ☎ 02.345.26.95

☆ LINEN HOUSE
♭D6
The best and most traditional linen. Makes and sells an impressive line of sheets, tablecloths and cushion covers.
10 rue Bodenbroeck, Le Sablon ☎ 02.502.63.02

MARTINE DOLY $B9

converted coach house is home to this Belgian household linen
een. She designs and sells a divine line of hand-finished linen and
ganza drapes, night-dresses and jimjams. Hand-finished touches
e embroidery and fab buttons make them hard to resist.
Chaussée de Waterloo, Ixelles (West) ☎ 02.512.46.28

odes $E6

ntage clothes shop Modes is worth a scout too – they have a small
ection of specialized table linen.
4 rue Blaes, Les Marolles ☎ 02.503.54.00

mes de Ménage $off map

mix of new and antique linen (including pyjamas), a bit pricey, but
od quality.
lace Brugmann, Ixelles (West) ☎ 02.344.32.95

ngerie & erotica

LES CHARMES D'HÉLÈNE $C6

xy lingerie to get your groove on. Dior, Ferré, Féraud and other
els are 1950s sexpot fabulous, and are sure to get a rise out of the
ht man.
rue Haute, Les Marolles ☎ 02.511.13.32

Erotische Verbeelding $off map

women-only here, where erotic underwear and sexual aids can be
ught by those who know what turns them on.
–12 Ijzerenwaag, Antwerpen ☎ 03.226.89.50

STIJL UNDERWEAR $E2

r impressing your nearest and dearest, there's unmentionables for
omen and men which are more sleek, aerodynamic minimalist
an Victoria's Secret frilly or Versace va-va-voooom.
rue Antoine Dansaert, Ste-Catherine ☎ 02.514.27.31

UNDRESSED $E11

tica accessories – crotchless knickers, peephole bras, and less-
vealing lingerie by Marlies Dekkers can be had here.
e de l'Aqueduc, Ixelles (West) ☎ 02.544.08.44

Grand' Place   ⚘F2/B6
The small daily flower market isn't the city's best, but it adds local
colour to the square.
Central

Marché du Midi   ⚘F5
A melting pot of ethnic food stalls, fruit, vegetables, plants, and cheap
clothes (Sunday mornings). It's a true celebration of Mediterranean
riches, with stalls selling salt cod, preserved lemons, cured meats,
fresh pasta, and Italian cheeses. Handfuls of fresh mint and coriander
are dirt cheap, and slabs of marinated lamb are a bargain. Belgian
Trappist-made cheeses like Orval and Chimay and hard goat's milk
cheeses mixed with herbs are also recommended. There's no better
insight into the soul of Brussels and its people than a trip to this massive street markett; kick-off is early Sunday morning – dawnish – and
it all winds down at midday.
Place du la Constitution, St-Gilles

Parvis St-Gilles   ⚘D9
Morning market for no-frills fruit, veg, and meat with a North African
spin (closed Mondays).
St-Gilles

☆ PLACE DU CHÂTELAIN MARKET   ⚘E11
Wild mushrooms, game, cheeses, and fruit and veg couldn't be fresher at this market (2–7.30pm Wed). This is more geared to busy professionals – delish quiches, pittas stuffed with falafels and wickedly
good tarts for easy bites. It's a cosy set-up in winter, with stalls selling
mulled wine, mussels, and snails.
Ixelles (West)

Place Flagey   ⚘C12
A local, no-frills, daily affair in the heart of the Portuguese community. Great for cut flowers, farm produce, and Italian delis and fab food
stalls selling salt cod, cured meats and regional cheeses.
Ixelles (East)

Place du Grand Sablon   ⚘D6
Weekend market, excellent for silver trinkets, jewellery, and antique
chairs; but no bargains here.
Le Sablon

...ce du Jeu de Balle *♀E6*

...rly-rising bargain-hunters find rummaging heaven at this daily ...a market good for vintage clothes, picture frames, and miscella-...ous junk. Spread out on tables, tarpaulins, and blankets are much ...sh and treasure. So prepare to do some serious sifting through ...es of clothes, costume jewellery, dishes, furniture, and other mis-...Manea. The best bargains are had during the week, but haggling ...n knock a few francs off already decent prices. Many of the items ...urface with much higher prices in Le Sablon. It is a melting pot of ...tures, with all sorts of junk on sale. Old books, vintage clothes, and ...ungy brocante are permanents.

...: Marolles

...enswear

...BALTHAZAR *♀B6*

...ls Paul Smith, Patrick Cox, and other sensible, stylish menswear.
...rue du Marché aux Fromages, Central ☎ 02.514.23.96

...DEGAND *♀off map*

...is traditional men's outfitter combines bespoke tailoring with ...xury gifts for the man who has it all – wooden desk accessories by ...vid Linley, silver cigar trimmers, and de-luxe board games.
...: avenue Louise, Ixelles (West) ☎ 02.649.00.73

...tre Terre Ciel *♀B10*

...tdoor types can try here – state-of-the-art camping equipment is ...stairs, hi-performance clothes below.
...place Stéphanie, Ixelles (West) ☎ 02.502.42.41

...menegildo Zegna *♀E7*

...le and Italian panache rule at the Brussels flagship, where suits ...d leatherwear are sold.
...blvd de Waterloo, Ixelles (West) ☎ 02.511.41.57

...KWASI *♀off map*

...'men who don't want to be fashion victims, but also don't want to ... dull and traditional,' says owner Robert Smith. Footwear and ...thes have just enough flash to impress.
...pl St-Géry, Ste-Catherine ☎ 02.511.85.89

☆ MICHIELS   *♦E6*
The threads are timeless, but the clothes are new at Michiels. This
men's shop, specializing in made-to-measure suits, has been open
since 1856 and the Belgian royal family are favoured customers.
195 rue Haute, Les Marolles ☎ 02.511.69.35

☆ SMADJA HOMME   *♦off map*
Fashion-conscious professionals head for Smadja Homme, which
sells Comme des Garçons, Paul Smith, and Joseph.
21 avenue Lepoutre, Ixelles (West) ☎ 02.513.50.13

Yoca   *♦E4*
Yoca offers many traditional labels to fashion- and money-conscious
blokes.
16 chaussée de Louvain, St-Josse & Schaerbeek ☎ 02.217.16.17

photography

Campion   *♦F7*
Photographers love Campion's two shops: one deals in secondhand
lenses and cameras from the 1930s, the other sells good-value brand-
new equipment.
13–15 rue St-Boniface, Ixelles (East) ☎ 02.512.13.31

shoes

Coccodrillo   *♦off map*
Footwear to complement cutting-edge designer fare.
9 Schuttershofstraat, Antwerpen ☎ 03.233.20.93

Degrif   *♦F3*
A small selection of footwear, but prices are cheap enough to make it
worth a look. It's luck of the draw as far as selection goes (turnover is
fast), but Patrick Cox, Charles Jourdan, and Pied-à-Terre have all been
known to feature in their women's lines.
11–25 chaussée de Louvain, St-Josse & Schaerbeek ☎ 02.219.64.59

☆ HATSHOE   *♦D1*
Footwear by the likes of Patrick Cox, Dries Van Noten, Robert Clergerie,
and other notables – but, alas, not hats.
89 rue Antoine Dansaert, Ste-Catherine ☎ 02.512.41.52

SHOE'S VICTIM.COM
$E2

putting your best foot forward – repros of classic trainers, new
me-grown models, and originals.
5 blvd Anspach, Central ☎ 02.502.81.00

LE SILLA
$E2

poker heels, sassy mules, club-kid clogs, and everything in between
r hot-stepping ladies.
rue Antoine Dansaert, Ste-Catherine ☎ 02.513.80.90

mô
$off map

e tiny but stylish Sumô stocks footwear by Prada, Bikkembergs, and
velko.
Mechelsestraat, Leuven ☎ 016.22.14.85

ys

Courte Echelle
$B6

rious dolls' house collectors should head here for miniature hand-
afted furniture.
rue des Eperonniers, Central ☎ 02.512.47.59

rneels
$A11

ussels' most up-market toy store, where rich mums and dads shop
r wooden puzzles, handmade dolls and soft toys by the likes
Steiff.
avenue Louise, Ixelles (West) ☎ 02.512.97.60

ntage clothes

Dépôt
$C4

ith clothes strewn all over the place, exploded laundrette is the
st way to describe this shop. But hunt it down for even cheaper
shions than Dod and Yoca – this is their warehouse for clothes from
asons of the recent past.
3 rue de Liedekerke, St-Josse & Schaerbeek ☎ 02.511.75.04

LES ENFANTS D'EDOUARD
$C11

st known for barely worn big-name men's and women's labels.
avenue Louise, Ixelles (West) ☎ 02.640.42.45

☆ GABRIELE ♀E2

Tops for 1940s gear like croc handbags and pill-box hats.
14 rue des Chartreux, Ste Catherine ☎ 02.512.67.43

L'Homme Chrétien ♀E2

For something a bit retro, L'Homme Chrétien has a huge choice of
gear for boys and girls from the 1950s to 1970s. Rails of vintage jeans
and jackets are there for the rummage alongside dressier evening
numbers from the 1970s.
27 rue des Pierres, Central ☎ 02.502.01.28

☆ IDIZ BOGAM ♀C2

Meaning 'go with God' in Russian. Offers yet another stylish option.
Owner Jacqueline Ezman sells vintage clothes going back to the
1930s, gathered from shopping trips throughout Europe, and alters
them to make one-of-a-kind pieces. The shop looks like a Paris salon
spread out over a warehouse-like space. Mink stoles, 1970s Italian
mules, classic costume jewellery – it's all here. She buys at auction
and scours the flea markets of Paris and New York for stylish classics.
Gladstone bags, flapper-style foxes and minks, slinky maxi-dresses,
distressed leather jackets and crimplene shirts are Ezman's staples.
It's also good for period footwear too – mostly unworn. This is as
expensive as it gets in Brussels, but most items are still a bargain.
76 rue Antoine Dansaert, Ste-Catherine ☎ 02.512.10.32

☆ LOOK 50 ♀F7

Vintage clothes and accessories are sold at Look 50, known for its
range of secondhand Levi's. It's a bit of a fleapit, but the place is full
of bargain-hunters oozing street cred.
10 rue de la Paix, Ixelles (East) ☎ 02.512.24.18.

Naughty I ♀off map

Vintage fashion from the 1960s and 1970s.
65–67 Kammenstraat, Antwerpen ☎ 03.213.35.90

☆ MODES ♀E6

One of the area's best: 1930s flapper dressers, 1940s dressing gowns,
headgear from top hats to bowlers, and other elegant vintage stuff.
The selection is so good that it's a regular port of call for costumers
from theatre companies throughout Europe. Unbeatable for old buttons – jet, plastic and Bakelite – men's braces from the 1940s, grandad
shirts, and hats for men and women from the 1920s.
164 rue Blaes, Les Marolles ☎ 02.503.54.00

NICOLAS WOIT
D1

Works on a retro tip: he does made-to-measure bias-cut dresses in vintage fabrics: perfect for getting a film noir femme-fatale swagger. Remakes women's classics from bygone eras using vintage fabrics and trimmings that he finds at auction. His Dansaert store is especially good for glam eveningwear, while men are catered for, too, with felt trilbies in winter and panamas during summer.

0 rue Antoine Dansaert, Ste-Catherine ☎ 02.503.48.32

LE PETIT RIENS
off map

This charity shop is a mecca for bargain clothes and furniture.

01 rue Américaine, Ixelles (West) ☎ 02.537.30.26

vintage furniture

Collector's Gallery
D6

The centrally located Collector's Gallery has the best high-class junk in town. Best for items that won't break the bank dating from the early 1900s to the 1970s, such as classic toys, vintage perfume bottles it even has a Barbie memorabilia section.

7 rue Lebeau, Le Sablon ☎ 02.511.46.13

Fiftie-Fiftie
off map

you're more 40s to 70s, Fiftie-Fiftie has plastic furniture on sale.

56 Kloosterstraat, Antwerpen ☎ 03.237.43.72

Fin des Siècles et Plus
E6

Furniture to fit out your penthouse with 1930s panache.

30 rue Haute, Les Marolles ☎ 02.502.66.35

MONT-DE-PIÉTÉ
C6

This is an auction that has been selling pawned objects since 1618. If you are lucky you may well pick up a fantastic bargain here on some typically Belgian furniture or other item.

9 rue St-Ghislain, Les Marolles ☎ 02.512.13.85

PALACE
E6

Tucked into a side street, Palace specializes in quirky furniture and vintage toys from the fabulous 1950s.

5 rue des Renards, Les Marolles ☎ 02.512.52.17

restaurants and cafés

Brussels' restaurants may not have the style of London or the culinary fame of Paris, but they sure make up for it in number and variety. Whether it's a Belge brasserie, a North African caff, or a modern fusion hangout, it's all good.

african/caribbean

Cantina Cubana $A6

If your palate yearns for something exotic, Cantina Cubana does the best Cuban cuisine in the area. The house specialities: black bean soup and lechón asado – suckling pig, oven-grilled in garlic and mojito sauce.

6 rue des Grands Carmes, Central ☎ 02.513.11.52 Ⓜ Anneessens ⓑ

L'Horloge du Sud $E8

One of few places where Euros and Africans mix in equal numbers. Try the fab African food if you're peckish.

141 rue de Trône, Ixelles (East) ☎ 02.512.18.64 Ⓜ Trone

Ile de Gorré $E7

The proliferation of central African eateries in the Matongé earned it the nickname Upper Kinshasa. Ile de Gorré, on place St-Boniface, is one of the best.

28 rue St-Boniface, Ixelles (East) ☎ 02.513.52.93 Ⓜ Porte de Namur ⓑ–ⓑⓑ

Les Jardins de Bagatelle $E7

There's a strong African flavour to the cooking here (which includes crocodile and antelope), but this sumptuously decorated restaurant is a cut above (in price and cuisine).

17 rue du Berger, Ixelles (East) ☎ 02.512.12.76 Ⓜ Porte de Namur ⓑⓑⓑ

american

Le Balmoral $off map

A laid-back, fifties-style milk bar, this American diner has a great children's menu of club sandwiches, burgers and pasta dishes. All can be washed down with milkshakes. It's a popular brunchtime haunt.

21 place Brugmann, Ixelles (West) ☎ 02.347.08.82 🚏 91, 92

Gazebo
♭D1

...ries for a cultural mix on its menu, but the overriding slant is ...merican. Owner Lee Better, part Jewish mother, part benevolent fag ...ag, dishes up top-notch versions of Yankee faves like key lime pie and ...hicken fried steak. It's a popular nexus for Brussels' gay population.

place du Nouveau Marché aux Grains, Ste-Catherine ☎ 02.514.26.96 Ⓜ Ste-Catherine ⓑⓑⓑ

Belgian

L'Atelier
♭off map

...ou'll find L'Atelier through an unassuming set of coach doors: the ...estaurant is in an old artist's studio with a pretty courtyard used for ...lfresco dining in summer. Inside or out, Belgian-French food is ...erved with flair and confidence.

8 rue Franklin, Quartier Européen ☎ 02.734.91.40 Ⓜ Schuman ⓑⓑⓑ

Au Brabançon
♭C4

...u Brabançon's pink dining room wall is covered with paintings of ...orses. But Black Beauty wouldn't last long here, since the menu is ...eavy with horse steaks, blood sausage, and other traditional Belgian ...ooking, just like your grandma used to make (if your grandma hap-...ened to be Belgian).

5 rue de la Commune, St-Josse & Schaerbeek ☎ 02.217.71.91 Ⓜ Botanique ⓑⓑ–ⓑⓑⓑ

Au Stekerlapatte
♭E6

...Brussels institution serving old-style Belgian cuisine to Eurocrowds ...which means lots of beef, potatoes and lashings of cream. The smell ...f butter in the air will lead you there.

4 rue des Prêtres, Les Marolles ☎ 02.512.86.81 Ⓜ Hotel des Monnaies ⓑⓑ–ⓑⓑ

☆ AU VIEUX ST-MARTIN
♭D6

...designer update of an old-style brasserie, with the works of con-...emporary Belgian artists on the walls. The expensive food – rabbit ...ooked in *kriek* (cherry beer), blood sausage, scampi croquettes – is ...ure Belge, and done with great refinement. *Atypique* Belgian food ...n a stacked plate. Local dishes like *waterzooi* (creamy fish stew) and *toemp* (vegetable mash) come alongside better-known exports like ...teak, *frites*, and pâté salads. Fresh produce and cream rule in the ...itchen, while in the dining room, equal numbers of pampered

Belgians and tourists pig out. Cheeky calorie cards are provided and doggy bags are common. Lingering is encouraged – a rack of magazines caters for art lovers and *Playboy* readers alike. But the decor and prices are definitely not so *atypique*.

38 place du Grand Sablon, Le Sablon ☎ **02.512.64.76** 🚋 **92, 93, 94**
🅑🄵–🄱🄵 🄱🄵 🄱🄵

Le Brassin

♪A11

A cosy spot to tuck into hearty Belgian food. It's a bit rough around the edges, but the regulars who hum along to Jacques Brel and drink fine beer don't seem to mind.

36 rue Keyenveld, Ixelles (East) ☎ **02.512.69.99** Ⓜ **Louise**

Breydel-De Konick

♪off map

Where chefs from Michelin-starred restaurants go on their days off.
Brugge

Cap de Nuit

♪B6

Basic Belgian and French cuisine that fills you up. The big draw here is that the kitchen is open until 7am: perfect for a post-clubbing bite.

28 place de la Vieille Halle aux Blés, Central ☎ **02.512.93.42**
🄱🄵 Ⓜ **Centrale**

Cargo

♪off map

A combination of Italian, French, and local food.

24b Leopold De Waelplaats, Antwerpen ☎ **03.260.60.10 by rail**

Chez Léon

♪F2

One of the best deals for kids is at this Belgian *frites et moules* institution. If parents buy a 495BF meal of mussels, chips and a beer, children under 12 get a free set menu that isn't limited to shellfish.

18 rue des Bouchers, Central ☎ **02.513.08.48** Ⓜ **Bourse; De Broukère** 🄱🄵

Chez Marie

♪E12

The standards of stylishly good food in a small, elegant room draw in a finely blended mix of expats and locals. Dishes often seen in cookery books but rarely attempted at home, such as stuffed baby courgette flowers, are efficiently dispatched to tables. Whether it's people or food you're into watching, the mirrors over each table give great cover, avoiding having to stare openly.

40 rue Alphonse de Witte, Ixelles (East) ☎ **02.644.30.31** 🚋 **71, 36**
🄱🄵 🄱🄵–🄱🄵 🄱🄵

Les Dames Tartines   *B3*

Excellent French and Belgian cuisine (horse, rabbit, and snails) that
has restaurant critics and diners reaching for superlatives.

**58 chaussée de Haecht, St-Josse & Schaerbeek ☎ 02.218.45.49
Ⓜ Gare du Nord**

In den Wittekop   *off map*

Sit at one of In den Wittekop's two tables to try the house specialities:
waterzooï (chicken or fish stew with white wine), bouillabaisse, or
Flemish stews (beef stewed in beers).

14 St-Jakobsstr, Brugge ☎ 05.033.20.59

In 't Spinnekopke   *F1*

Dates back to 1762 and is popular with ale-lovers round the world: it
serves over 100 Belgian beers, and does a large part of its cooking in
Belgian brews.

1 place du Jardin aux Fleurs, Ste-Catherine ☎ 02.511.86.95 Ⓜ Bourse
ⒷⒻⒷⒻⒷⒻ

☆ 'T KELDERKE   *F2*

This cellar restaurant, previously a 17th-century prison, has ditched
the jail vibe in favour of quiet and cosy. The menu is stick-to-your-ribs
Belgian cooking, such as *stoemp*, a mix of mashed potatoes and veg.
Greasy, buttery, decadent. Long wooden benches and a vaulted
ceiling give the 'little cellar' a suitably homely feel. This is unfussy
home cooking with a very definite Belgian twist. Go local on the
steaks or *moules*. Always busy, so book ahead or be prepared to wait.

15 Grand' Place, Central ☎ 02.513.73.44 Ⓜ Bourse; De Brouckère
ⒷⒻ–ⒷⒻⒷⒻ

☆ LOLA   *D6*

Black and white and red all over, the clean, sleek space feels like the
set of an American soap, but the mix of Belgian and French cuisine
(roast beef with rocket and buffalo mozzarella, rank lobster, smoked
salmon and foie gras) is actually very good.

33 place du Grand Sablon, Le Sablon ☎ 02.514.24.60 🚊 92, 93, 94 ⒷⒻⒷⒻ

☆ MAISON D'ANTOINE   *F8*

Brussels' most famous *friterie*, whose chips are double-fried and the
sauces double-dolloped.

1 place Jourdan, Quartier Européen ☎ 02.230.54.56 Ⓜ Schuman ⒷⒻ

☆ LE PAON ROYAL $E2

The Royal Peacock does Belge and French faves like lamb braised in beer and *chateaubriand* from the grill, in a great colonial town-house setting. Great choice of beers, some becoming ingredients in this rustic, traditional tavern that's a favourite of local notables.

6 rue du Vieux Marché aux Grains, Ste-Catherine ☎ **02.513.08.68**
🚋 **34, 95, 96** ⓑⓕ–ⓑⓕⓕ

☆ LE PETIT BOXEUR $E2

It's hard to find anything to dislike about this quaint renovated restaurant near trendy place St-Géry. Innovative dishes like mushroom terrine and squid lasagne are sure to liven up palates bored with trad Belgian fare. Starters and main courses are just the right size, but beware of industrial-strength rich desserts. Warmed by candlelight and mellow jazz, it's the perfect place for a romantic meal.

3 rue Borgval, Ste-Catherine ☎ **02.511.40.00** Ⓜ **Bourse** ⓑⓕⓕ–ⓑⓕⓕⓕ

Plattesteen $A6

Within spitting distance of six gay bars, Plattesteen is on the downtown gay circuit. A tavern with pinball machines and neon beer signs, it also does basic Belge, along with substantial salads and pastas.

41 rue du Marché au Charbon, Central ☎ **02.512.82.03** Ⓜ **Bourse; Anneessens** ⓑⓕ

☆ PRÉ-SALÉ $D1

Excellent homestyle Belgian cooking in a dining room vaguely resembling an old butcher's shop. Cabaret shows, with the whole restaurant getting into the act, are often staged here.

20 rue de Flandre, Ste-Catherine ☎ **02.513.43.23** 🚋 **63** Ⓜ **Bourse; Ste-Catherine** ⓑⓕⓕ

La Quincaillerie $off map

From the two tiers of balconies, smaller parties can look down on the meals of other eaters in this converted hardware shop, the refurbishment of which was overseen by Antonio Pinto. Plates of fresh seafood, huge salads, steaks, and other traditional dishes are prepared masterfully without sticking to the culinary staight-and-narrow. With an oyster bar downstairs, and four dining rooms, booking is rarely necessary, but service can be impersonal – the lone diner can be forgotten on the upper balcony.

45 rue du Page, Ixelles (West) ☎ **02.538.25.53** 🚋 **81, 82** ⓑⓕ–ⓑⓕⓕ

ns Vins ♪F7

it's modern French/Belgian cooking you're after, try Vins Vins. The
enu is adventurous – check out the marinated salmon *ceviche* for
arters – and there's a chatty neighbourhood feel.

8 chaussée de Wavre, Ixelles (East) ☎ 02.502.61.65 Ⓜ Porte de
amur ⓖⓕ ⓖⓕ ⓖⓕ

aterzooï ♪off map

icklers for tradition will love Waterzooï, one of the oldest restaurants
Gent. Order the namesake dish, Gent's special addition to cuisine, a
licious, creamy and filling soup-cum-stew with chicken or fish.

St-Veerlepl, Gent ☎ 09.225.05.63 by rail

rasseries & bistros

L'AMADEUS ♪D10

osy and candlelit L'Amadeus is located in Rodin's former workshop.
are ribs are about the best thing on an otherwise predictable
enu, but the wine list is impressive and the atmosphere lively. It
ay be noisy, pricey, and a little yuppie, but a visit here is still a bit of
event: from the dark, candlelit conservatory (a former Rodin work-
op) to the even darker 'cosies' near the kitchens. The menu is
spectable brasserie fare (like goat's cheese and basil tart) without
uch flourish, but with a good choice of wines, and a sommelier on
nd if you're really stuck. The yuppie community comes here in
oups, but it's not averse to couples on a romantic night out.

rue Veydt, Ixelles (West) ☎ 02.538.34.27 Ⓜ Louise ⓖⓕ ⓖⓕ–ⓖⓕ ⓖⓕ

BRASSERIE LA PAIX ♪off map

Brussels institution – this family restaurant has been opposite the
autiful glass structure of the old abattoirs (now a market) since
82. It's Belgian in every possible way, from the richly sauced meat
shes to the blown up photos of family weddings on the walls.
iendly and familiar; the maître d' may just sit down and have a chat
d cigarette break at your table.

rue Ropsy-Chaudron, Anderlecht ☎ 02.523.09.58 Ⓜ Clemenceau
–ⓖⓕ ⓖⓕ

asserie Michel-Ange ♪E13

informal place to tuck into *moules-frites* and Belgian beer, with a
ont terrace in the summer.

ave Michel-Ange, Quartier Européen ☎ 02.733.82.16 Ⓜ Schuman ⓖⓕ

☆ LES BRASSERIES GEORGES
♫off map

Parisian-style bistro in one of the leafiest areas of western Ixelles. If you're after an evening of pure self-indulgence, it's worth the trek through the woods, though, because the surf and turf takes some beating.

259 avenue Winston Churchill, Ixelles (West) ☎ **02.647.21.00** 🚋 **23, 90** ⒷⒻⒷⒻ–ⒷⒻⒷⒻ

☆ CANTERBURY
♫off map

Book a table for you and your dog (yes, they cater for pooches too) at this busy modern brasserie with good food and high prices. Popular with families, business people and locals. Everyone's welcome, even dogs – bowls of water are provided for them on the leafy terrace. Staff are friendly and efficient, food is of a high quality, and the portions are generous. Specialities include chicken *waterzooi* (a thick creamy chick en soup with vegetables and potato). Try the fish & chips *comme à Liverpool* (the likes of which you'll never taste again, even in Liverpool) or the Irish entrecôte steak with red wine-flavoured butter. There's a good selection of Belgian beers, aperitifs, and spirits, or try a glass of peach-flavoured champagne – the house favourite. It's very expensive

2 avenue de l'Hippodrome, Ixelles (East) ☎ **02.646.83.93** 🚋 **71** ⒷⒻⒷⒻ–ⒷⒻⒷⒻ

Cosmopolite
♫F13

All bleached wood and halogen, offers designer salads and classics with a twist, including foie gras with shrimps.

36 avenue de Cortenburg, Quartier Européen ☎ **02.230.20.95** Ⓜ **Schuman** ⒷⒻ–ⒷⒻⒷⒻ

De Kaai
♫off map

Brasserie fare is available in a mirrored warehouse that doubles up as a late-night dancing joint.

94 Rijnkaai, Hangar 26, Antwerpen ☎ **03.233.25.07 by rail**

☆ DE LA VIGNE À L'ASSIETTE
♫C11

Sitting alone in a residential street, this fine little restaurant is a fave with the business crowd at lunch and those in-the-know in the evenings. Simply but carefully designed, the wooden tables are scrubbed up a treat along with pale lemon chairs to match the walls. Cloudy glass globes complete the flung-together look. The menu is small but intense, combining flavour and texture to produce memorable combinations such as lamb with Chinese five-spice. Co-owner Eddy Dandrimont is a sommelier at heart (Belgium's No. 1 in 1995) and is rightly proud of his reassuringly well-priced wine list.

51 rue de la Longue Haie, Ixelles (East) ☎ **02.647.68.03** 🚋 **93, 94** ⒷⒻⒷⒻ–ⒷⒻⒷⒻ

☆ EAT ♪E11

Equally appealing to veggies and carnivores; the salad composé never fails to impress. It's not open in the evenings, but is the perfect place for a light lunch and a chit-chat. Specializing in substantial salads, this young, funky eatery feeds the hungry lunchtime crowds. Menus written up on blackboards avoid commitment to paper, allowing daily changes to benefit from fresh produce. Classic salad combinations, like deep-fried brie and plum, are imaginative enough to elevate them from the bog standard. Good intentions of just a light lunch are then efficiently dispelled by a tempting array of home-made cakes and tarts, which you can also take away.

103 rue de L'Aqueduc, Ixelles (West) ☎ 02.537.22.90 🚊 93, 94 ⑧⑨

☆ L'ÉCOLE BUISSONNIÈRE ♪B3

Offers serious value-for-money continental grub. The school cafeteria interior's nothing to write home about, but the mix of businessmen, students, and locals make it a fun dining experience.

13 rue Traversière, St-Josee & Schaerbeek ☎ 02.217.01.65 Ⓜ Botanique ⑧⑨–⑧⑨⑧⑨

La Galettière ♪E2

This hole-in-the-wall crêperie does wicked buckwheat and blue-wheat pancakes stuffed with a variety of fillings as in Brittany – light and scrumptious.

53 rue des Pierres, Central ☎ 02.512.84.80 Ⓜ Bourse

Pakhuis ♪off map

Design freaks should make a beeline for Pakhuis, a flamboyant ware-house conversion by Antonio Pinto (of Quincaillerie fame), where the cavernous green roof and scores of whirring fans give an Apocalypse Now feel; the comfy leather chairs and classy brasserie fare, however, hold no horrors at all. It's closed on Sundays.

4 Schuurkenstr, Gent ☎ 09.223.55.55 by rail

Le Pavillon ♪C11

Definitely not for herbivores, a cosy bistro where just about anything that moves is served up with a tasty sauce. The wine list is resolutely French at this cheap and cheerful *bon viveurs'* haunt, but thankfully the beers are brewed locally.

64 rue Defacqz, Ixelles (West) ☎ 02.538.02.15 by rail ⑧⑨–⑧⑨⑧⑨

☆ **TAVERNE DU PASSAGE** ♪*F2*

The hint of formality in the Taverne's 1920s setting makes it a favourite with a slightly older crowd. The food is every bit as crisp and well-presented as the waiters' shirts, and trad French and Belgian cooking is *de rigueur* (*waterzooï* is on the menu, as are *moules*). The service is friendly and professional, and if you can overcome the feeling of being a bit-part in an Orient Express re-run, you'll enjoy the genteel atmosphere and fine food.

30 galerie de la Reine, Central ☎ **02.512.37.32** Ⓜ **Bourse** ⑧⑧–⑧⑧⑧⑧⑧⑧

Le Temps Délire ♪*F10*

Lower prices and simple fuss-free Franco-Belgian fare are on offer, with classic brasserie fare including *moules et frites*. Jazz and blues concerts are held here on Saturday nights.

175–177 chaussée de Charleroi, St-Gilles ☎ **02.538.12.10** ⑧⑧⑧⑧⑧⑧

breakfast & brunch

Brood-Huys ♪*off map*

Start the day in style here, where they serve excellent, hearty breakfasts, brunches, and salads.

12 Jakobijnenstr, Gent ☎ **09.225.77.65 by rail**

De Foyer ♪*off map*

Grand and theatrical, with as much neo-classicism as you can handle in the foyer of an old theatre, it has legendary brunches, for which you must book weeks in advance.

18 Komedieplaats, Antwerpen ☎ **03.233.55.17 by rail**

★ **LE PAIN QUOTIDIEN** ♪*E2*

Breakfast and brunch continental-style are always on offer in the mornings at any of the city-wide branches of this faux rustic café chain. The croissants and breads are divine, and the java nice and strong. There are lots of chocolate spreads to choose from. It has one huge central table that diners share and lots of diddies for daytime intimacy. Although the drinks and light meals are expensive, the price does filter out a certain element you might not want to cosy up to. An added bonus on sunny days is the large terrace out back.

16 rue Antoine Dansaert, Ste-Catherine ☎ **02.502.23.61** Ⓜ **Bourse** ⑧⑧

☆ **HET WARM WATER** ♪*E6*

Veggie snackery that suits the mood after a ramble through the flea market.

19 rue des Renards, Les Marolles ☎ **02.513.91.59** ⊟ **20, 48** ⑧⑧

☆ L'AMOUR FOU   *B11*

This local mainstay is a great place to chat, chill-out, and admire the art. Although the decor of this uptown bar has changed more times than its menu, the clientele of students and young professionals has remained faithful. And with its cheap and cheerful grub, backroom lounge-bar and internet access, you can see why.

185 chaussée d'Ixelles, Ixelles (East) ☎ 02.514.27.09 Ⓜ Porte de Namur

☆ L'ARCHIDUC   *E2*

Elite is the operative word here, an Art Deco café catering to late twenty- to fortysomethings and folks who traded in bohemia for corporate salaries ten years ago. Live jazz is sometimes an extra pull. The snob factor is so discreet (there's no door policy, for example) that if you bring your own posse, it's easy to ignore. You do have to buzz in as the night wears on, though.

6 rue Antoine Dansaert, Ste-Catherine ☎ 02.512.06.52 Ⓜ Bourse

L'Arlequin   *F8*

For something more new millennium, L'Arlequin is a trendy, glass-fronted café-restaurant, with reasonably priced drinks and good modern brasserie-style food.

45 rue Froissart, Quartier Européen ☎ 02.280.41.11 Ⓜ Schuman

L'Art du Café   *E4*

An upscale affair, taking its coffee very seriously; freshly ground beans make up the java, and the interior, if a tad twee, is a relief from Starbuck's.

**98 chaussée de Louvain, St-Josse & Schaerbeek ☎ 02.280.47.12
Ⓜ Madou**

De Blauwe Kater   *off map*

Known for its jazz and blues concerts.

Hallengang, Leuven ☎ 016.20.80.90 by rail

La Bodeguita   *off map*

A down-to-earth café that serves up salsa for Latin lovers.

21 Ernest Van Dijckkaai, Antwerpen ☎ 03.226 01 12 by rail

Brasserie Verschueren
D9

There's always a lively scene in this unpretentious neighbourhood café. It may be due to the bar's graceful Art Deco curves or the cheery music, but it's more likely because of the locals who return night after night to do what les *Bruxellois* do best – chill out over a cool beer.
11–13 parvis St-Gilles, St-Gilles ☎ 02.539.40.68 Ⓜ Parvis St-Gilles

Café Chez Marcel
E6

Native *Bruxellois* tend to opt for this a hole-in-the-wall joint for flea market salesmen to grab a beer. Marcel also serves the meanest onion soup you've ever tasted – just don't make any dates for afterwards.
20 pl du Jeu de Balle, Les Marolles ☎ 02.511.13.75 Ⓜ Porte de Hal

Café Gambrinus
off map

Run by the same family since 1896, this sumptuous café has fancy woodwork, cosy booths, and a terrace with great views of the Stadhuis.
13 Grote Markt, Leuven ☎ 016.20.12.38 by rail

☆ CAFÉ MÉTROPOLE
D2

The *belle époque* café is part of the Métropole, the hotel where international film stars camp out while in town. Chain hotels now outdo the Métropole in services offered, but they can't beat its absolute luxury: defiantly glamorous in cinnamon browns with swirly, decadent Art Nouveau flourishes. The piano bar off the hotel lobby, in lush creams and whites, feels like a Merchant-Ivory production. It's all about aesthetics: plush upholstery, antique furniture, and a *fin de siècle* ceiling with huge chandelier. Beers are available, along with an impressive range of whiskies and cognacs.
31 place de Brouckère, Central ☎ 02.219. 23.84 Ⓜ De Brouckère

Café Tartine
E2

Designers, DJs, and those with business in the neighbourhood jockey for a window seat at Café Tartine: it's a good place for a potent pick-me-up espresso. People-watching is the biggest attraction here.
35 rue du Midi, Central ☎ 02.503.10.15 Ⓜ Bourse

Café Vlissinghe
off map

Soak up the history at the oldest bar in town (from 1552).
2a Bleekerstr, Brugge ☎ 050.34.37.37 by rail

Cafedraal
off map

Have lamb or seafood in the cosy Cafedraal. This eaterie's green terrace is an ideal spot for lunching al fresco.
38 Zilverstraat, Brugge ☎ 05.034.08.45 by rail

☆ LE CIRIO
♭E2

Caters to women with lap dogs and crusty older men, and has a weathered charm. Cirio is where you go not to be seen.

18 rue de la Bourse, Central ☎ 02.512.13.95 Ⓜ Bourse

Le Coq
♭E2

A seemingly ordinary café that is very untrendy but perversely always packed. Everyone looks like they're either recovering from a hangover or heading for one here. There's a taxi stand right outside, in case you want to bolt while your drinking partner is in the loo.

14 rue Auguste Orts, Ste-Catherine ☎ 02.514.24.14 Ⓜ Bourse

Damberd
♭off map

World music and swinging ambience are assured at Damberd, which has been a café since the 15th century.

9 Korenmarkt, Gent ☎ 09.225.84.33 by rail

☆ EL METEKKO
♭A6

El Metekko is a fave of hairdressers and older gay dudes viewing the romantic possibilities cruising along boulevard Anspach.

256 blvd Anspach, Central ☎ 02.512.46.48 Ⓜ De Brouckère

L'Espérance
♭D2

Incognito – this was the place where cheating lovers rendezvouzed before retreating upstairs to rooms rented by the hour. Rumour has it that the Deco bar can still get you a spot to do the dirty deed, but the café has a streamlined cool worth staying downstairs for.

1 rue Finistère, Central ☎ 02.217.32.47 Ⓜ Rogier

Fair Food
♭off map

If you're into organic stuff this has it all. Honest, healthy, and affordable.

50 Graaf van Egmontstraat, Antwerpen ☎ 03.238.92.96 by rail

☆ LE FALSTAFF
♭E2

Everyone knows this amazing Art Nouveau café, and most can direct you there blindfolded. Despite the bus fumes, the terrace is one of the best for people-watching – or cruising cuties – in the city. Surly service, though. It's a great place to soak up the atmosphere of turn-of-the-century Brussels. Liveried waiters glide between potted palms, while silver-haired ladies tuck into classic Belgian fodder. The attached Monte Christo bar has regular latin DJs.

17–21 rue Henri Maus, Central ☎ 02.511.87.89 Ⓜ Bourse

Galerie 18   *E6*
Galerie 18 has a mix of bric-a-brac and antiques in a setting
where everyone seems to be recovering from a hangover at the
weekend.
18 rue du Chevreuil, Les Marolles M Porte de Hal

☆ LE GREENWICH   *E2*
A decaying café dating back to 1900, where patrons come to play
chess. Very far from the madding crowd, it is atypique Bruxelles – and
all the better for it.
7 rue des Chartreux, Ste-Catherine ☎ 02.511.41.67 M Bourse

Hungry Henrietta   *off map*
Serves an eclectic menu to students and professors alike.
19 Lombardenvest, Antwerpen ☎ 03.232.29.28 by rail

Indigo   *E6*
The floral mural on the wall here is as close as you can get to an LSD
experience without actually taking it. Totally East Village Manhattan
in vibe, it serves scrumptious quiches and wicked, wicked desserts.
**160 rue Blaes, Les Marolles ☎ 02.511.38.97 ⑧ M Porte de Hal; Hôtel
des Monnaies**

Kladaradatsch! Cartoons   *off map*
Live music, food, café, and cinema – you get it all here. Get there early
or you won't get in.
4–6 Kaasstraat, Antwerpen ☎ 03.232.96.32 by rail

Lenny's   *off map*
Set in an old grocery shop, Lenny's dishes out the best salads in town.
47 Wolstraat, Antwerpen ☎ 03.233.90.57 by rail

Literair Café Henry van de Velde   *off map*
Designed by the Belgian architect of the same name, this is the place
for coffee.
4 Rijschoolstr, Leuven ☎ 016.50.16.72 by rail

Lollapalooza   *off map*
Combine a dive into cyberspace with a non-virtual snack.
28 Pelgrimstraat, Antwerpen ☎ 03.227.41.42 by rail

☆ MAPPA MUNDO ♭E2
Three floors, but lots of cozy corners too. The decor tries to conjure up a pub where you might hear sea shanties, but the public – frat boys, Commission types, upwardly mobile uptowners, and other professionals in their casual Friday gear – is strictly landlubber.
2–6 rue du Pont de la Carpe, Ste-Catherine ☎ 02.514.35.55 Ⓜ **Bourse**

Mokafé ♭F2
Bruxellois of all stripes flock to this Art Deco café before dinner or after a movie as it's smack dab in the middle of the Galerie de la Reine. Snacks are served (the cakes and tarts are the draw), but most people go for the terrace, prime people-watching territory.
9 Galerie du Roi, Central ☎ 02.511.78.70 Ⓜ **Brouckére**

☆ LE PAIN QUOTIDIEN ♭D1
The flagship café that started a world chain. The idea: breaking bread (or croissants) over the same table as fellow diners in a faux rustic setting. Even those who dismiss the concept on an anti-chain principle have to admit the coffee, croissants, and light organic menu of desserts and salads are delicious, if overpriced. One exception to the never-a-chain rule.
16 rue Antoine Dansaert, Ste-Catherine ☎ 02.502.23.61 ⓦ Ⓜ **Bourse**

Patisserie Alsacienne Bloch ♭off map
It may not look like much, but this Jewish bakery tempts Belgians from all over; its croissants and coffee are the business.
60–62 Veldstr, Gent ☎ 09.225.70.85 **by rail**

Popoff ♭off map
For the best desserts ever, hit Popoff, in the shade of the cathedral. Try their home-made hot chocolate and cheesecake.
18 Oude Korenmarkt, Antwerpen ☎ 03.232.00.38 **by rail**

La Porteuse d'Eau ♭B9
A beautiful Art Nouveau-styled café/bar with a light, airy atmosphere. Enjoy a quiet beer with the locals or sample one of the scrumptious patisseries with some tasty, strong coffee.
48a avenue Jean Volders, St-Gilles ☎ 02.537.66.46 Ⓜ **Parvis St-Gilles**

☆ LE ROY D'ESPAGNE ♱F2

High on the historical quotient, this is in one of the grandest guild-houses (the bakers') on the Grand' Place, with a gorgeous view from upstairs. Inflated pigs' bladders hanging from the ceiling look suspiciously like condoms. And the huge fireplace in the centre of the ground floor gives a waiting-for-Dracula vibe. A *très* cosmopolitan crowd flocks to the terrace in good weather.

1 Grand' Place, Central ☎ 02.513.08.07 Ⓜ Bourse

De Skieven Architek ♱E6

Murals of Brussels cityscapes and a limited menu of sandwiches and soups. The big draws are the international newspapers and mags sold here, so you can catch up on what's going on round the world.

50 place du Jeu de Balle, Les Marolles ☎ 02.514.43.69 Ⓜ Porte de Hal

☆ L'ULTIME ATOME ♱E7

The elegant place St-Boniface is dominated by one of the city's most buzzy cafés, it's packed with expat yuppies and local *artistes*, some of whom come here to people watch, others to tuck into value-for-money grub, some for the staggering array of beers and spirits, all to soak up the café's easy-going vibes.

14 rue St Boniface, Ixelles (East) ☎ 02.511.13.67 Ⓜ Porte de Namur

De Vagant ♱off map

Don't miss this fine example of one of Antwerpen's trad old cafés, especially as De Vagant has 400 different kinds of *jenever* (gin).

25 Reyndersstraat, Antwerpen ☎ 03.233.15.38 by rail

Vooruit ♱off map

Culture vultures congregate at the Art Nouveau building, erected as a workers' cultural centre and now the city's main avant-garde arts venue; the café's decor is sparse and proletarian, although the switched-on punters are anything but.

23 St-Pietersnieuwstraat, Gent ☎ 09.223.82.01 by rail

☆ ZEBRA ♱E2

Small, old, and eclectic: world music of the Peter Gabriel/Sting variety dominates, with a clientele that looks well acquainted with the joys of ganja. Panini and other light fare are served, and there's a large terrace area for people-watching.

35 place St-Géry, Ste-Catherine ☎ 02.511.09.01 Ⓜ Bourse

chinese

☆ LA CANTONNAISE
off map

Fast but still special, this lunchtime favourite hums in the evening, serving quality Chinese tasties.

110 rue Tenbosch, Ixelles (West) ☎ 02.344.70.42 🚌 93, 94 ®F–®F®F

Chinoise-Riz
E11

A dark and atmospheric eaterie packed with Chinese folk tucking into sizzling platters of seafood and punters worrying about the unfeasibly large knives wielded by the chefs.

94 rue de l'Aqueduc, Ixelles (West) ☎ 02.534.91.08 Ⓜ Hôtel des Monnaies ®F–®F®F

french

À Table
B3

For dinner-proper, try upscale À Table, which has an elegant dining room serving typical French cuisine prepared with flourish. Some of the seating comes from old cinemas.

290 rue Royale, St-Josse & Schaerbeek ☎ 02.223.48.68 Ⓜ Botanique ®F–®F®F®F

Le Bermuchet
E6

Chef Pascal Fellemans also does a take on French cuisine for a young, trendy clientele. Specialities include ostrich, and spaghetti Bermuchet, with a sauce of ham, cream and Fellemans' special secret spices.

198 rue Haute, Les Marolles ☎ 02.513.88.82 Ⓜ Loiuse ®F–®F®F

Het Blauwe Huis
off map

Excellent French cuisine always draws the crowds here.

17 Drabstraat, Gent ☎ 09.233.10.09 by rail

Bonsoir Clara
D1

This restaurant's cutting-edge interior makes it worth a visit in itself. Set smack in the middle of trendy Ste-Catherine, stylish and arty types squabble over the tightly squeezed tables, thanks to the excellent modern French and Italian cuisine. Don't leave without trying the puff pastry filled with a spiced biscuit mousse or the oven-baked apples. It's far better than most Brussels' restaurants for vegetarians. Book ahead at weekends.

22–26 rue Antoine Dansaert, Ste-Catherine ☎ 02.502.09.90 Ⓜ Bourse ®F®F–®F®F®F

Les Brasseries Georges *⌀off map*

The red velvet curtains at its entrance set the affected tone of this Paris-style brasserie. Not surprisingly then, its clientele mainly comprises the well-heeled professionals living in Uccle, just to the south. Red meat features strongly on the menu, although shellfish, oysters, and other *fruits de mer* are also recommended. Vegetarians beware: you might have to make do with a plate of mushrooms and chips.

259 avenue Winston Churchill, Ixelles (West) ☎ **02.647.21.00** 🚊 **23, 90** ⒷⒻ ⒷⒻ–ⒷⒻⒷⒻⒷⒻ

Les Capucines *⌀B10*

High in quality and innovation, the Phillipe Starck-designed Les Capucines is all dark wood and blue lighting. The fine cuisine is French in flavour and hot on sauces that are unmatched anywhere else in town. The place attracts business people, rich ladies, as well as foodies. The old adage 'you get what you pay for' is all too true here in the evenings, but catch a table for lunch and it's far better value.

22 rue Jourdan, St-Gilles ☎ **02.538.69.24** Ⓜ **Louise** ⒷⒻⒷⒻⒷⒻ

☆ CHELSEA *⌀D10*

The Chelsea serves high-quality French cuisine and offers garden dining for balmy, summer evenings, a wide-ranging menu, and an excellent wine list. Supporters of its footballing namesake are probably the last people you'll encounter in this restaurant-cum-wine bar. Decorated with a curious mix of oriental carpets and minimalist modern paintings, it is capped by a smoking room (a wide range of Cuban cigars is available), where patrons are welcome to unwind after a hefty feed. The menu is French, with foie gras, beef (from Argentina) and salmon (from Scotland) featuring heavily.

85 chaussée de Charleroi, St-Gilles ☎ **02.544.19.77** 🚊 **92** ⒷⒻ ⒷⒻ–ⒷⒻⒷⒻ

☆ CHEZ MARIE *⌀E12*

This is the place if you're ready for an assault on the taste buds, and don't mind forking out for it. Although part of the ultra-trendy Kasbah and Bonsoir Clara stable (it was started up by the same guy), this local restaurant is smaller and more intimate than its downtown siblings. The largely French cuisine is meticulously prepared, and the wine list one of the finest in the city.

40 rue Alphonse de Witte, Ixelles (East) ☎ **02.644.30.31** 🚊 **71, 36** ⒷⒻ ⒷⒻ–ⒷⒻⒷⒻ

Chez Moi   *♪D7*
Classy, modern and efficient, with friendly staff and honest authentic French country cooking.
66 rue du Luxembourg, Quartier Européen ☎ 02.280.26.66 Ⓜ Trône
ⒷⒻ ⒷⒻ ⒷⒻ

☆ **COMME CHEZ SOI**   *♪C6*
At the top end of the market: a three-star Michelin restaurant and possibly the best in Brussels. Its Art Nouveau interior is as delicious as the French food they serve, which is prepared to perfection by master chef Pierre Wynants, with an excellent wine cellar to boot. The name means 'like you're at home', but the prices are anything but. It revels in its reputation, but getting a hip operation is quicker than securing a table here. However, the French food is without blemish. If it's haute cuisine you're after, you can't get any hauter. For expense accounts, special occasions and pure hedonism, this is quite simply the best.
23 place Rouppé, Central ☎ 02.512.29.21 Ⓜ Anneessens ⒷⒻ–ⒷⒻⒷⒻⒷⒻ

☆ **LA DÉCOUVERTE**   *♪E6*
Framed butterfly prints on clean white walls are a cute touch here. There is one set menu nightly: take it or leave it. That might seem a tad arrogant, but it pulls it off for two reasons – the food is French and is always excellent.
26 rue de l'Épée, Le Sablon ☎ 02.513.43.11 🚋 20, 48 ⒷⒻ

☆ **DE LA VIGNE À L'ASSIETTE**   *♪C11*
Another local joint whose reputation has spread far and wide. The name means 'from the vine to the plate', and the food is always as fresh as the pale-lemon colour scheme. Pricey, but worth splashing out for the adventurous combinations of modern French cuisine on offer.
51 rue Longue Haie, Ixelles (East) ☎ 02.647.68.03 🚋 92; Ⓜ Loiuse
ⒷⒻ ⒷⒻ–ⒷⒻ ⒷⒻ ⒷⒻ

☆ **LES DEUX FRÈRES**   *♪off map*
Although some distance from the centre, this expensive restaurant is frequently packed, and especially popular for corporate dinner parties. While multi-era images of the female nude cling to its walls, there's nothing seedy about it. Waiters are almost annoyingly helpful, not even allowing you to pour your own wine. Fish, fowl, and beef feature heavily, with all the dishes (like veal sautéed with calamari and olives) immaculately presented.
2 avenue Vanderaey, Uccle ☎ 02.376.76.06 🚋 55 ⒷⒻⒷⒻ

L'École Buissonnière ♭B3

This restaurant, whose name means 'playing truant', was once a youth hostel canteen. Its owner, Alain Corbion, has kept up the the laid-back vibe, and prides himself on the informal food and atmosphere. Packed with local business folk looking for a quick fix, it's renowned for fast service (a record 17 minutes for the 3-course lunch). Alain gets your measure on the house wine, too, leaving a litre on the table and charging by the centimetre (even emptying the bottle works out cheap). In the evening, a young, international crowd chats across the wooden tables whilst tucking into one of 12 special salads, or a wide range of bargain fish and meat. Playing hooky was never this good.

13 rue Traversière, St-Josse & Schaerbeek ☎ 02.217.01.65 Ⓜ Botanique ⓑⒻ–ⓑⒻⓑⒻ

Le Gourmandin ♭E6

Le Gourmandin takes itself very seriously. And so it should: the food is as refined as its dining room is intimate, thanks to master chef Jean-Bernard van Hauw, renowned for his way with cod and monkfish.

152 rue Haute, Les Marolles ☎ 02.512.98.92 Ⓜ Hôtel des Monnaies ⓑⒻⓑⒻ

☆ L'IDIOT DU VILLAGE ♭C6

Has the royal seal of approval: Queen Paola has eaten Alain Gascoin's creative interpretations of French mainstays like rabbit and raisins, and tuna grilled with artichokes. Fantastic food and a relaxed atmosphere lead to protracted nights of gossip and laughter in this favoured haunt of celebs. In the scarlet warmth of walls covered with flea-market paintings, relaxed staff hum along to French film soundtracks. The food, while elaborate, remains earthy. The rabbit and leek stew respects its ingredients and, bizarrely, a lightly salted meringue with ice cream and caramel sauce works blissfully.

19 rue Notre Seigneur, Les Marolles ☎ 02.502.55.82 Ⓜ Hôtel des Monnaies ⓑⒻⓑⒻ–ⓑⒻⓑⒻⓑⒻ

Inada ♭D10

Elegant surroundings, outstanding, beautifully arranged food, and fine wines are top priorities at Inada, an expensive but exquisite French restaurant named after its Japanese chef/proprietor, who often emerges from the kitchen at the end of a hard night's cooking to mingle and chat with his guests. Delicate Eastern influences grace both the light spacious interior and the menu.

73 rue de la Source, St-Gilles ☎ 02.538.01.13 Ⓜ Hôtel des Monnaies ⓑⒻⓑⒻⓑⒻ

Kapsiki   *♪off map*

Named after an African tribe, Kapsiki has a New York Soho feel thanks to its radiant silver walls. The chef is as much at ease with classic French cooking as he is with world food.

34–36 Parijsstr, Leuven ☎ 016.20.45.87 by rail

Lola   *♪D6*

This elegant, long-roomed restaurant serves French brasserie-style cuisine with a lightness and delicacy that seems fitting for its stylish clientele. Rumour has it that this was Georgio Armani's regular lunchtime spot when he was overseeing the finishing touches of his Emporio Armani store a couple of doors down. Brasserie classics like rabbit and duck are served with a creative twist and delicate fragrant sauces. Mouth-watering salads and fish dishes, as well as some vegetarian options, are also available.

33 place du Grand Sablon, Le Sablon ☎ 02.514.24.60 Ⓜ Centrale ⑱⑲

☆ LE PAIN ET LE VIN   *♪off map*

The trail to suburbia ends, in summertime, with aperitifs on Le Pain et le Vin's leafy terrace. Heading inside to eat, the sparsely stylish dining room purrs with happily munching Belgians. Light courgette mousse, foie gras with a quince chutney, and classic steaks infuse the menu with creativity and breadth. The wine list spans the globe and there's something for all pockets. Savvy staff offer decent drinking advice, fuelling speculation that their friendliness stems from obligatory wine-tasting.

812 chaussée d'Alsemberg, Uccle ☎ 02.332.37.74 🚃 55 ⑱⑲–⑱⑲⑳

☆ LE PETIT BOXEUR   *♪E2*

Gets the balance right between atmosphere and appetite: the decor is 1930s sleek with rococo Roman flourishes. Wild pigeon (not from the street, they promise), snails, and nettles make it onto the menu, along with more traditional edibles like duck and salmon done up in French-Italiano style.

3 rue Borgval, Ste-Catherine ☎ 02.511.40.00 Ⓜ Bourse ⑱⑲–⑱⑲⑳

☆ RICOTTA & PARMESAN   *♪F2*

Rustic, but calculatedly so, this restaurant marries French refinement with robust Italian dishes. The redwood interior features plate-glass displays of vintage cooking utensils, in keeping with the faux-peasant appeal. Choice dishes are salmon with buffalo mozzarella and veal *pappardelle*.

31 rue de l'Ecuyer, Central ☎ 02.502.80.82 Ⓜ Centrale ⑱–⑱⑲

Les Salons de L'Atalaïde
♭D10

Few establishments reward the eyes on first sight more than the kasbah-styled Les Salons de L'Atalaïde, with its Italian-influenced French menu. Opulent drapes, murals, and candlelights scale down the baroque grandeur of this former auction hall to an intimate level. Among the highlights on the menu are the Irish entrecôte with Roquefort sauce and the fillet steak with marrow bone.

89 chaussée de Charleroi, St-Gilles ☎ 02.537.21.54 Ⓜ Hôtel des Monnaies ⒷⒻⒷⒻⒷⒻ

Totem
♭A6

A popular nexus for Brussels' gay population, where the menu is more modern European – south of France and Tuscany redone to fit an international palate. The house speciality is *vitello à la Claudine* (finely sliced veal with charlotte potatoes in chervil, garlic, and coriander). The restaurant doubles as a gallery space, with exhibits changing often.

6 rue des Grands Carmes, Central ☎ 02.513.11.52 Ⓜ Anneessens ⒷⒻ–ⒷⒻⒷⒻ

☆ TOUR D'Y VOIR
♭D6

Bare-brick-walled decor is so seven years ago, but Tour d'y Voir is a 14th-century abbey – so it's forgiven. Flattering lighting, French cuisine and an ambience so intimate it feels illicit. Adventurous folk order the chef's surprise: you don't know what you're getting until it arrives on your table. Sort of like Russian roulette. Stained-glass windows and cherubic paintings lend an ecclesiastic feel to this luxurious restaurant, where diners often sport the latest Gucci or Armani numbers. Duck, beef, pork, salmon – even walrus – are among the varied delights on the menu. No main-course vegetarian options are listed, although meat-free dishes can be prepared on request. The wine list is superb, though pricey.

6 place du Grand' Sablon, Le Sablon ☎ 02.511.40.43 🚃 92, 93, 94 ⒷⒻⒷⒻ–ⒷⒻⒷⒻ

frites

☆ LA BARRIÈRE ST-GILLES
♭F9

Bruxellois always opt for the *friterie* on the Barrière.

3 chaussée d'Alsemberg, St-Gilles ☎ 02.538.34.48 Ⓜ Horta ⒷⒻ

Maison d'Antoine
♭F8

The best chips in Brussels? Expats certainly seem to think so.

1 place Jourdan, Quartier Européen ☎ 02.230.54.56 🚃 80 ⒷⒻ

Balthazar 　　　　　　　　　　　　　　　　　　　*E13*

Balthazar has kept the feel of a house but with an ultra-modern look. The food is French fused with Pacific; a traditional base spiced up by look and flavour, such as scampi risotto with *galangal* or calf's liver with ginger and soya.

63 rue Archimède, Quartier Européen ☎ 02.742.06.00 Ⓜ Schuman
ⒷⒻⒼⒻ

Farine's Food & Future 　　　　　　　　　　　　*off map*

Seats everybody together at one big table and spoils them for choice with an array of world cuisines.

40 Vlaamse Kaai, Antwerpen ☎ 03.238.37.76 by rail

Fast Food/Global Design 　　　　　　　　　　　*off map*

Trendy and homey, with an open fire in winter; in summer you can wine and dine on the canal.

36 Jan Breydelstraat, Gent ☎ 09.225.29.41 by rail

Funky Soul Potato 　　　　　　　　　　　　　　*off map*

Tuck into a Soul Fingers ratatouille or a Boogie Wonder Lamb.

76 Volkstraat, Antwerpen ☎ 03.257.07.44 by rail

Grand Café Leroy 　　　　　　　　　　　　　　*of map*

Lives up to its name in terms of both food (mostly fusion) and decor.

49 Kasteelpleinstraat, Antwerpen ☎ 03.226.11.99 by rail

Ici-Même 　　　　　　　　　　　　　　　　　　　*E6*

An even more eclectic menu is on offer here, where you don't need to plump for just one dish: its global tapas menu means the 480BF special of the house includes a taste of seven dishes from around the world.

204 rue Haute, Les Marolles ☎ 02.502.54.24 Ⓜ Louise Ⓑⓕ

La Manufacture 　　　　　　　　　　　　　　　　*F1*

Something of a showplace: it's the former workhouse of Delvaux, Belgium's answer to Louis Vuitton. The space is all rich woods and metal rendered in linear chic, with enough warmth to save it from feeling like a museum. Sushi nibbles, ostrich *carpaccio* and langoustine ravioli are some of the worldly items on the ever-changing menu, one of the more expensive ones on this side of town.

12 rue Notre Dame du Sommeil, Ste-Catherine ☎ 02.502.25.25 Ⓜ Bourse ⒷⒻⒼⒻ

☆ LE LIVING ROOM
D10

For a touch of snob value, impress your date with the upscale decor at Le Living Room. The bold menu is varied and includes fried red mullet with anchovy paste, as well as sashimi and sushi. And if that's not eclectic enough, you can finish with an assorted dish of Le Living Room desserts (think tiramisu with strawberries, or home-made upside-down apple pie). With its fantasy baroque decor, low tables with armchairs, candelabras, seductive lighting, and blood red and purple walls, you'd be forgiven for thinking you'd just stepped into a Peter Greenaway film set.

50 chaussée de Charleroi, St-Gilles ☎ **02.534.44.34** 🚊 **92** ⑧⑧–⑧⑧⑧

☆ L112
E11

Simple and unfussy, this fuses the best of French and Far Eastern cuisine and serves it up to an affluent thirtysomething crowd. It is a hidden jewel on the Brussels restaurant trail, and an easy one to miss if you're not in the know. The decor and fragrant garden area hint at an individual spirit; this charm is reflected in the cuisine, prepared by chef Bernard André. A delicate alchemy of flavours is in every dish: grilled prawns with saffron and red peppercorns, chicken with lemon and honey, or chocolate mousse with a hint of cinnamon, served with bittersweet redcurrants.

112 rue Lesbroussart, Ixelles (East) ☎ **02.640.83.43** 🚊 **92, 93, 94** ⑧⑧

greek (see also mediterranean)

Ouzerie
D11

The Ouzerie is another place where it's best to order meze. The food in this inexpensive Greek joint is excellent, the service impeccable and the sound of Greek voices reassuring. Don't expect plate-smashing or cheesy music though – owner Stefanos Svanias is way too classy for that.

235 chaussée d'Ixelles, Ixelles (East) ☎ **02.646.44.49** Ⓜ **Porte de Namur** ⑧⑧–⑧⑧⑧

Parnassos
E2

Near the Grand' Place, it serves kebabs, meze, and the ubiquitous moussaka.

29 rue au Beurre, Central ☎ **02.512.03.95** Ⓜ **Bourse** ⑧

Restaurant Thassos
B9

Cheap and cheerful Greek joint which specializes in *petits os* (spare ribs) for 200BF.

118 chaussée de Forest, St-Gilles ☎ **02.537.26.53** ⑧⑧

STROFILIA $♭C2$

skips the Apollo statues and fake grapevine decor and has a dramatic 17th-century wine cellar that adds ambiance. Thirty Greek wines are served in the striking bare-brick dining room at ground level, along with Greek mainstays like grilled squid, baked figs with walnuts and sesame, and yes, moussaka, but all a notch above normal Greek fare. Stefanos Svanias had already established his reputation with the Ouzerie. But not content to rest on his vine leaves, he now runs this stunner of a Greek restaurant. Built in the remnants of an old pig market, the tiled and terracotta'd front room gives way to a New York-style brick and stone floor loft at the back. The menu is heavy on meze (although there is a small selection of large main courses available), encouraging sharing among friends. And the wines are all Greek – no cheapo retsinas here, these vintages are handpicked. Efficient service and a pride in pleasing the punters make this restaurant popular with a relaxed, youngish crowd in the evenings.

**8 rue du Marché aux Porcs, Ste-Catherine ☎ 02.512.32.93
Ⓜ Ste-Catherine ⒷⒻ–ⒷⒻⒷⒻ**

ealthfood and organic cafés

De Blauwe Zon $♭off map$

If you've got cash to blow (on an organic steak, maybe), this is the place to go.

5 Tiensestraat, Leuven ☎ 016.22.68.80 by rail

De Lotus $♭off map$

For a health fix, De Lotus is the place. But you only have the choice of one organic dish at lunch.

Wapenmakersstraat, Brugge ☎ 050.033.10.78 by rail

Indian

Amarkali $♭F7$

If you prefer a more carnivorous eastern experience, pitch up at this Pakistani joint and jostle for a table. You can eat as much chicken *bhuna* and lamb tandoori as you like for less than 500BF. They'll also throw in a dessert and coffee for those who have the room.

8 rue de la Longue Vie, Ixelles (East) ☎ 02.513.02.05 Ⓜ Porte de Namur ⒷⒻⒷⒻ

★ LA PORTE DES INDES
♭off map

Easily the poshest Indian restaurant in town. The dishes are from the French, not British, former colonies and the emphasis is quite firmly on seafood. Run by the well-established Blue Elephant chain of Thai restaurants, La Porte des Indes equals its sister restaurants in quality (and cost). The menu boasts dishes from the former French colonies of South India, with an inclination towards seafood rather than curry. Like most of the restaurants along avenue Louise, it attracts a bourgeois clientele, with no expense spared on decorative canopies and gilded images of Hindu deities. Buffets are laid on every Thursday and Saturday evenings for the less well-banked to sample the finer side of life.

455 avenue Louise, Ixelles (West) ☎ **02.647.86.51** 🚋 **93, 94** ⓑⒻ ⒷⒻ–ⒷⒻⒷⒻ

Raj
♭off map

Somewhat more exotic, at least for Belgian palates, the flock-free Raj is all cushions, red velvet and mysterious candlelight, and the food is luscious and authentic Indian (closed Mondays).

43a Kraanlei, Gent ☎ **09.225.18.95** **by rail**

italian (see also pasta & pizza)

Ciao
♭D6

Make sure you reserve a good week in advance for Ciao: it's hard to get a table at this little Italian eaterie. The food is classic Italian served in a clean, white-table-clothed setting.

28 rue Joseph Stevens, Le Sablon ☎ **02.513.03.23** Ⓜ **Centrale** ⒷⒻ–ⒷⒻⒷⒻ

Convivio
♭E11

A popular trattoria famed for its inexpensive antipasti and sizzling grilled fish. Unfortunately, the two sisters who run it are equally famed for their erratic service.

6 rue de l'Aqueduc, Ixelles (West) ☎ **02.539.32.99** Ⓜ **Louise**
ⒷⒻ ⒷⒻ–ⒷⒻⒷⒻ

Cosi
♭off map

An altogether more traditional Italian ristorante. The food isn't cheap, but the extensive range of grilled vegetable entrées and adventurous pasta dishes is of top quality. It also has a cheaper sister restaurant – Pizza Cosi – several doors down the street.

95 rue Américaine, Ixelles (West) ☎ **02.534.85.86** Ⓜ **Louise** ⒷⒷⒻⒷ

Crèche des Artistes ♪B11

though it's tiny inside, don't be surprised if there's a fleet of Mercs
tside: the chef has quite a fan club among moneyed food buffs.
rue de la Crèche, Ixelles (East) ☎ 02.511.22.56 Ⓜ Porte de Namur
⑧⑨

nieli il Divino ♪off map

tch those francophone tastes and focus on Italian flavours here.
e seafood is to die for, as are the Art Deco interior and the garden.
Beukenlaan, Antwerpen ☎ 03.825.37.38 by rail

Dieu des Caprices ♪E13

e of Brussels' classics; a typical Italian menu in a very Italian setting.
rue Archimède, Quartier Européen ☎ 02.736.41.16 Ⓜ Schuman ⑧⑨⑧

LA FIN DE SIÈCLE ♪off map

e clientele is well-heeled and a table quite difficult to get. But the
lian food is top-notch, the baroque decor suitably OTT, and the
rden a treat in summer.
avenue Louise, Ixelles (West) ☎ 02.648.80.41 ⊟ 92, 93, 94 ⑨–⑧⑨

Mezzogiorno ♪off map

you're talking Italian, Il Mezzogiorno is waiting, with bright-
loured walls and extravagant antipasti.
Baudelokaai, Gent ☎ 09.224.33.29 by rail

no a Mano ♪F7

ways packed, but once you've tasted their crisp pizzas and
venturous pastas, you'll know why.
ue St-Boniface, Ixelles (East) ☎ 02.502.08.01 Ⓜ Porte de Namur
⑧–⑧⑨⑧

rbacco ♪F10

r country Italian cooking, head to Perbacco, a relaxed, no-frills
nteen-style resto where the menu changes daily.
chaussée de Charleroi, St-Gilles ☎ 02.537.67.99 Ⓜ Hôtel des
nnaies ⑧⑨⑧

tto Ripa ♪C8

lk into the theatre set that is Sotto Ripa and enjoy modern Italian
d amongst the dripping candles and outrageous drapes.
rue du Luxembourg, Quartier Européen ☎ 02.230.01.18 Ⓜ Trône
⑧⑧

restaurants and cafés

☆ SAMOURAI ♪F2

Opinion varies on whether the interior of this Japanese restaurant i Zen minimalist or just plain unimaginative. Three small room stacked on top of each other mean you have to tuck your elbows in But despite its size, the restaurant is crammed with a raft of chef who turn out the freshest sushi, tempura and sashimi, with imagi native menu combinations. An impressive French wine list at ever more impressive prices should entice you to go native and stick with the saké. Tucked into a passageway, Samourai has a loyal following o local regulars. This is easily the best Japanese resto in town.
28 rue du Fossé aux Loups, Central ☎ 02.217.56.39 Ⓜ De Brouckère
ⒺⒻ–ⒺⒻⒺⒻ

Wasabi ♪D6

The latest hot resto serving sashimi, sushi, and other Japanese faves with a slight hint of fusion. The decor looks more like a magazine spread: prism coloured walls here, zebra-print banquettes there, and a trolley on the ba leading back to the kitchen. It's very impressive and pretty inviting.
12 rue Joseph Stevens, Le Sablon ☎ 02.511.96.93 Ⓜ Centrale

Yamato ♪E7

Always packed with Japanese businessmen and students, but it' worth the wait for the enormous bowls of pork and noodle soup, an the delicious ravioli-like *gyoshi*.
11 rue Francart, Ixelles (East) ☎ 02.502.28.93 Ⓜ Porte de Namur ⒺⒻ–ⒺⒻⒺ

☆ YAMAYU SANTATSU ♪B11

There's no messing around with Chef Yu Aoki. After all, you are in one of the best sushi restaurants in Belgium. The Brussels-base Japanese community spreads its wings here: just check out the whisky bottles labelled with the company's names. Have Yo Sushi fol lowed by a Japanese ice cream for dessert – and don't forget the saké Book your table ahead or sit at the counter.
141 chaussée d'Ixelles, Ixelles (East) ☎ 02.513.53.12 Ⓜ Porte de Namur ⒺⒻ–ⒺⒻⒺ

jewish

Hoffy's ♪off map

Smack in the middle of the Jewish quarter, kosher fish, meat, an vegetables are the Hoffman brothers' specialities. Hoffy's will tak great pains to explain to you the ins and outs of their cuisine.
52 Lange Kievitstraat, Antwerpen ☎ 03.234.35.35 by rail

BONSOIR CLARA *♪E2*

Downtown's ultra-chic set head here for spiced baby duckling and mustard marrow broth with egg, mushrooms, and bacon, and other exotic dishes. Jazz and soft Latin provide the soundtrack, while a patchwork quilt of stained glass provides a technicolour backdrop.

rue Antoine Dansaert, Ste-Catherine ☎ 02.502.09.90 Ⓜ Bourse
⑧–⑧⑧

Chez Fred *♪off map*

Down-to-earth Mediterranean dishes at decent prices.
Kloosterstraat, Antwerpen ☎ 03.257.14.71 by rail

La Cour des Miracles *♪F5*

Better known for its kaleidoscopic kitsch decor. The ground floor is a bar with a red baby grand piano, a dance floor, seashells, harps, and a pool with carp and bass with a chandelier hanging over it. The first floor has dining rooms serving Mediterranean, Middle Eastern and North African cuisine – fancy a little couscous with lamb? Veal kebabs? Baklava? And the second floor is a tearoom à la Aladdin: several candle-lit areas with plush seating surrounded by dazzling throw cushions.

rue de l'Hectolitre, Les Marolles ☎ 02.513.92.94 Ⓜ Porte de Hal ⑧

La Découverte *♪E6*

As tiny and friendly as Mum's front room; you get what you're given and don't complain at this intimate joint. Not that there'd be reason to – the set menu is pieced together from the best that markets and farms have to offer that day. Where choice is lacking, quality and imagination step in. Raspberries on tender duck, for example, are lip-smackingly good. Vegetarians are not a problem to the chefs-cum-waiters, amazingly for Brussels. Phone, ask what's on today, and reserve your table.

rue de L'Epée, Le Sablon ☎ 02.513.43.11 Ⓜ Louise ⑧–⑧⑧

Fils de Jules *♪off map*

New York hits Brussels via France and Spain in this trendy 1930s retro bisto. Sporting the latest in black, the staff bring Basque influences to the tables set with knife, fork, and (often) mobile phone. Impenetrable names for dishes belie the honesty and flair in the cooking (which is big on foie gras and fish). At lunch, business folk do their deals; in the evening, a disposable-income set takes over. All yes, all professional, all-inspiring.

rue du Page, Ixelles (West) ☎ 02.534.00.57 🚋 92, 93, 94 ⑧⑧

☆ LA FIN DE SIÈCLE   *♪off map*

La Fin's cuisine is more eclectic: pasta, mezze, falafel, and other Mediterranean and North African dishes pop up often. Fish cooked so delicately it melts on the tongue and pasta al dente are winners. Baroque rules in this candlelit, red-velvet-decked townhouse. But don't let this mislead you – there's no need to get out your gold card. A young and stylish crowd gathers for fine Italian dishes (think aubergines and parmesan with a tomato coulis), topped off with exquisite gelatos. In summer, a tranquil garden serves as the perfect background for romantic endeavours. If you don't book ahead, you'll be shown the door, so try its sister on avenue de l'Armée.
423 avenue Louise, Ixelles (West) ☎ 02.648.80.41 🚊 92, 93, 94 ⓑⒻ–ⓑⒻⒻ

☆ LA FIN DE SIÈCLE   *♪E2*

La Fin de Siècle is the place to head for if you want home-grown atmosphere in this area of high trend. In the afternoon, locals play chess; in the evenings, this rustic bistro with roughly painted walls and old wooden tables can fill to bursting point with all types. The menu is varied, offering tandoori chicken alongside *tabouli*. Belgian specialities include rabbit with cherry beer and *stoemp* (potato and vegetable mash with country sausages). No relation to the La Fin de Siècle on avenue Louise.
9 rue des Chartreux, Ste-Catherine ☎ 02.513.51.23 Ⓜ Bourse ⓑⒻ–ⓑⒻⒻ

Ombre et Soleil   *♪off map*

To forget Belgium's wintry chills, warm up with some Mediterranean food at Ombre et Soleil – best to sit by the open fire upstairs.
20 Muntstraat, Leuven ☎ 016.22.51.87 by rail

Senza Nome   *♪off map*

Reserve a table before trekking to this cosy St-Josse restaurant – it gets very busy, especially when audiences from the nearby Halles de Schaerbeek come for a post-show feed. The menu changes regularly and depends on the freshest ingredients available (try the sautéed mushrooms for a full-on taste sensation), resulting in a wide selection of light, tangy dishes bursting with flavour (like the veal in the *tagliata di filetto*). Tomato heaven. But a non-smoker's hell.
22 rue Royale Ste-Marie, St-Josse & Schaerbeek ☎ 02.223.16.17 🚊 92, 93 ⓑⒻⒻ–ⓑⒻⒻ

À Toi Mauricette (ATM)   *♪B10*

A popular, informal lunchtime place: a bright, contemporary space where you can munch on inventive, Mediterranean-style salads (the dressings are divine) and light snacks.
29 chaussée de Charleroi ☎ 02.534.70.18 Ⓜ Louise ⓑⒻⓑⒻ–ⓑⒻⒻ

mexican

MONKEY BUSINESS
♪C11

raucous anglophone expat drinking den off avenue Louise. though trying a bit too hard to be an all-American sports bar, the rumptious Tex-Mex fare more than compensates.
● rue Defacqz, Ixelles (West) ☎ 02.538.69.34 Ⓜ Louise

ablo's
♪C7

jitas, tortillas, and other favourites are served in the large, open, d very noisy dining room to an international crowd. Generous rtions of food make up for the thimble-sized margaritas.
rue de Namur, Le Sablon ☎ 02.502.41.35 Ⓜ Porte de Namur ⓑ

iiddle eastern

Barmaki
♪B6

banese resto Al Barmaki allows you to sample various specialities from e homeland of the Kalach family, who have been running it for three cades now. Chicken kebabs, fried aubergine, and other meze are meant be eaten with your fingers, as is the wide selection of veggie dishes.
rue des Eperonniers, Central ☎ 02.513.08.34 Ⓜ Centrale ⓑ

xpress
♪B6

banese-run L'Express serves refreshingly unfatty pittas with gener- s falafels, meat, or chicken fillings, lashings of mixed salad, and sty garlic sauce. It's always crowded, but the service is good and fast.
rue des Chapeliers, Central ☎ 02.512.88.83 Ⓜ Centrale ⓑ

ORIENTALIA
♪off map

me say this is the best Lebanese in Europe. Others just appreciate e range of cheap tasty dishes.
9 chaussée de Mons, Anderlecht ☎ 02.520.75.75 Ⓜ Anneessens ⓑ

LES PYRAMIDES
♪C12

der a tableful of Egyptian and Lebanese dishes, such as *tabouleh* or lafel, sit back and, if it's the weekend, watch the belly-dancer shake r stuff. Despite the tacky images adorning its window, this is an cellent place for Egyptian and Lebanese food. Couscous and mixed ills are among the main-course specialities; but the meze is the best tion. It tends to get crowded on weekend evenings, when a belly- ncer delights diners, but service still remains efficient and friendly.
8 chaussée d'Ixelles, Ixelles (East) ☎ 02.644.03.55 ▯ 71 Ⓜ Porte de amur ⓑ–ⓑⓑ

restaurants and cafés

Art Sauvage
F7

Decadent, but not pricey, this is a magical Moroccan restaurant; *tajines*, couscous, and *pastilla* are authentic and the rich red interior brings a splash of warmth.

12 rue de Naples, Ixelles (East) ☎ **02.513.68.85** Ⓜ **Porte de Namur** ⓑⓕ–ⓑⓕⓑⓕⓑⓕ

Aux Mille & Une Nuits
C10

A Tunisian couscous joint with a fantastically kitsch Arabian Nights interior, it's the place for a young and vibrant Congolese/North African crowd.

7 rue de Moscou, St-Gilles ☎ **02.537.41.27** Ⓜ **Parvis St-Gilles** ⓑⓕ ⓑⓕ ⓑⓕ

Beni Znassen
D9

One of Brussels' most authentic Moroccan restaurants. Started around 25 years ago as a local café, it used to give away free couscous on Friday nights. With the unstoppable growth of its reputation, the place slowly transformed into a restaurant. But it's still cheap, which is why this St-Gilles institution remains a favourite haunt of students, artists, and the local Moroccan community.

81 rue de l'Église, St-Gilles ☎ **02.534.11.94** Ⓜ **Parvis St-Gilles** ⓑⓕ ⓑⓕ–ⓑⓕ ⓑⓕ ⓑⓕ

☆ EL YASMINE
C11

With its Arabian-Nights decor, this is a great traditional North African joint, and you won't find a fresher mint tea or tastier Tunisian salad this side of the Sahara. It's hard to know what to put top of the list at this Moroccan/Tunisian restaurant: good prices, tasty food, the Bedouin decor, or the friendly service. El Yasmine offers all this in a picture-postcard setting. It's tasty, it's fun (with great music) and even the plates are for sale (they'll provide clean ones). Since moving to this new location, the *tajines*, couscous, and delightfully fresh salads seem even tastier. Finish off with an invigorating mint tea.

7 rue Defacqz, Ixelles (East) ☎ **02.647.51.81** 🚃 **92, 93, 94** ⓑⓕ–ⓑⓕ ⓑⓕ

☆ KASBAH
E2

A sky of Moroccan lamps with red bulbs inside hang from the ceiling making the ambiance as memorable as the menu – try the North African lamb and traditional *tagines* which are out of this world. The Kasbah would be a dark, romantic place to mull over the fine food of North Africa (like couscous *merguez* or chicken *tajine* with lemon) if it wasn't so *crowded*. Being reasonably priced, and in the trendiest street in town, means that elbows have to be tucked in. There's buckets of atmosphere, thanks to the trad Moorish lighting. But it's not very authentic.

20 rue Antoine Dansaert, Ste-Catherine ☎ **02.502.40.26** Ⓜ **Bourse** ⓑⓕ–ⓑⓕ ⓑⓕ

riental (see also chinese, japanese, thai, vietnamese)

i Kegi
♪off map

stylish Oriental canteen. From *ebi tempura* to *chawan moshi*, baked oodles and rice; you name it, they serve it – and at very reasonable prices.
–36 Minderbroedersrui, Antwerpen ☎ 03.213.22.26 by rail

asta & pizza (see also italian)

nanas & Ramanas
♪off map

f the beaten track, but oh-so-trendy, Ananas & Ramanas is an timate joint for salad or pasta.
Vaartstraat, Leuven ☎ 016.22.01.73 by rail

e Grote Avond
♪off map

r more down-to-earth Italian fare, try the spaghetti at De Grote vond, a typical old café with a great outdoor terrace.
Huydevetterskaai, Gent ☎ 09.224.31.21 by rail

Paradiso
♪B6

e ceiling mural of the resto's boss and wife ascending to heaven is kitsch masterpiece, but the food ain't no joke – excellent, freshly ade tortellini, rigatoni, and other pastas.
rue Duquesnoy, Central ☎ 02.512.52.32 Ⓜ Centrale ®

termezzo
♪F2

termezzo also does decent pasta, but its claim to fame is being the sto of choice for the after-opera crowd. Great value for money, it so draws businessmen at lunchtime.
rue des Princes, Central ☎ 02.218.03.11 Ⓜ De Brouckére ®®

i Tango
♪E4

cked into a quiet residential street, Mi Tango, run by Walter from gentina, is the area's best-kept secret. Lunchtimes are buzzy, and ndlelit tables in the evenings are often booked out owing to the eat-value pasta, sangria, and Riojas.
rue de Spa, Quartier Européen ☎ 075.25.27.20 Ⓜ Arts-Loi ®®®

zzeria Mirante
♪E2

r a truly authentic Italian, head straight here. The surliest service in Brus-ls, but they get away with it as they know they've got a good thing going: dividual pizzas done as in Italy, topped with whatever your heart desires.
Plattesteen, Central ☎ 02.511.15.80 Ⓜ Bourse ®

90

restaurants and cafés

☆ SENZA NOME
off map

If freshly prepared pasta is your thing, this is the place. The candy-pink walls border on tacky, but who cares? Chances are you'll keep your eyes on your *plat du jour* in any case.

22 rue Royale Ste-Marie, St-Josse & Schaebeek ☎ 02.223.16.17 ⊞ 92, 93 ⊛⊕⊕

portuguese

Le Forcado
F10

Iberian tastes are satisfied at Le Forcado, a well-established, up-market Portuguese restaurant serving traditional cuisine like great salt cod.

192 chaussée de Charleroi, St-Gilles ☎ 02.537.92.20 Ⓜ Horta ⊛⊛⊛⊕

Mar Bravo
B9

Serves up a Portuguese version of paella that benefits from the large jug of Porto accompanying it.

397 rue Haute, Les Marolles ☎ 02.538.04.14 Ⓜ Porte de Hal ⊕–⊛⊕

russian

Les Ateliers de la Grande Île
A6

If your palate wants to travel a little further, Mother Russia is the inspiration for this popular joint. It has all the weepy romance of Dr Zhivago, thanks in no small party to the 40-odd vodkas served. *Blinis*, *pierogies*, salmon soup, *borscht*, and other Russian specialities also figure on the menu, and a gypsy string trio adds to the atmosphere.

33 rue de la Grande Île, Ste-Catherine ☎ 02.512.81.90 Ⓜ Anneessens ⊛⊕⊕

Au Grand Mayeur
D6

This 17th-century building brings the romance of the Steppes to its dining room, with a nightly gypsy band and a menu of beef stroganoff, *borscht*, and *blinis*. A guilty pleasure – you know it ain't really authentic, but after a few vodkas, who cares?

43 place du Grand Sablon, Le Sablon ☎ 02.512.80.91 Ⓜ Centrale ⊛⊕–⊕⊛⊕

Catherine de Russie
F1

Mixes Russian and French cuisine in a more refined, cobalt-blue setting. In a former nunnery, the resto serves stuffed cabbage, baked potatoes topped with caviar and, what else, vodka.

26 rue des Riches-Claires ☎ 02.502.82.45 Ⓜ Anneessens ⊛⊕⊕

☆ AUX ARMES DE BRUXELLES *F2*

A fave of the late Jacques Brel, this Art Deco stunner has quality seafood at reasonable (but by no means cheap) prices. Lunchtime is more of a bargain, with one standout being the stingray in hazelnut butter cream sauce and capers. In a street overflowing with fish restaurants ready and waiting for the constant flow of tourists, and many eateries overpriced for what they offer, Aux Armes de Bruxelles stands alone. With its old-world charm, high-quality service and cuisine – try baked cod served with spinach, or lobster bisque (the best in town) – it doesn't need to throw the line out. This really is one of Brussels' best fish restaurants, and the one to head for if you find yourself washed up on the shores of rue des Bouchers. Of course, *moules* are on the menu, and you can even have them with mustard sauce.

13 rue des Bouchers, Central ☎ 02.511.55.98/50 Ⓜ De Brouckère ⑨⑧⑨–⑧⑨⑧⑨⑧⑨

☆ LA BELLE MARAÎCHÈRE *C2*

Oysters are the thing here. Run by two Devreker brothers, one of whom is a master chef, it's low on flash but high on quality cuisine. Fish *waterzooi*, the Gent speciality creamy stew of cod, carrots, and potatoes, is cooked to perfection. Slap bang in the middle of the fish district around place Ste-Catherine, this big fish restaurant is run by brothers Freddy and Eddy Devreker, both officially Master Chefs of Belgium. Still a family affair, Freddy's son now does the cooking deeds, which includes a magnificent *marmite des pêcheurs*. Unfettered by fashion, the decor doesn't seem to have changed in 30 years, nor the style of cooking, which is no bad thing. Waiters, young and old, are on hand with seamless service. Serious eating, serious punters, serious prices. A Brussels institution.

11 place Ste-Catherine, Ste-Catherine ☎ 02.512.97.59 Ⓜ Ste-Catherine ⑨⑧⑨–⑧⑨⑧⑨

☆ BIJ DEN BOER *C2*

Less splendiferous. The joint's name means 'at your neighbours'. Big portions are the rule; *boulliabaisse*, monkfish with oyster mushrooms, and scampis are highly recommended. Red-clothed tables in rows, panelled walls, and mussels in steaming casseroles. A classic.

60 quai aux Briques, Ste-Catherine ☎ 02.512.61.22 Ⓜ Ste-Catherine; ser ⑧⑨⑧–⑧⑨⑧⑨

☆ LA BONNE HUMEUR *A13*

Like Au Brabançon (said to be the inspiration of the Belgo chain), La Bonne Humeur is easy to miss: the nondescript window looks like

just any other café. But inside, the place serves some of the city's best *moules et frites* in a diner setting. When you see *Spécialité de Moules* hand-painted in a window, you know you've arrived. 1960s Formica furniture – for real, not retro chic.
244 chaussée de Louvain, St-Josse & Schaerbeek ☎ 02.230.71.69 🚊 59 ⓑⓑ

Jacques ♪C2
Another no-frills affair, with delish seafood; the prawns in garlic butter are worth the aftermath of a snogless evening.
44 quai aux Briques, Ste-Catherine ☎ 02.513.27.62 Ⓜ Ste-Catherine ⓑⓕⓑⓑ

☆ LA MARÉE ♪C2
Down to earth, a true value-for-money seafood joint off the beaten track, but definitely worth beating a path to its door for the marvellous *moules* prepared in lots of ways. Scrubbed-pine interior and fish tanks. A tad more expensive than others, but *moules* afficionados don't care.
99 rue de Flandre, Ste-Catherine ☎ 02.511.00.40 🚊 63 ⓑⓑ

☆ LA QUINCAILLERIE ♪off map
Probably the best-known restaurant in the area thanks to the sumptuous wrought-iron decor and legendary seafood. Some believe the brasserie rests on its laurels, while fleecing customers in the process. Make up your own mind – if you can afford to.
45 rue du Page, Ixelles (West) ☎ 02.538.25.53 🚊 81, 82 Ⓜ Ste-Catherine
ⓑⓑ–ⓑⓑⓑ

Rugbyman ♪C2
Lobster-lovers can choose their meal while it's still alive and crawling at Rugbyman, with two locations on the quai au Briques.
2 quai aux Briques ☎ 02.512.37.60 Ⓜ Ste-Catherine ⓑⓕⓑⓑ

☆ SEA GRILL ♪F2
Purists balk at the idea of going to a 5-star hotel to eat, but push all principles aside and make this place a must-go. Sit in utter luxury among glass-etched Norwegian fjords and marvel at the Christoffle lobster press as it squeezes your *Homard Breton à la Presse* to a mere shadow of its former self. Fêted chef Yves Mattagne, heavily laden with medals, will even sell you his recipes and pictures on CD-Rom. Cushioned waiters, unashamed elegance, two Michelin stars (earned on the back of innovative cooking where fish is prepared to trad meat recipes), and an affordable set menu. Sounds like heaven? It is.
Radisson SAS Hotel, 47 rue du Fossé aux Loups, Central
☎ 02.219.28.28 Ⓜ De Brouckère ⓑⓑⓑⓑ

☆ TAVERNE DU PASSAGE $F2

An Art Deco stunner, is also tops for seafood. Waiters wear white smocks with epaulets and serve huge bowls of *moules et frites* to punters who lounge on leather banquets feeling thoroughly 1920s.
30 Galerie de la Reine, Central ☎ 02.512.37.32 Ⓜ Centrale ⑱

La Truite d'Argent $C2

More of the high-sheen variety: an early 1900s dining room that looks too good to be true, and what's more the crab, lobster and other seafood live up to the snazzy decor.
23 quai au Bois à Brûler, Ste-Catherine ☎ 02.219.95.46 Ⓜ Ste-Catherine ⑱⑱⑱

La Villa Rosa $B9

Located in what was the Spanish quarter, La Villa Rosa has been the place for paella in Brussels for 50 years.
395 rue Haute, Les Marolles ☎ 02.537.33.21 Ⓜ Porte de Hal ⑱–⑱⑱

Visnet $C2

The most recent trendy fish resto is Visnet, the latest offering from Brussels' most successful restauranteur Frederic Nicolay.
23 place Ste-Catherine, Ste-Catherine ☎ 02.218.85.45 Ⓜ Ste-Catherine

spanish

El Madrileño $E13

Intimate El Madrileño is a family-run Spanish eaterie that specializes in paella, *petit cochon de lait*, and *jamón serrano*, plenty of which hangs from the bar. Excellent tortilla too. It lures a mixed crowd of locals and Commission workers.
10 chaussée de Waterloo, St-Gilles ☎ 02.537.69.82 Ⓜ Parvis St-Gilles
⑱⑱–⑱⑱⑱

☆ LE FILS DE JULES $E11

This Starck- and Art Deco-influenced eaterie serves delicious Basque and Landais dishes. The warm foie gras is the size of a bookend and the grilled squid dish big enough to keep an ink factory in business.
35 rue du Page, Ixelles (West) ☎ 02.534.00.57 🚏 92, 93, 94 ⑱⑱

Le Jardin d'Espagne $E13

Frequented by Commission types of all nationalities.
65 rue Archimède, Quartier Européen ☎ 02.736.34.49 Ⓜ Maalbeek
⑱⑱⑱

thai

Le IIème Elément $F7

A modern Thai restaurant with metallic tables, esoteric murals, and sharp lighting. The Thai chefs make authentic, delicious food, and, unusually for a Thai place, inexpensive.

7 rue St-Boniface, Ixelles (East) ☎ 02.502.00.28 Ⓜ Porte de Namur ⓑⓕⓓⓓ

☆ LES LARMES DU TIGRE $E6

The place to go for Thai cuisine. A ceiling of rice-paper parasols cover both smoking and non-smoking dining rooms, and the menu – which includes rice noodles in peanut sauce with chicken, seafood or beef – is a revelation. The Sunday buffet is especially popular, and reservations are a must. Marc Beukers and sibling Muriel have established this Thai restaurant as one of Brussels' best. Walk into the classic townhouse and admire the hundreds of parasols hanging from the ceiling above the clean, white interior. It's all about sleek service and intensely authentic food, with the giant prawns in red curry sauce proving that size really does matter. The lunchtime crowd is professional with a hint of legal; in the evening, there's more of an international buzz. Perfect for hotting up those post-acquittal celebrations.

21 rue Wynants, Les Marolles ☎ 02.512.18.77 Ⓜ Louise ⓑⓕⓑⓕ

Phat Thai $E2

Many excellent southeast Asian restaurants line the rue Jules van Praet, but this is arguably the best. Carved cherrywood trellis and terracotta-tiled floors add authenticity, at least for western eyes. The menu of seafood, chicken, and veggie dishes is in both English and French, taking the Russian roulette aspect out of ordering.

30 rue Jules van Praet, Ste-Catherine ☎ 02.511.82.43 Ⓜ Bourse ⓑⓕⓑⓕ–ⓓⓑⓕⓓ

vegetarian

☆ DEN TEEPOT $F1

Veggie in the bean-and-lentil order of evolution. While wholesomely fibrous, tastiness isn't relinquished.

66 rue des Chartreux, Ste-Catherine ☎ 02.511.94.02 Ⓜ Ste-Catherine ⓓ

☆ DOLMA $C12

The vegetarian buffet at this Tibetan health-food joint is excellent. It's very chilled, with brushed yellow walls, photos of Tibetan monasteries, and piano music in the hall. If you accept that quorn and tofu don't have to be bland, then Dolma could prove a treat. Next to a health food shop, its main attraction is a buffet where you can pile your plate

with as much pasta, salad, and savoury pastries as you like, while still keeping the calorie count low. The choice of puddings is more limited, with chocolate cake and fruit salad the staple fare. The only major flaw is a pianist who makes elevator music sound lively by comparison.
31 chaussée d'Ixelles, Ixelles (East) ☎ 02.649.89.81 🚌71, 81, 82, 366 ⑧⑤–⑧⑤⑧⑤

☆ LA TSAMPA ⚘E11
Has an astonishing selection of imaginative dishes. This is where Yin meets Yang on a plate. Chef Silva Jorge dazzles your taste buds with dishes from all over the world in a down-to-earth setting behind an organic food shop. Have the Tibetan ravioli followed by a Japanese *pot-au-feu*; or why not try the *pirojki* (vegetable and yoghurt in puff pastry)? And don't skip the puddings – the raspberry soufflé or chocolate chestnut cake are just too good to be true. Wash it all down with one of the organic wines.
109 rue de Livourne, Ixelles (West) ☎ 02.647.03.67 🚌93, 94 ⑧⑤–⑧⑤⑧⑤

vietnamese

☆ LA CANTONNAISE ⚘off map
It doubles as a take-away – but the Chinese/Vietnamese über-cheap food is a delight.
10 rue Tenbosch, Ixelles (West) ☎ 02.344.70.42 🚌93, 94 ⑧⑤–⑧⑤⑧⑤

Da Kao ⚘E2
For Vietnamese food, Da Kao is the cheapest resto in the city: a main course of rice and chicken is 120BF, with a three-course meal a little more than double that. Popular with dancers, intellectuals, artists, and anyone else out for a bargain.
38 rue Antoine Dansaert, Ste-Catherine ☎ 02.512.67.16 Ⓜ Bourse ⑧⑤ ⑧⑤–⑧⑤⑧⑤⑧⑤

☆ POUSSIÈRES D'ETOILE ⚘off map
The best in a row of Vietnamese joints on chaussée de Boondael, with its innovative (and cheap) menu. Veggie options in Brussels are few and far between. Twinkling lanterns (normal ones as well as those made out of old oil cans) are everywhere – and it's not only the painstakingly detailed interior that puts this head and shoulders above the rest. Lightly steamed raviolis reveal spiced tender strips of meat, and the shock of finding that deep-fried coconut balls with banana ice cream is actually delicious takes a bit of getting over. There are further surprises at the cash desk – this place is really, really cheap.
37 chaussée de Boondael, Ixelles (East) ☎ 02.640.71.58 🚌93, 94 ⑧⑤

bars

Drinking in Brussels is one of life's pure, unadulterated joys – the variety of bars is dizzying, the opening hours elastic, the price of drinks cheap for a major city, and the beers arguably the best in the world. In fact, the only real dilemma is which watering hole to stagger to next.

club/bars

☆ L'ACROBAT   ♪E2
This self-styled speakeasy plays everything from bossa nova to vintage Michael Jackson. The interior is multicultural kitsch: Indian murals, twinkly lights, and papier mâché squid. Dress to sweat when the dance floor in the back is open (Fri–Sat); it's as well-ventilated as a Turkish steambath.
14 rue Borgval, Ste-Catherine ☎ 02.513.73.08 Ⓜ Bourse

Café Locale   ♪off map
Good if you're not so confident on the dance floor.
25 Waalse Kaai, Antwerpen ☎ 03.238.50.04 by rail

☆ CANOA QUEBRADA   ♪A6
Latinos, Africans and pasty-faced north Europeans all throng to this Brazilian bar to dance samba and down the meanest (and maybe the priciest) *caipirinhas* this side of Rio.
53 Rue du Marché au Charbon, Central ☎ 02.511.13.54 Ⓜ Bourse

☆ CARTAGENA   ♪A6
If you know how to dance salsa and merengue, this tiny Columbian joint is the best place to practice. If you don't, sit at the bar with a *Mojito* in your hand and feast your eyes. It avoids the out-to-get-laid aim by playing salsa – the sounds let you work up a flirtatious sweat on the mini-dancefloor, but the gents know how to take no for an answer.
70 rue du Marché au Charbon, Central ☎ 02.502.59.08 Ⓜ Bourse

☆ LE CERCLE   ♪D6
There's something for everyone in this Sablon bar. Sounds of salsa and the Congo keep the dance floor full at weekends. Other nights run the gamut from world music to jazz, with Sunday afternoons dedicated to Café Philo, excursions into Sartre, Nietzsche, and other

deep thinkers. The crowd is *très* international, especially on Friday and Saturday nights. The pricey *plat du jour* changes daily.
20–22 rue Ste-Anne, Le Sablon ☎ 02.514.03.53 Ⓜ Gare Centrale 🚃 92, 93, 94

El Pablo Disco Bar
🖋*A6*

Major DJs spin a mix of house, ambient and garage at this hyper-trendy bar, but you won't see much dancing. Punters are too busy tucking into shakes, cocktails and 60 kinds of vodka. A lot of Red Bull is drunk as Brussels' beautiful young things liven themselves up for a dance. Ravers waiting for the weekend file in nightly for club-friendly genres, all in a trippy, multicoloured decor.
60 rue du Marché au Charbon, Central ☎ 02.514.51.49 Ⓜ Bourse

drinking dens

☆ L'ATELIER
🖋*off map*

Legendary student hangout (it's next to the university, ULB), with over 200 types of beer, loud music and even louder chit-chat. Sometimes there's live music on; but if not, there are always animated discussions of life and love to get involved in, or games of pinball and table football to watch.
77 rue Elise, Ixelles (East) ☎ 02.649.19.53 🚃 93,94 🚌 74

☆ CHEZ RICHARD
🖋*D6*

A bite-size slice of madness on an otherwise sedate square, Chez Richard is something of an institution for thirtysomething party-goers who still dance on tables and sing along to soppy ballads and rock classics until the wee small hours of the morning. *Très* French indeed.
2 rue des Minimes, Le Sablon ☎ 02.512.14.06 Ⓜ Centrale

☆ COASTER
🖋*E2*

The centrepiece of this small but perfectly formed bar is a giant operating-theatre lamp – and after a boozy night in this barfly's hangout, it might come in handy. Your stamina (and liver) is put to the test by the regulars. Fun-loving DJs and a local crowd who like to party till dawn (it's been known to stay open until gone 8am) make this buzzing bar one of Brussels' best-kept secrets. It boasts its own challenge to your larynx: neon-coloured cocktails served in shakers. Peach Bull, *Mojitos* and Long Island Iced Tea actually resemble colours that occur in nature, but other drinks are so bright they'd show up in an X-ray. With its boat hanging from the ceiling and video projection screen, is more Janet Jackson/Madonna-fan friendly.
28 rue des Riches Claires, Ste-Catherine ☎ 02.512.08.47 Ⓜ Bourse

☆ LE CORBEAU $D2

If you're after a quiet drink, it's best to avoid this boozers' paradise. The music is ear-splitting, the customers young and rowdy, and the beer comes in a chevalier, a half-metre glass that makes taking a sip challenging. If you've never danced on a table to Bonnie Tyler before, this may be the place to make your debut. There's a high tourist element, mixed with locals on the weekend, so proceed with caution.
18–20 rue St Michel, Central ☎ 02.219. 52.46 Ⓜ De Brouckère

Old Hack $B8

With the vast International Press Centre in the heart of the area, many bars are filled with quaffing journos and BBC reporters. This is one such place: a small, simply furnished bar with understated decor and a big following.
176 rue Joseph II, Quartier Européen ☎ 02.230.07.95 Ⓜ Schuman

☆ PORTE NOIRE $C6

For a crash course in Belgian beers, let the barman of this smoky, dimly lit bar be your guide. With a dozen local brews on tap and over 120 in the fridge, your only headache (until the next morning, of course) will be deciding which one to sample first.
67 rue des Alexiens, Les Marolles ☎ 02.511.78.37 Ⓜ Anneessens

☆ ROCK CLASSIC $A6

Though this good-time bar blasts out hard-core music, the atmosphere inside is much gentler. A huge portrait of David Bowie guards the entrance to the black-and-white tiled toilets and most of the customers seem more interested in playing pinball, table football, or chess than playing air guitar to AC/DC. Not as tough as it thinks it is.
55 rue du Marché au Charbon, Central ☎ 02.512.15.42 Ⓜ Bourse

☆ TELS QUELS $A6

There's a relaxed feel to this hub of Brussels' lively gay and lesbian scene. People drift in and out for a beer and a chat, a game of pinball, or simply to find out what's going on elsewhere from the bar's noticeboard.
81 rue du Marché au Charbon, Central ☎ 02.512.32.34 Ⓜ Bourse

Het Waterhuis aan de Bierkant $off map

Beer monsters' heaven, with a splendid canalside terrace and more than 100 beers on offer; the 'menu' provides notionally humourous explanations of each brew in four languages (the jokes are different in each language, though not necessarily more amusing).
9 Groentenmarkt, Gent ☎ 09.225.06.80 by rail

Archiduc ♫E2

Sumptuous Art Deco lounge-bar with slinky stairwell and curvaceous balcony. Try the Georges Simenon cocktail (mainly grapefruit, gin, and campari) in a vibe reminiscent of his *noir* pennings. Sometimes piano players and jazz bands keep punters happy late into the night. At peak times, ring the bell to enter.
5 rue Antoine Dansaert, Ste-Catherine ☎ 02.512.06.52 Ⓜ Bourse

☆ AU SOLEIL ♫A6

Dates back a long time, but at first it was just a tailor's shop. Today, it quenches the thirst of downtown's alternative crowd as well as yuppies slumming it. During the day, this former clothes store is a quiet place to sample local brews and read the paper. But at night a mixed crowd of barflies and artsy locals spills out onto the bar's sprawling terrace on one of the city's liveliest streets.
86 rue du Marché au Charbon, Central ☎ 02.513.34.30 Ⓜ Bourse

Bar Tabac ♫off map

In the early hours, join the fashion crew, writers, designers, and actors who come here.
43 Waalse Kaai, Antwerpen ☎ 03.238.19.37 by rail

Bauhaus ♫off map

International crowds here lounge on leopard-skin seats behind wooden carved tables.
133–137 Langestraat, Brugge ☎ 050.34.10.93 by rail

Bazaar ♫E6

The joint of choice for much of Brussels' bohemia. A hot-air balloon made of brocade curtains hangs over the bar, old gilt mirrors reflecting subdued lighting show you to your best advantage, and comfy old armchairs give it a laid-back atmosphere. On weekends, disco, salsa, trip-hop, and other dance beats mix it up in the cellar. During the week, take in the light menu of couscous, tapas, and mint tea.
63 rue des Capucins, Les Marolles ☎ 02.511.26.00 Ⓜ Hotel des Mônnaies

☆ BEURSSCHOUWBURG ♫E2

This cavernous drinking hall is downtown central for a hip Flemish crowd. It hosts concerts and DJs, with everything from drum 'n' bass to tea dances playing Belgian *chansons*. Low-maintenance decor contributes to the alternative vibe. Grab a *witbier* and fight for a trestle table.
20–28 rue August Orts, Ste-Catherine ☎ 02.513.82.90 Ⓜ Bourse

Le Châtelain
♱E11

Don't be put off by the local yuppies; the steaks are the best in town and the place is jumping after the Thursday-night street market in the place.

17 place du Châtelain, Ixelles (West) ☎ 02.538.67.94 Ⓜ Louise

't Ei
♱off map

Salsa and tapas await at this trendy hangout.

13 Eiermarkt, Brugge ☎ 050.33.20.85 by rail

L'Entrepôt du Congo
♱off map

Philosophize day and night here – note the ironic inclusion of a portrait of King Baudouin, the only thing hanging on the walls.

42 Vlaamse Kaai, Antwerpen ☎ 03.238.99.32 by rail

☆ EL METEKKO
♱E2

In spite of its makeover, this trad bar next to the Stock Exchange still attracts chain-smoking intellectual types. Always lively, and with a fine selection of pasta dishes on offer, El Metekko is a perfect starting point for a night on the tiles.

86–88 boulevard Anspach, Central ☎ 02.512.46.48 Ⓜ De Brouckère

☆ LE JAVA
♱E2

A snaking mosaic-encrusted bar takes up over half the space in this tiny café, making contact between trendy expats and local artistes that much easier. Famed for its cocktails (all the usual suspects), Le Java has a small Brazilian restaurant upstairs.

31 rue St Géry, Ste-Catherine ☎ 02.512.37.16 Ⓜ Bourse

Kulminator
♱off map

Kulminator (Antwerpen) is the best beer bar in the city, with about 600 brews on offer. Fine modern architecture by Bob Van Reeth makes it seem like you're floating on the Scheldt in Zuiderterras.

32 Vleminckveld, Antwerpen ☎ 03.232.45.38 by rail

Lebozo
♱off map

The snob spot at the edge of the docks. Enjoy the music on the plush red velvet.

50 Godefriduskaai Willemdok, Antwerpen ☎ 03.238.41.45 by rail

☆ MAPPA MUNDO
♱E2

With music ranging from raï to rap, food spanning bagels to bolognese, and young hipsters hailing from all four corners of the globe,

Mappa is the most international of the place St-Géry bars. It is also the most laid-back – people come here to enjoy themselves, not to pose.
2 rue du Pont de la Carpe, Ste-Catherine ☎ 02.514.35.55 Ⓜ Bourse

Le Perroquet   *♪D6*
A corner bar with Art Nouveau decor that's a nice backdrop for drinking and flirting. The service is slow, but no matter: the motto here is chill.
31 rue Watteeu, Le Sablon ☎ 02.512.99.22 Ⓜ Louise

☆ LE ROI DES BELGES   *♪E2*
With Zebra and Mappa Mundo on either side, it was only a matter of time before the brushed steel and cherry wood fittings in this former Indian store became a bar. Downstairs is warm and smoky, while the 1970s-style salon upstairs is very Austin Powers.
35 rue Jules van Praet, Ste-Catherine ☎ 02.503.43.00 Ⓜ Bourse

SiSiSi   *♪F10*
Attracts a trendy multi-national twentysomething crowd who come for the cheap beer and to watch the St-Gilleois at work and play.
174 chaussée de Charleroi, St-Gilles ☎ 02.534.14.00 Ⓜ Horta

Trefpunt   *♪off map*
Poetic souls should head here, a more intimate hub for the culturally inclined.
18 Sint-Jacobs, Gent ☎ 09.233.58.48 by rail

☆ DE ULTIEME HALLUCINATIE   *♪B3*
Knocking back a few beers or shots of *jenever* (gin) is possible at De Ultieme Hallucinatie, a local landmark and a period gem. In an Art Nouveau house dating back to 1850, it also serves excellent, if a tad expensive, French and Belgian cuisine. Suits and Eurocrats dine up front in the posh dining room, while other punters have drinks and snacky food in the winter garden out back. Stepping into 'The Ultimate Hallucination' is like entering a dreamworld.
316 rue Royale, St-Josse & Schaerbeek ☎ 02.217.06.14 🚋 92, 93, 94

☆ WILDE   *♪E2*
Although this spanking new lounge-bar is owned by an Irishman and serves a mean Kilkenny, there are no false nicotine-stained ceilings in this studiously cool hangout. The decor may be 1950s retro, but the tunes spun by the resident DJs are definitely up-to-the-minute. Oscar Wilde wouldn't know what to make of his namesake bar. It is supposed to be in the celebrated wit's spirit but the slamming house

grooves are more Kim Wilde than Oscar. Unlike most bars with dance tunes, the music here is low enough for you to carry on a conversation without straining your vocal chords.

79 boulevard Anspach, Central ☎ 02.513.44.59 Ⓜ **Bourse**

☆ ZEBRA   ♪E2

With its cool metallic fittings and sprawling terrace, the Zebra helped turn place St-Géry from a sleepy backwater into Brussels' most hip and happening place to go out. Six years on, it's still the place to be seen downtown, as anyone who has ever tried to find a table here will vouch.

33 place St Géry, Ste-Catherine ☎ 02.511.09.01 Ⓜ **Bourse**

irish bars

The Bank   ♪E11
Tastefully decorated uptown joint catering to an expat crowd.
79 rue du Bailli, Ixelles (West) ☎ 02.537.52.65 ▯ **93, 94**

Celtica   ♪E2
The latest faux import from Ireland. More intimate than most of Brussels' other Irish pubs, with chart-friendly tunes in a down-to-earth environment.
55 rue du Marché aux Poulets, Central ☎ 02.514.22.69 Ⓜ **Bourse**

James Joyce   ♪E13
Good, honest food and beer.
34 rue Archimède, Quartier Européen ☎ 02.230.98.94 Ⓜ **Schuman**

Kitty O'Shea's   ♪B8
Packed at all times and serving wholesome pub grub.
42 boulevard de Charlemagne, Quartier Européen ☎ 02.230.78.75 Ⓜ **Schuman**

MacSweeney's   ♪B10
Popular Irish bar MacSweeney's is a safe bet for anglophones, especially those suffering withdrawal from Sky Sports. The terraces are particularly pleasant in the summer. MacSweeney's is a typical Irish pub and, with its big screens, is an excellent place to watch sport on rainy afternoons.
24 rue Jean Stas, St-Gilles ☎ 02.534.47.41 Ⓜ **Louise**

O'Dwyers ♪E13
One of the newer kids on the block, more of a bar than a pub, with its long room leading through to the garden.
55 rue Archimède, Quartier Européen ☎ 02.735.10.09 Ⓜ Schuman

☆ **O'REILLY'S** ♪E2
Cavernous and often raucous Irish mega-pub. Excellent country cooking. It has chain franchise written all over it. Heavily lacking in authenticity, it still manages to draw in some Irish folk: the Guinness at least is real, as are the sports events broadcast regularly.
1 place de la Bourse, Central ☎ 02.552.04.80 Ⓜ Bourse

☆ **WILD GEESE** ♪B8
This ever-popular watering hole brings some much-needed *craic* to an otherwise soulless office area. Popular with wannabe Eurocrats on the pull.
2–4 avenue Livingstone, Quartier Européen ☎ 02.230.19.90 Ⓜ Maelbeek

music on tap

The Bar Room ♪off map
For Latino in fab settings, head for the Bar Room. If red velvet and cocktails are your thing, the Bar Room has a great lounge to while away the hours.
30 Leopold De Waelplaats, Antwerpen ☎ 03.257.57.40 by rail

Café Hopper ♪off map
The best jazz venue in town.
2 Leopold De Waelstr, Antwerpen ☎ 03.248.49.33 by rail

Rococo ♪off map
Incurable romantics will feel right at home here, an informal but eccentric candlelit bar with a piano in the corner.
57 Corduwaniersstraat, Gent ☎ 09.224.30.35 by rail

Foyer Zuiderpershuis ♪off map
Set in an old factory, converted by architect Bob Van Reeth, Foyer Zuiderpershuis provides food for stomach and soul – check out their cultural agenda for world music concerts, expositions, and dance.
Waalse Kaai, Antwerpen ☎ 03.248.70.77 by rail

Sounds *♭B11*
A jazz venue-cum-bar with live music (Wed–Sat). It's oh-so-cool, with purple velvet and black and white photos of all the greats.
28 rue de la Tulipe, Ixelles (East) ☎ 02.512.92.50 Ⓜ Porte de Namur

Volle Gas *♭B11*
Used to be a jazz bar and still has occasional live acts. But it's gone more up-market and now bills itself as a soft-lit bistro. As befits this area, there are dozens of bars pumping out reggae and serving up African dishes.
21 place Fernand Cocq, Ixelles (East) ☎ 02.502.89.17 Ⓜ Porte de Namur

neighbourhood caffs

Brasserie de l'Union *♭C10*
A legendary bar that draws a bit of a dodgy, underbelly-of-the-city crowd, as well as rowdy bohos.
55 parvis St-Gilles, St-Gilles ☎ 02.538.15.79 Ⓜ Parvis St-Gilles

☆ BRASSERIE VERSCHEUREN *♭D9*
Come and admire the Art Deco curves of this down-to-earth café whilst supping on a cold beer. Vastly popular with the locals, the vibe at this café is not to be missed.
11–13 parvis St-Gilles, St-Gilles ☎ 02.539.40.68 Ⓜ Parvis St-Gilles

Lokkedize *♭off map*
A great local joint with fab *jenevers* (gins).
33 Korte Vulderstraat, Brugge ☎ 050.33.44.50 by rail

☆ MOEDER LAMBIC *♭F9*
Although the neighbourhood has seen better days, and the decor inside is tatty, this tiny bar probably has more beers on offer – between 800 and 1000 (most of them Belgian, with a few exotic imports) – than any other in town. So pluck a comic from the shelves, order a platter of Belgian cheese and get to work. But don't expect a comfy seat inside – it's small (the beer gets more space than the customers), pretty chaotic, and comfort plays second fiddle to the brews. Punters are mainly boys on a boisterous night out.
68 rue de Savoie, St-Gilles ☎ 02.539.14.19 Ⓜ Albert

De Tap en de Tepel   *off map*
A rambling joint with a blazing fire and a marvellously secluded garden, serving excellent wines and platters of pungent cheese.
7 Gewad, Gent ☎ 09.223.90.00 by rail

Tierra del Fuego   *B10*
A popular, colonial-styled Latin American bar/café. It serves some of the best *caipirinhas* in town, but there's also a good selection of rums, tequilas, and South American grub.
14 rue Berckmans, St-Gilles ☎ 02.537.42.72 Ⓜ Hôtel des Monnaies

sports bars

The Ceílidh   *B8*
Quiet, but with its own following, which comes here for the live sport on satellite TV.
37 rue du Taciturne, Quartier Européen ☎ 02.280.49.37 Ⓜ Schuman

JJ's   *A10*
For American football, darts, and snooker, try JJ's, an American cocktail bar with Tex-Mex food on the menu. But beware – it's a bit of a meat market in the evenings.
28 rue Jourdan, St-Gilles ☎ 02.538.78.28 Ⓜ Hôtel des Monnaies; Louise

Monkey Business   *C11*
A good-time beer bar popular with Americans and young Brits. Shows major sporting events and serves damn fine Tex-Mex food.
30 rue Defacqz, Ixelles (East) ☎ 02.538.69.34 🚊 92, 93, 94

Sports Avenue   *E7*
High-tech sports bar with basketball memorabilia and a gigantic screen.
4–5 avenue de la Toison d'Or, Ixelles (West) ☎ 02.500.78.38 Ⓜ Porte de Namur; Louise

traditional bars

☆ À LA BÉCASSE   *E2*
Down a narrow alley lies a bar which doesn't seem to have changed since Brueghel's days. The waiters look like monks, the food is served on wooden platters, and the local Lambic beers come in ceramic jugs. Very medieval. It could be tourist central, but its location, tucked down this alley, makes it too much of a best-kept secret for that.
11 rue de Tabora, Central ☎ 02.511.00.06 Ⓜ Bourse

☆ À LA MORT SUBITE ♪F2

Mort subite means 'sudden death', and if you drink enough of this legendary bar's fruit beers, such a fate might befall you. Smoke-stained ceilings and surly waitresses add to this institution's charm. It's as smoky as hell, so don't forget your eye drops. A decent, if limited, menu of pastas, soups and salads is also served.

7 rue des Montagnes aux Herbes Potagères, Central ☎ 02.513.13.18 Ⓜ De Brouckère

Bier Circus ♪F3

The long beer list includes *gueuze*, Trappist beers, wheat beers, organic beers, and many ales from Belgian micro-breweries. Tintin and other Belgian cartoon favourites decorate the walls of the bar in the back, and a limited menu is served.

89 rue de l'Enseignement, Central ☎ 02.218.00.34 Ⓜ Parc

't Brugs Beertje ♪off map

For a fine real beer experience and a good range of brews.

5 Kemelstraat, Brugge ☎ 050.33.96.16 by rail

Café Beveren ♪off map

For old-fashioned, knees-up-style entertainment, Café Beveren has an authentic 1933 organ belting out old tunes.

2 Vlasmarkt, Antwerpen ☎ 03.231.22.25 by rail

Chez Bernard ♪E2

A classic Brussels bar, all dark wood and mirrors, with a good choice of beers and bar snacks. Perfect for that pre-dinner sip or post-digestif.

47 place Jourdan, Quartier Européen ☎ 02.230.22.38 Ⓜ Schuman

☆ LE CIRIO ♪E2

Coiffured old ladies and their well-trimmed dogs come here to drink strong Trappist ales and *half en half* – a champagne/white wine mix. A beautiful oasis of calm in one of the city's most bustling areas.

18 rue de la Bourse, Central ☎ 02.512.13.95 Ⓜ Bourse

't Dreupelkot ♪off map

Take a trip down memory lane (well, a medieval alley) for mind-clearing *jenevers* in chilled glasses.

12 Groentenmarkt, Gent ☎ 09.224.24.55 by rail

t Galgenhuisje
♪off map

The Gallows House is the smallest and most crowded bar in the city, set in 14th-century cellars opposite the square where public executions once took place.

5 Groentenmarkt, Gent ☎ 09.233.42.51 by rail

Un Grain de Sable
♪D6

Find a spot on the terrace at Un Grain de Sable; this bar-resto has yellow-coloured walls that drive you nuts after a few drinks.

15–16 place du Grand Sablon, Le Sablon ☎ 02.514.05.83 Ⓜ Centrale

☆ LE GREENWICH
♪E2

Unfazed by the yuppification taking place around it, Le Greenwich remains the same as when Magritte tried to hawk his paintings here in the 1920s. The only sound you're likely to hear in this graceful mirrored establishment is that of chess players slapping their top-clocks.

7 rue des Chartreux, Ste-Catherine ☎ 02.511.41.67 Ⓜ Bourse

The Hairy Canary
♪E13

The Hairy Canary (a Victorian-style boozer), is as traditional as they come, and seems to have been *en place* forever.

12 rue Archimède, Quartier Européen ☎ 02.280.05.09 Ⓜ Schuman

☆ LE ROY D'ESPAGNE
♪F2

Karl Marx and Engels are said to have supped a few here while taking breaks from penning the Communist Manifesto. The only revolutionary thing about it these days is the stuffed horse. With a roaring fire in winter, and sunny terrace in summer, it's the best place to watch the comings and goings on the Grand' Place.

Grand' Place, Central ☎ 02.513.08.07 Ⓜ De Brouckère

e Zavel
♪D6

Decently priced daily specials (and the *moules et frites* are top notch). The crowd is older, less into posing and more into relaxing – a firm fave.

place du Grand Sablon, Le Sablon ☎ 02.512.16.80 Ⓜ Centrale

bars

☆ **LE CERCEUIL** ♪*F2*

With coffins serving as tables, the beer served in skull-shaped mugs and skeletons hanging from the ceiling, this dark and dingy bar with its ultraviolet lighting is something of a goths' paradise. Wear black and make sure your wallet's full, as the pricey beers are enough to make Count Dracula turn in his grave. Like death, however, once is more than enough.
10–12 rue des Harengs, Central ☎ 02.512.30.77 Ⓜ **Bourse**

D'Adario ♪*off map*

For an arty trip, this is a refuge for soul-searching philosophers, with live jazz on Saturday.
21–33 Ravenstr, Leuven ☎ 016.29.01.23 **by rail**

Le Comiqu'Art ♪*B9*

Serves Belgian food and good brews to the starving audiences of the local comic/theatre often on offer here.
1 rue de la Victoire, St-Gilles ☎ 02.537.22.75 Ⓜ **Port de Hal**

Dali's ♪*F2*

Dali's gives up serious club beats, with decor inspired by and in homage to the Surrealist artist: red lip-shaped sofas, easel-shaped settees, melted clocks, portraits of the mad Spaniard, repros of his paintings, and brightly-coloured walls. It is small, but dancing is possible on weekends, when they open up the first floor. Downstairs there's a dance floor and chill-out room, with regular live jungle, trip-hop, and acid jazz sessions.
35 Petite rue des Bouchers, Central ☎ 02.511.54.67 Ⓜ **Bourse; De Brouckère**

Het Elfde Gebod ♪*off map*

End the day with a prayer in the 16th-century Het Elfde Gebod ('The Eleventh Commandment') – it's chocka with religious statues. May the saints be with you.
10 Torfbrug, Antwerpen ☎ 03.289.34.65 **by rail**

☆ **LA FLEUR EN PAPIER DORÉ** ♪*A6*

'Every man has the right to 24 hours of freedom a day,' a Dadaist poet wrote above the entrance to this thesps' hangout. Regulars Magritte and Delvaux certainly thought so (check out their doodlings on the walls). These days there are more tourists than artists, but there's still a surreal feel to the place.
53 rue des Alexiens, Les Marolles ☎ 02. 511.16.59 Ⓜ **Anneessens**

☆ GOUPIL LE FOL   *♭B6*

Belgian flavour is served up here, or should we say French flavour: the music is French chanson with the likes of Edith Piaf, Charles Aznavour, and hometown boy Jacques Brel. The decor screams two words – fire hazard. Sheet music, albums, and other colourful junk pack its two floors. Beware, the drinks are pricey. It's a former brothel, a boho bar with deep, battered sofas and junk shop bric-a-brac. There'll also probably be an intellectual reading Rimbaud, and a group of bemused Japanese tourists sipping the café's famed fruit wine. Unmissable.

22 rue de la Violette, Central ☎ 02.511.13.96 Ⓜ Bourse

☆ KAFKA   *♭E2*

Quirky downtown bar filled with Kafka memorabilia and Flemish intellectuals. A stone's throw from the UGC De Brouckère cinema, it's just the place to discuss the night's movie over a Trappist ale or one of the bar's impressive array of Russian vodkas. It's full of leftist intellectuals, young Marxists, and older leftovers from Paris 1968. And if you don't know about Paris 1968, someone there will be more than happy to fill you in on all the details. Franz would have loved it.

6 rue de la Vierge Noire, Ste-Catherine ☎ 02.513.54.89 Ⓜ De Brouckère

Le Pantin   *♭E12*

One of the area's most eccentric bars. Beatniks, pub philosophers, and chess-players swarm to this joint like barflies.

355 chaussée d'Ixelles, Ixelles (East) ☎ 02.640.80.91 Ⓜ Porte de Namur

Pink Flamingo's Lounge   *♭off map*

Kitsch rules here – 100 statues of the Virgin Mary and a collection of old records by corny local singer Eddy Wally.

55 Onderstraat, Gent ☎ 09.233.04.56 by rail

☆ LA TENTATION   *♭C2*

Don't be surprised to see bagpipers or whirling Celtic dancers here, as this gloriously restored red-brick building is home to the city's large Galician diaspora. Entrance fees are charged when bands are on.

28 rue de Laeken, Ste-Catherine ☎ 02.223.22.75 Ⓜ De Brouckère

clubs

The Brussels-Antwerp clubbing scene is international in flavour. The children of Europe meet on the dancefloor, with casual as the dress code and relaxed as the mood; there's no point in breaking out your Gucci here – unless you want to feel over-dressed, that is. Whether you're up for hip-hop, drum 'n' bass, deep house or sassy salsa, the vibe is always *très* laid back.

Café d'Anvers
♪off map

Smack bang in the middle of Antwerp's red light district, Café d'Anvers used to be a church ministering to the working girls in the area. Bits of the gothic atmosphere remain intact, but today it serves up chunky house, garage and other club grooves. The crowd is more H&M than VIP, from teens to thirties, and all the better for it. A huge space with cozy corners, low lighting and a second level for getting intimate if you want to.

15 Verversrui, Antwerpen ☎ 03.226.38.70 w www.café-d-anvers.be 🚗 from Centraal Station

☆ CHEZ JOHNNY
♪E4

The Belgian answer to an Essex boy (or Guido), a Johnny wears his gold jewellery with pride, loves his car and leaves a whiff of Brut trailing after him wherever he goes. This club is his home. Sort of a joke, actually, as the club is long on kitsch appeal: loads of Abba and French pop music from all decades, with the legendary Claude François – the francophone Cliff Richard – being a real favourite. Carnavalesque decor and a very packed house, it handles the not-so-chic overflow from the Mirano next door well. It's half-nostalgic (1970s French pop), half-ironic (resort-from-hell decor: hammocks hanging from the ceiling, rubber chickens hanging around, lifebuoys), with most punters missing the joke decor.

24 chaussée de Louvain, St-Josse & Schaerbeek ☎ 02.227.39.99 Ⓜ Madou

☆ FUSE
♪F5

Kevin Saunderson, Stacey Pullen, and Dave Clarke are just some of the big-name DJs who've put the needle on the record at Brussels' temple of techno. Paris's famed Respect is Burning party series often takes up residence, as do other party nights, like Fuse (every Saturday) and La Démence. People come from all over Europe for the no-nonsense, hard-edge trance/techno. No prizes for the interior, but the punters don't seem to mind. Belgium's premier techno stomping ground has two dance floors to handle the thousandplus crowds on Fridays (free before midnight) and Saturdays. Every third Sunday is turned over to La Démence, the city's uninhibited gay mega-party series, with house and garage as the soundtrack. Mad Club @ Fuse is a monthly extravaganza courtesy of DJ Rudy and Brussels' own Cecil B Demille. Beach parties, carnivals, Christmas in July: Rudy & Co push these themes and more to the limit to the sound of commercial house and kitsch disco. It's handbag heaven.

208 rue Blaes, Les Marolles ☎ **02.511.97.89 w www.fuse.be M Porte de Hal**

☆ MIRANO CONTINENTAL ♪E4

This is the disco that just won't die. Mirano is Brussels' answer to Stringfellows and Studio 54. This former cinema is the club of choice for the city's BCBG – *bon chic bon genre*; in other words, the Ralph Lauren set. It's very Francophone – and all very glam in a *Hello!* magazine kind of way. The music is radio-friendly house, with excursions into funk and garage. The revolving dance floor makes staying sober a very good idea. Put on your best Gucci knock-off and head out to where Brussels' beautiful people flock for a Saturday night boogie.

38 chaussée de Louvain, St-Josse & Schaerbeek, ☎ **02.227.39.70 M Madou**

Red & Blue ♪off map

From muscle boys to hairdressers to common or garden variety gay, Red & Blue handles 'em all on Saturdays. Formerly a supper club, spacious R'n'B kept the faux deco interior of its previous incarnation, with tables and chairs surrounding the dance floor – so you can chill out without being too far from the action. The music ranges from dodgy house to just-shy-of-kitsch disco. But the tunes ain't the drawing card here: it's the mating place. Up goes the sleaze factor the first Saturday of every month for R'n'B's Club Flesh night.

11–13 Lange Schipperskappelstraat, Antwerpen ☎ **03.213.05.55 w www.redandblue.be 🚌 from Centraal Station**

Sonïk ♪A6

This techno-house-garage club has the worst ventilation of any club in Brussels – you may as well dance in a sauna. Thankfully the grooves – courtesy of the DJ trio who founded the club – satisfy. The only prob: the punters are slow to hit the dancefloor.

112 rue du Marché au Charbon, Central ☎ **02.511.99.85 M Anneessens**

☆ LE SPARROW
♭B6

The Sparrow rose from the ashes of the former tourist-trap disco, Le Garage. It's now just about the funkiest dance club in Brussels. The soundtrack consists of the very best hip-hop flavoured soul and R'n'B, mixed with the sounds of Africa. It caters to an older crowd that never works up too much of a sweat, despite its silky soul grooves. The high Congolese quotient means that the African sounds are mixed with Puff Daddy and Babyface. Bring your own partner – this is mostly a couples crowd. The Sparrow's only drawback: the larcenous drinks prices can leave you high and dry. ♪ Salsa takes over Sunday nights.

18 rue Duquesnoy, Central ☎ 02.512.66.22 Ⓜ Centrale

☆ STUDIO LIVE
♭A6

On Saturday nights house-lovers head for theatre space, Studio Live. This is the new incarnation of the much-lamented former Who's Who's Land. Fierce, groovy house, two-step, deep garage, and other beats channelled from an invisible DJ bring in the throngs. The decor is recording-studio-meets-Alice-in-Wonderland: huge keyboards and giant mikes provide the backdrop. Less techno than Fuse, bigger beats than Mirano. A winner – if it survives for long enough.

17 rue du Poinçon, Central ☎ 02.512.52.70 Ⓜ Anneessens

☆ LE SUD
♭F2

Walk Like an Egyptian, anyone? A truly guilty pleasure, this joint serves up sounds of the 1980s for a young crowd who were probably only just teething back then. It's a dingy club, with ramshackle bric-a-brac, musty old sofas, and candle-lights that serve at least to make you look better – no matter how wasted you are. The doormen are some of the dimmest you'll find in Brussels and look like they've a dodgy tale or two to tell.

45 rue de l'Écuyer, Central ☎ 02.513.37.65 Ⓜ De Brouckère

Zillion
♭off map

Four dance floors belching dry ice, four different flavours of house to mess with your mind, and too damned much to deal with just on nature's intended chemicals. Antwerp's mega-club brings in the faux Versace and platform-trainer crowd – although trainers are supposedly a no-no at the door. A dance-club monstrosity, Zillion is best enjoyed if you bring your own posse. Video-walls, fog-machines, and moving robots entertain to deep house, techno,

oul, and funk. What used to be an old church and then cinema
as turned into a funky hall hung with chandeliers.
   **Jan van Gentstraat, Antwerpen ☎ 03.248.15.16 w www.zillion.be
   ◗ from Centraal Station**

Practical information

 few rules for clubbing in Belgium: if you can't speak French or
lemish, use an American accent – America trumps Britain in coolness
ue to distance – and doormen think Yanks have more money.

● Clubs open around 11pm but only hard-up students arrive before
nidnight – when entrance is usually free. Things hot up around
am, so pace yourself.

▩ Tip the doorman on your way out – 50BF is usually the minimum,
ut the soft hush of a 100BF note paves the way for easy access next
ime. Bigger clubs take credit cards, but only at the bar.

✿ Generally casual so avoid being overdressed. Babes have no
roblem getting in. Guys should avoid arriving in large groups.

● To find out about the newest clubs and what's going on, pick up
 copy of *Out Soon* at music shops, or check out **w** www.noctis.com
n English) for up-to-date listings, and **w** www.café-cool.be (in
rench and Flemish).

gay scene

bars

☆ LE BELGICA
A5

Big on demolition decor, but Brussels' trendiest gay bar is often so packed you don't notice. The calendar on the wall is stuck at July 21 – Belgian National Day – as a token of national pride. The house drink, Le Belgica, is a potent little shot glass of lemon *jenever* (gin) that makes life a little more lovely after you've had a few. This loud and proud gay bar has always raised a metaphorical finger at authority and continues to do so. Its selection of fruit-flavoured *jenevers* is unrivalled in Brussels.
rue du Marché au Charbon, Central ☎ 02.673.13.82 Ⓜ Bourse

Chez Maman
A6

The area's main drag bar. The mistress of ceremonies is Maman, a dazzling menopausal mix of your favourite Bond girl and First Lady, depending on what wig she's wearing. Armpit-small, but an enjoyable night out.
7 rue des Grands Carmes, Central ☎ 02.502.89.96 Ⓜ Anneessens

Le Comptoir
B6

A guppie (read gay yuppie) joint whose clientele is borderline hairdresser, as opposed to Le Belgica's lumberjack lad/fashion victim.
24–26 place de la Vieille Halle aux Blés, Central ☎ 02.514.05.00 Ⓜ Centrale

Planète Chocolat
A6

Popular with the gay crowd, the café also does excellent coffee, complemented by chocolates made by proprietor Frank Duval.
24 rue du Lombard, Central ☎ 02.511.07.55 Ⓜ Bourse; Anneessens

☆ TELS QUELS
A5

Just about the only bar in town where lesbians and gays mix easily. It publishes a monthly mag, has an archive of gay publications, and offers a nondescript environment where people meet and chat rather than meet and mate.
81 rue du Marché au Charbon, Central ☎ 02.512.32.34 Ⓜ Bourse

clubs

Le Cabaret @ Le Siècle
F2

Some Brussels clubs are really only worth their weight on specific nights. Le Siècle is one such spot; it plays host to Le Cabaret, one of the

est gay nights in town, on Sundays. This is a rarity: a girl-friendly gay
night in Belgium (though a gay posse escort is a must). Happening at
the otherwise suspect Le Siècle club (yuppie central), weekly Le
Cabaret plays diva-powered house with large doses of Gloria Gaynor
and Donna Summer. If it's in a drag queen's repertoire, you'll hear it
here. Deliciously rank.

1 rue de l'Écuyer, Central ☎ 02.513.08.10 Ⓜ De Brouckère

La Démence @ Fuse ♪F5

Bus-loads of boys from Amsterdam and Paris flock to Belgium's
hottest gay party, held every few Sundays and the night before any
major public holiday. Bypass the ground floor's sad techno-house.
The real deal is upstairs, with slamming deep garage and stellar
house. An amusing side-trip is the lounge outside the darkroom,
with all the ambience of a doctor's waiting room.

208 rue Blaes, Les Marolles ☎ 02.511.97.89 w www.fuse.be Ⓜ Porte de Hal

Different @ Sonik ♪A5

The real deal at Sonik is at Different, a monthly event where gays and
lesbians mix it up to vintage disco, soul, and house. The gender blend
cancels out the pick-up vibe rampant in boys-only/girls-only clubs.
Lousy ventilation keeps you knocking back the drinks – it makes a
sauna seem airy

12 rue du Marché au Charbon, Central ☎ 02.511.99.85 Ⓜ Anneessens

Phil Collins Club @ Red & Blue ♪off map

On Saturdays, join the hordes of gay men who come from all over to
dance to kitsch disco tunes and score at Red & Blue. The name's a
joke: Mr Collins of Genesis fame features nowhere on the playlist.
Instead, Antwerp's only weekly club night blends funk, raggae, house,
garage, and almost every other dance flavour for every stripe of club
kid. The night recently changed promoters, so the jury's still out on
whether the same funky, fierce vibe can be maintained.

**11–13 Lange Schipperskappelstraat, Antwerpen ☎ 03.213.05.55 w
www.redandblue.be 🚂 from Centraal Station**

5. Club Cigare ♪C7

This uptown prides itself on being an exclusive hang-out for pretty
boys in tight T-shirts and too much of whatever the latest fragrance
is. It's presided over by ageless fairy godmother Gervaise, an ebony
nightlife institution who brings a little Studio 54 into the lives of
everyone she touches.

9 rue du Pépin, Le Sablon ☎ 02.511.63.22 Ⓜ Porte de Namur

entertainment

Whether you're after theatre, cinema, dance or cutting-edge sounds, Brussels can supply the goods.

newspapers

Brussels' newsstands reflect the cultural diversity of the city in the plethora of foreign dailies on offer from *El País* to *Die Welt*. *Le Soir*, the top-selling French-language broadsheet is a more liberal read than its competitor *La Libre Belgique*, once the most influential Catholic daily. For popular Flemish quality reads, check out *De Morgen*, which used to be funded by the Socialist party and has a reputation for political scoops. *De Standaard*, Flanders' biggest-selling broadsheet, is right of centre and has good political and foreign news. Colourful tabloid reads include the French language *La Dernière Heure*, low in eye-candy but high in sports coverage. The sensationalist *Het Laatste Nieuws* is the highest-selling tabloid in Flanders, although *Het Nieuwsblad* has better sports coverage. Top financial reads are the French-language *L'Écho* and the Flemish *De Financieel Economische Tijd*. For an insider's view on EU politics, the English-language weekly, *European Voice*, is best.

listings magazines

A must is the English-language expat weekly *The Bulletin*. Its insert, *What's On*, has extensive listings of happenings in Brussels and beyond. The satirical Flemish *Humo* beats any other TV/radio listings mag for its current affairs and cultural coverage (both are out Thursdays). *Télémoustique* is a French-language TV mag which carries *Mosquito*, a free weekly ents agenda (out Wednesdays). *Kiosque* is the most comprehensive French-language entertainment guide. *The Ticket*, a free music agenda, in French or Flemish, lists events nationwide, as well as club info. French-language *Mofo* features concert dates, band interviews and album reviews. Both are monthly and available in most music stores. One of the best listings is *Mad*, the entertainment and cultural supplement of *Le Soir* (Wednesdays).

radio

Small indie broadcasters compete for the airwaves against public-funded radio stations. The hip **Studio Brussel** (100.6 FM) has an eclectic mix of jazz, acid, African, hip-hop and rock. Real rock fans should check out the French-language **Radio 21** (93.2 FM). Of the three public Flemish stations, **VRT1**

91.7FM) offers political debates, **VRT2** (93.7 FM) middle of the road chart its, and **VRT3** (89.5 FM) highbrow classical music. On the French side, **RTBF Musique 3** (91.2 FM) plays popular classical numbers and **La Première** (91.5 M) is a talk station worth tuning into for political debates. Exercise your anguage skills with **BFM** (107.6 FM), the all-talk French-language station, nd the city's news station, **Bruxelles Capitale** (99.3 FM). Neither **Bel RTL** 04 FM) nor **Radio Contact** (102.2 FM) offer anything extraordinary.

elevision

n average 30 channels are available on cable, including **Euronews**, urosport, **BBC1**, **BBC2** and **CNN**. There are two public Flemish chanels: **VRT** for light entertainment, and the more up-market Ketnet/Canvas for documentaries and cultural programming. Of the hree private Flemish stations, **VTM** is the most commercial; **Kanaal 2** as cartoons and movies; and **VT4** screens mediocre US comedy and novies, as well as soft porn. Both the French public stations, RTBF1 (La Jne) and **RTBF2** (La Deux), show news, documentaries and films, but a Deux is more highbrow. **RTL-TVi**, a Luxembourg-based station, out-uts American made-for-TV films and soaps. Meanwhile, **Club RTL** creens cartoons, game shows, and international movies (usually ubbed), and **Télé-Bruxelles** (French)/ **TV Brussel** (Flemish), the twin ublic-access stations cover local community news and events.

vebsites

here is a plethora of useful Brussels sites: **w** www.bruxelles.irisnet.be he local government site, with good entertainment links; **w** www.tib.be tourist info site which lists hotels, events and sports; **w** www.belgium-ourism.net (good info for visitors); **w** www. timeout. com/brussels (for vhat's on this month); **w** www. idearts.com (for more specific cultural nd arts info); **w** www.skynet.be (entertainment links and up-to-date ravel info); and **w** www.resto.be (for restaurant bookings).

heatre

here is no centralized booking facility for theatre tickets; ring indi-idual venues. Credit-card bookings can entail a 3% commission harge. Last-minute tickets are usually available on the door.
) There is no hard-and-fast rule about performance nights, lthough you can expect Monday and Tuesday nights to be quieter nan weekends. Matinée performances are sometimes on offer. here is a definite theatre season, with most closing Jun–early Sep.

🏨 Prices vary but are cheaper than in other capitals, even for the bigger houses. Expect to pay between 500BF–950BF.

❶ The best place to check for theatre info is the English-language *The Bulletin. Kiosque*, a French monthly listing, is also a must. National newspapers run listings. For English theatre information try: **w** www.theatrefactory.com.

cinema

It's not usually necessary to book ahead for seats, and few cinemas have credit-card booking facilities. The exceptions are: **Kinepolis** ☎ 02.474.26.00 and the two **UGC cinemas** ☎ 0900.104.40 (booking lines in Flemish and French).

☽ Programmes change on Wednesdays, and most of the larger cinemas show films four times a day – at 2.15–2.45 pm, 4–5 pm, 7.15–7.45 pm and 9–10.15 pm. There are usually 20 minutes of adverts and trailers before the feature starts. At midnight on Fridays and Saturdays there are late-night screenings at **De Brouckère**.

🏨 Tickets are cheapish, ranging from 200BF–280BF, with reductions on Mon for students, OAPs and if you pre-pay for four films at once at UGC cinemas.

❶ Check listings in the weekly English-language magazine *The Bulletin* or any national paper on Wednesdays. Cinebel.be has scheduling details and reviews of virtually everything that's on, and **w** www.idearts.com has general cultural and arts info.

music

Tickets are generally available on the door, although for popular acts it's best to buy in advance. If you're stuck Brussels' touts are surprisingly altruistic, rarely selling tickets above face value. Among the outlets selling tickets for a wide variety of gigs are **FNAC** ☎ 02.209.22.39 and **Virgin Megastore** ☎ 02.219.90.04.

☽ There are gigs most nights of the week, and most start between 8 pm–9 pm (8 pm if there's a support act, 9pm if not). Performances tend to be punctual but for sessions in clubs and bars don't bother arriving before 10pm.

🏨 Expect to pay 500BF–800BF per ticket for gigs in main venues but for clubs and bars just turn up and pay the cover charge of 200BF–300BF.

❶ For Anglophones, the best rock listings are contained in the weekly *The Bulletin* or *The Ticket*. Those who can understand French should get the *Mad* supplement of *Le Soir* (Wed), monthly mag *Kiosque*, freebie *Rif-Raf* (available in cafés and record shops), or *The Ticket*, monthly gig guide (also free from most bars and cafés). The Dutch-language newspaper *De Morgen* and magazines *Humo* and *Knack* have good music coverage. For the most up-to-date and comprehensive info on jazz in Brussels check out the excellent website **w** www.jazzinbelgium.org.

classical

Most venues have their own box office. It is usually possible to buy tickets at the door, but it's best to reserve ahead. The tourist office in the Grand' Place ☎ 02.513.89.40 also sells tickets for recitals, or try the book/music store **FNAC** ☎ 02.209.22.39

⏱ Classical concerts tend to take place Mon–Sat. Curtains normally rise at 8 or 8.30pm, although lunchtime events are not uncommon.

⊞ Prices vary widely: in some smaller venues tickets can cost less than 200BF, but opera performances at La Monnaie and recitals in the Palais des Beaux-Arts reach 2500BF.

❶ For listings, it's best to buy the English-language weekly *The Bulletin* or *Mad*, the Wednesday supplement to French-language daily *Le Soir*. The monthly magazine *Kiosque* is also an excellent source of info. Web sites **w** www.gmn.com and **w** www.agenda.be are also worth checking out for the latest music info.

dance

Tickets for major productions are often available from **FNAC** ☎ 02.209.22.39, or direct from venue box offices; most take credit cards. Places are often limited at smaller venues, so it's best to book; few take credit cards but you can usually phone ahead and reserve.

⏱ Shows usually start at 8 or 8.30pm. Smaller venues close Jul–Aug, but the majors stay open.

⊞ Expect to pay 500BF–1000BF for tickets at larger theatres; smaller venues in the region of 300BF–500BF.

❶ For reviews and listings try: *The Ticket* (monthly cultural guide), *Mad* (Wednesday supplement in *Le Soir*), the Flemish press, and the English-language *The Bulletin*. For info on contemporary dance in Brussels see **w** www.users.skynet.be/sky80013/dance.

events

What's on when in Europe's adopted capital...

spring

Musique et Lumière (Muziek & Lichtshow) *♪F2*
Sound and light show in the wonderful Grand' Place. Sit and sip a beer as the Hôtel de Ville is magnificently illuminated.
Grand' Place, Central Ⓜ De Brouckère ◑ Easter–Sep: daily 🎫 free

Printemps Baroque du Sablon (Barokke Lente van de Zavel) *♪6/7*
Music, theatre and festivities in the finest Sablon settings.
Various locations in Le Sablon ☎ 02.507. 82.00 🚃 91, 92, 93, 94 ◑ mid Apr 🎫 free

Foire du Livre Antique (Beurs van het Oude Boek) *♪B6*
An international event for book enthusiasts, particularly those who love old maps, first editions, and secondhand books.
Salle de la Madeleine, 14 rue Duquesnoy, Central ☎ 02.512.44.472 Ⓜ De Brouckère ◑ end Apr 🎫 200BF

Serres Royales de Laeken (Kon Serres van Laken) *♪off map*
The spectacular royal glasshouses are open for a few weeks so the public can admire exotic tropical plants, azaleas, and fuchsias. One day is reserved for the disabled.
ave du Parc Royal, Laeken ☎ 02.551. 20.20 🚃 53 ◑ end Apr–beg May 🎫 50BF–100BF

Queen Elisabeth Music Competition *♪A7*
A landmark event in Belgium's classical music scene that is now a musical institution. It's the most gruelling classical competition in the world; only the very best make it through.
Palais des Beaux-Arts, 5–7 rue Ravenstein, Le Sablon ☎ 02.513.00.99 Ⓜ Central ◑ May 🎫 prices vary

Dring Dring Festival *♪A/B14*
A week-long celebration of cycling in Brussels. On the first Sunday, avenue Tervuren is car free. There are guided tours and sales of new and old bikes.
Parc du Cinquantenaire, Quartier Européen ☎ 02.502.73.55 Ⓜ Schuman ◑ beg May 🎫 bike hire varies

Fête du Port (Havenfeesten) ♪off map
Festivities in Brussels' port, with a display of sailing boats and war-ships. Lots of activities including water-skiing, tours of the harbour in riverboats, concerts, and fireworks.
quai de Heembeek & Brussels, Royal Yacht Club, 1 chaussée de Vilvoorde, Voorhaven ☎ 02.421.66.51 Ⓜ Yser ◑ *beg May* BF free

KunstenFESTIVALdesArts ♪throughout town
Avant-garde dance, music, theatre, and films.
Various Brussels locations ☎ 070.22.21.99 w www.kunstenfesti-valdes arts.be ◑ *May* BF prices vary

Fête de l'Iris (Irisfeest) ♪A/B14
Multicultural outdoor event with activities for all age groups. Make-up work-shops for children and European food specialities followed by an evening concert and a fireworks display. It's the official Brussels Region festival.
Parc du Cinquantenaire, Quartier Européen Ⓜ Schuman ◑ *mid May* BF free

Bruxelles (Brussel) 20km ♪A/B14
The capital's most important road race attracts runners from all over the world.
Parc du Cinquantenaire, Quartier Européen ☎ 02.511.90.00 Ⓜ Schuman ◑ *end May* BF free

Jazz Marathon ♪throughout town
The capital's famous annual jazz jamboree.
Various locations in Brussels ☎ 02.456.04.86 ◑ *last weekend May* BF 450BF

Carnaval à Binche ♪off map
A world-famous Lenten carnival in Binche, highlighted by Mardi Gras (Shrove Tuesday) with *gilles* (giants) in fancy-dress costumes. It ends in the square with *gilles* throwing oranges at the crowds.
Binche, Wallonia ☎ 06.433.68.96 ◑ *Shrove Tuesday* BF free

Ars Musica ♪througout town
Inventive, contemporary classical music festival with lots of premieres.
Various locations in Brussels & Antwerpen ☎ 02.219.26.60 ◑ *mid Mar–beg Apr* BF prices vary

La Bataille de Waterloo (Slag Bij Waterloo) ☼off map
Spectacular re-enactment of the battle between Wellington's and Napoleon's armies is fought by military enthusiasts.
Waterloo (Wallonia) ☎ 02.352.98.82 ● *Jun (every five years; next one 2006)* ⓑⓕ free

Fête de la Musique ☼throughout town
The French-speaking community celebrates the arrival of summer with a three-day multicultural musical event.
Various Brussels locations ☎ 02.209.10.90 ● *21 Jun & nearest weekend* ⓑⓕ free

Couleur Café ☼off map
A multicultural world music event.
Tour & Taxis, 5–7 rue Picard, Molenbeek ☎ 02.672.49.12
Ⓜ Ribaucourt ● *end Jun* ⓑⓕ 700BF–1600BF

Ecran Total ☼F2
A mix of international film classics, documentaries, recent releases, and new movies are shown at this annual festival.
Arenberg-Galeries Cinema, 26 Galerie de la Reine, Central ☎ 02.512.80. 63 Ⓜ Centrale ◖ *end Jun–beg Sep* ⓑⓕ 260BF

Festival de Wallonie ☼throughout town
This Francophone extravaganza is a staggered series of classical music events in castles, abbeys, and churches.
Various locations in Brussels & Wallonia ☎ 08.173.37.81 ● *Jun–Oct* ⓑⓕ 300BF–850BF

Brosella ☼off map
A small, but established, outdoor folk and jazz festival.
Théâtre de Verdure, Parc Osseghem, Heysel ☎ 02. 548.04.54
Ⓜ Heysel ◖ *beg Jul* ⓑⓕ free

Klinkende Munt ☼E2
Avant-garde series of pop/jazz/world/rock festival of concerts. And the best thing is it's free.
Various locations, including Beursschouwburg ☎ 02.513. 82.90
Ⓜ Bourse ◖ *6 days beg Jul* ⓑⓕ free

Ommegang ♪F2/B6
Medieval pageant re-creating a 16th-century celebration in honour of Emperor Charles V and his son Philip II; people parade with giant effigies on their shoulders and there's a mock battle fought on stilts.
Grand' Place, Central ☎ 02. 548.04.54/02.512.19.61 Ⓜ De Brouckère
◑ 1st Thu Jul & preceding Tue ⓑⓡ 850BF–2550BF

Rock Werchter ♪off map
Belgium's biggest open-air rock festival.
Werchter festival site, near Leuven, Flanders ☎ 016. 60.04.06 ◑ 1st weekend Jul ⓑⓡ 1600BF–3100BF

10 Days Off ♪throughout town
One of the biggest annual dance festivals in Belgium, this summer fling attracts the very best international DJs and acts.
Location varies each year w www.dma.be/p/5voor12/ ◑ beg Jul
ⓑⓡ varies

Fête Nationale Belge (Belgische Nationale Feestdag) ♪A/B7
Remembering the day in 1830 when Léopold I was crowned first king of the Belgians. A host of events and military parades ending with a spectacular firework display.
Various locations around Parc de Bruxelles ☎ 02. 511.90.00 🚋 91, 92, 93, 94 ◑ 21 Jul ⓑⓡ free

Sfinks Festival ♪off map
A four-day world music festival in a park crammed with exotic food stalls and workshops.
Oude Steenweg, Boechout, near Antwerpen (Flanders)
☎ 03. 455.69.44 ◑ last weekend Jul ⓑⓡ 1000BF per day

Gentse Feesten ♪off map
The medieval city of Gent hosts a 10-day festival of music, street theatre, jazz, and dance in its squares and quays.
Gent (Flanders) ☎ 09.225.36.76 ◑ end Jul ⓑⓡ free

Les Dimanches du Bois de la Cambre ♪off map
Relaxed series of outdoor jazz and classical concerts in the Bois de la Cambre.
Pélouse des Anglais, Bois de la Cambre, Ixelles (West)
☎ 02.218.40.86 🚋 23, 90, 93, 94 ◑ Jul–Aug: every Sun ⓑⓡ free

La Foire du Midi (Zuidkermis) *D5/F5/B9*
Huge funfair with over 2km of Ferris wheels, merry-go-rounds, and roller coasters. Try local delicacies like the famous *smoutebollen* (a kind of doughnut) or grilled *boudin* sausage.
boulevard du Midi, Les Marolles ☎ 02.279.40.76 Ⓜ Gare du Midi
◑ mid Jul–end Aug 🚇 100BF per ride

Meyboomplanting *B6/F2*
Commemoration of the Brussels bourgeois' win over a challenge by their Leuven counterparts in 1308 with the planting of a Meyboom (May tree) and an afternoon parade on the Grand' Place.
Grand' Place, Central ☎ 02.217.39.43 Ⓜ De Brouckère ◑ beg Aug 🚇 free

Tapis aux Fleurs (Bloementapijt) *B6/F2*
800,000 flowers carpet the Grand' Place in a three-day tribute to Belgium's world-famous begonias.
Grand' Place, Central ☎ 02.513.89.40 Ⓜ De Brouckère ◑ mid Aug
every 2 years (even-numbered years) 🚇 free

Marktrock *off map*
A mixed bag of Belgian and international rock and pop acts plays at this three-day event.
Various locations across Leuven, Flanders ☎ 016.29.08.23 ◑ mid
Aug 🚇 free–500BF

Recyclart *C6*
Cultural and urban-renewal group Recyclart presents a festival of music, painting, sculpture, street theatre, and juggling.
Chapelle Station, Les Marolles ☎ 02.502.57.34 Ⓜ Centrale Aug
🚇 free

Memorial Ivo Van Damme *off map*
An annual track-and-field meet bringing together internationally renowned athletes.
King Baudouin Stadium, Heysel ☎ 02.474.72.30 Ⓜ Heysel ◑ end Aug
🚇 500BF–2200BF

Grand Prix de Belgique de Formule I *off map*
Formula I Belgian-style on one of the most scenic circuits in the world.
Francorchamps, Wallonia ☎ 08.727.51.46 ◑ end Aug 🚇
5000BF–14,000BF

Les Nuits Botaniques ♫*B3*
Rock, pop, *chanson*, and world music in Le Botanique.
Le Botanique, 236 rue Royale, St-Josse & Scharbeek ☎ 02.218.37.32
Ⓜ Botanique ◗ *mid Sep* 🚇 *250BF–1600BF*

Journées du Patrimoine (Open Monumentendag) ♫*throughout town*
Historic buildings, artists' studios, and Art Nouveau gems that are
rarely open to the public welcome visitors for the weekend.
Various locations across Brussels ☎ 02.204.14.20 Ⓜ Porte de Hal
◗ *2nd or 3rd weekend Sep* 🚇 *free*

Brueghel Festival ♫*map 5*
A celebration of local artist Pieter Brueghel the Elder who lived in the
Marolles until his death in 1669. There's a parade, street parties, and
live music.
Various locations in Les Marolles ☎ 02.512. 19.00 Ⓜ Porte de Hal
◗ *3rd Sun Sep* 🚇 *free*

Fête de la Communauté Française ♫*throughout town*
Walloons and some *Bruxellois* celebrate their Francophony with
street parties, music, and free theatre performances.
Various locations across Brussels ☎ 02.413.23.110 27 ◗ *Sep* 🚇 *free*

Festival van Vlaanderen ♫*throughout town*
Classical music marathon held in medieval abbeys, cathedrals, and
city halls.
Various locations in Brussels & Ghent ☎ 02. 548.95.95 ◗ *Mar–Dec*
🚇 *600BF–3000BF*

Armistice (Wapenstilstand) ♫*F3*
The end of WWI is commemorated all over Belgium. Military parades
take place at the tomb of the Unknown Soldier.
place Madou, Central Ⓜ Madou; Botanique ◗ *11 Nov* 🚇 *free*

winter

St-Nicolas (Sinterklaas) ♫*throughout town*
Belgian children get their pressies for the festive season (it's a much
bigger deal than Christmas). They also scoff spicy *speculoos* (ginger-
bread biscuits) and marzipan.
◗ *6 Dec*

Le Marché de Noël (Kerstmarkt)   *⊘B6/F2*
International Christmas market, with stalls from many EU countries in a warm and friendly atmosphere. A shopper's delight.
Grand' Place, Central Ⓜ **De Brouckère** ◖ *beg–mid Dec*

Brussels on Ice   *⊘B6/F2*
The Grand' Place is transformed into a huge ice-skating rink. Rent some skates or sit back and watch the professionals (in both sporting and artistic shows).
Grand' Place, Central ☎ **02.513.89.40** Ⓜ **De Brouckère** ◖ *end Dec–beg Jan* ⒝Ⓕ 150BF

Fête de la St-Sylvestre (Oudejaarsavond)   *⊘throughout town*
Festivities across the capital as New Year is the one time of year Belgians really let rip. Catch the fireworks from place des Palais.
☎ **02.513.89. 40** 🚍 **free public transport** ◖ *New Year's Eve*

Brussels International Film Festival   *⊘throughout town*
Ten days of international films and documentaries.
Various cinemas ☎ **02.227.39.89 w www.brussels filmfest.be** ◖ *Jan* ⒝Ⓕ 180BF–280BF

Gay & Lesbian Film Festival   *⊘B3*
A popular annual event with international long and short films and documentaries.
Le Botanique, 236 rue Royale, St-Josse & Schaerbeek ☎ **02.218.37.32** Ⓜ **Botanique** ◖ *mid Jan* ⒝Ⓕ 180BF

sights, museums & galleries

Forget Brussels' dreary Eurocrat image: scratch the city's surface to find a bewitching blend of Baroque splendour, fin-de-siècle flamboyance, and monumental pomposity.

landmarks

Arc de Triomphe (Triomfboog) _A/B14_
The BBC's backdrop of choice for EU stories, the arch was inspired by Paris's Arc de Triomphe and Berlin's Brandenberg Gate. Léopold II built it to celebrate 50 years of Belgian independence in 1880, eventually having to use his plundered Congo fortune to complete the arch in 1905.
Parc du Cinquantenaire, Quartier Européen ☎ 02.737.78.11
Ⓜ Mérode 🅱️ free

Atomium _off map_
This model of an iron atom, magnified 165 billion times (standing at 102m), was built for the 1958 Exposition _Universelle_ (World Fair) and has an appropriately dated, Flash-Gordon feel. Despite local affection for the distinctive grey balls, nobody seems willing to capitalize on its touristic potential: bar the view, there's little worth seeing inside.
boulevard du Centenaire, Heysel ☎ 02.474.89.77 Ⓜ Heysel 🅱️ 200BF

Basilique du Sacré Coeur (Heilig Hert Basiliek) _off map_
This chunky Art Deco basilica, another big-is-beautiful Léopold II project, is the fifth-largest church in the world and took 66 years to complete (1970). Some call it monstrous, others appreciate its surreal grandeur. A bizarrely tacky red-neon crucifix glows on top of its green copper dome at night.
1 parvis de la Basilique, Koekelberg ☎ 02.425.88.22 Ⓜ Simonis, then
🚌 87 🅱️ free

Le Botanique _B3_
This airy early 19th-century glasshouse (one of the city's lovelier landmarks) is now the Centre Culturel de la Communauté Française, with a cinema, theatre, and exhibition halls. The French-style gardens feature statues by Meunier, but are known as a night-time haunt for drug dealers; better to join the arty crowd in the centre's café.
236 rue Royale, St-Josse & Scharbeek ☎ 02.226.12.11 Ⓜ Botanique
🅱️ 180BF ⏰ 11am–6pm Tue–Sun ♿

La Bourse (Beurs)
E2

The flamboyant Neoclassical stock exchange, which boasts sculptures by Rodin, stands in splendid isolation on the shoddy boulevard Anspach. It's still active and its steps, flanked by two imposing lions, are a favourite haunt for activists and demonstrators.
2 rue Henri Maus, Central M Bourse

Cathédrale St-Michel-&-St-Gudule (St-Michiels & St-Goedele Kathedraal)
E3

Out on a limb between the upper and lower towns – and surrounded by soulless modern buildings – this masterpiece of Brabant Gothic architecture dates back to 1226. Curiously, for such a dreamily medieval pile, it's only been a cathedral since 1962.
parvis St-Gudule, Central ☎ 02.217.83.45 M Centrale ☞ free ⊟ none ◑ 8am– 7pm daily ♿

Colonne du Congrès (Congreszuil)
E3

Completed in 1859 to celebrate the founding of Belgium's constitutional monarchy, this poignant monument is the focus for memorial services on Armistice Day (11 Nov). An eternal flame burns at the base of the 47m-high column in memory of the Unknown Soldiers of the two world wars.
place du Congrès, Central ⊟ Place du Congres

Eglise Ste-Marie (Kon. Ste-Mariakerk)
off map

An eclectic, eccentric 19th-century church at the northern end of rue Royale; the architect was inspired by London's St Paul's Cathedral and Istanbul's Haghia Sofya, which explains the bizarre neo-Byzantine influence. Regularly threatened with demolition, it was saved by local action groups and restored in 1996.
rue Royale, St-Josse & Schaerbeek M Botanique ☞ free ◑ varies

Grand' Place (Grote Markt)
B6/F2

Yes, it's touristy, but Brussels' centrepiece has too much magic to be ruined by the hordes who traipse its cobbles. Louis XIV's artillery razed the square in 1695, aiming for but missing the Hôtel de Ville. Brussels' burghers rebuilt the rest in Flemish Renaissance Baroque style, in three years. Visit at night, when gentle lighting illuminates the gilt edges of the guildhouses.
Central M Bourse

Manneken Pis & Jeanneke Pis   🎧A6/F2

Brussels' no. 1 postcard image is the disappointingly small (30cm) statue of a boy peeing; even worse, he's only a copy of the 1619 original which was stolen and smashed in 1817. A female equivalent, the Jeanneke Pis, crouches round the corner; the result of an entrepreneurial restaurant owner trying to woo tourists his way.

Manneken Pis: corner of rue du Chêne & rue de l'Etuve, Central; Jeanneke Pis: Impasse de la Fidélité, Central 🚇 Bourse 🎫 free 🍴 none ⏰ 24 hours daily

La Monnaie (De Munt)   🎧F2

The city's elegant Neoclassical opera house (1817) was built on the site of a 17th-century theatre. It saw revolution in 1830 when, fired by a nationalistic Auber opera, theatre-goers poured onto the square and raised the Brabant flag, the first step in Belgium's fight for independence.

place de la Monnaie, Central 🚇 De Brouckére

Palais de Justice (Poelaert)   🎧F6

The construction of this mock-classical law court (the highest in the land) required mass local evictions. A typically overstated Léopold II project, it was conceived as the largest building on the continent. Candles burn outside to remember Julie and Mélissa, alleged victims of Belgium's notorious paedophile, Marc Dutroux.

place Poelaert, Le Sablon 🚃 Place Poelaert

Palais Royal (Koninklijk Paleis)   🎧C7

This is where tourists who don't read Hello! discover that Belgium has a royal family. Its members prefer to hang out at their Laeken pad, away from the public eye, although they deign to appear at the balcony of this Léopold II-era mock-Louis XVI affair on special occasions, like the Belgian National Day.

place du Palais, Le Sablon 🚃 Place Royale

Place des Martyrs (Martelaarsplein)   🎧D2

Built in 1775, this Neoclassical square, which honours the 450 citizens killed in the 1830 uprising, is a sad symbol of the divide that has flogged Belgium since the 1960s. Those in favour of a united Flemish and Francophone country were horrified when the Flemish Regional Government planted its headquarters, awash with their flags, here.

Central 🚇 De Brouckére

Place Royale (Koningsplein)
♯C7

An opulent 18th-century square built over the Habsburg emperors' 15th-century palace. At its centre is a statue of Godefroid de Bouillon, a crusader king who captured Jerusalem; behind is the Eglise St-Jacques-Sur-Coudenberg; and in front is Calder's *Whirling Ear* sculpture brought out for Brussels' stint as European City of Culture in 2000.

Le Sablon ⊞ Place Royale

Porte de Hal (Hallepoort)
♯B9

This lonesome tower, sole survivor of the city's second medieval wall, provides a mournful contrast to the office blocks on boulevard du Midi. It served as a prison from the 16th to the 18th centuries, but is now home to the Musée du Folklore. It's one of few medieval remnants not ruined by modern developments.

boulevard du Midi, Les Marolles ⊞ Port de Hal

Tour et Taxis (Thurn et Taxis)
♯off map

This colossal, derelict 19th-century customs depot is the focus of an acrimonious battle between heritage enthusiasts and developers who want to turn it into an entertainment complex. Meanwhile, it's a suitably grand venue for the Couleur Café festival, and an impressive place for an illicit stroll.

5–7 rue Picard, Molenbeek ⊞ Ribaucourt

Tunnels
♯throughout town

Both the bane and the joy of motorists, the tunnels that bypass central Brussels were built for the 1958 Exposition *Universelle*. They ease traffic, but when there's an accident, drivers get stuck in polluted underground jams. Newcomers often struggle to navigate the underground whirl.

around central Brussels

government buildings

Parlement Européen (Europees Parlement)
♯E13

Built for 600+ MEPs, many of whom complain about the rabbit-warren corridors and pokey rooms, this glass-and-steel edifice earned its nickname of *Les Caprices des Dieux* for two reasons: one, locals thought it pretentious, hence the 'whim of the gods'; two, it resembles the French cheese of the same name.

rue Wiertz, Quartier Européen ⊞ Trône

Résidence Palace ♭D8

This yellowbrick Art Deco complex, in the European quarter, was conceived as a luxury residential complex for the bourgeois set of the 1920s, with an on-site restaurant, theatre, hairdresser, and a gorgeous mock-Moorish indoor swimming pool. It now houses the country's fearsome immigration office.

rue de la Loi, Quartier Européen Ⓜ Schuman

St-Gilles Hôtel de Ville (Stadhuis St-Gillis) ♭F9/E10

The *St-Gillois* are proud of their ornate, Renaissance-style 19th-century town hall, the most impressive in Brussels bar the one on the Grand' Place. It's a sign of the bygone wealth of this neighbourhood, now one of the poorer parts of the city, with a large immigrant population.

place Maurice van Meenen, St-Gilles Ⓜ Horta

viewpoints

Arc de Triomphe ♭A/B13

Climb to the top of the Arc de Triomphe through the Musée Royal de l'Armée et d'Histoire Militaire for fantastic views over the Quartier Européen.

Parc du Cinquantenaire, Quartier Européen ☎ 02.737.78.11 Ⓜ Mérode 🚌 free

Atomium ♭off map

The top pod of this 102m-high landmark (model of an iron atom, magnified 165 billion times) provides a fantastic view over the whole of Brussels' cityscape.

boulevard du Centenaire, Heysel ☎ 02.474.89.77 Ⓜ Heysel 🚌 200BF

Basilique du Sacré-Coeur ♭off map

Climb right to the top of the dome in this landmark basilica for a fantastic panorama of Brussels city centre from further afield.

parvis de la Basilique, Koekelberg ☎ 02.425.88.22 Ⓜ Simonis, then 🚌 87 🚌 free

Hilton Brussels ♭F6

The Hilton towers over Brussels' most exclusive shopping district and overlooks Egmont Palace. Head to the 27th floor for the best outlook.

boulevard de Waterloo, Ixelles (West) ☎ 02.504.11.11 Ⓜ Porte de Namur 🚌 free

Manhattan Center
♭B2

Take the lift to the top of this humongous office-block complex which houses many multinational companies, three floors of shops, and a multi-storey car park. The view's all about distance, not detail, as this place towers way above its neighbours.

21–34 avenue du Boulevard, St-Josse & Schaerbeek ☎ 02.23.36.36 Ⓜ Rogier 🎫 free

Mont des Arts
♭B6

Just a little way down the hill from place Royale is this little piece of serenity. Sit on the fountain's wall and gaze down onto the *jardin* and across the lower town.

rue Montagne de la Cour, Le Sablon Ⓜ Centrale 🎫 free

Magasin Old England
♭A7

This one-time department store has shut up shop for good and now houses the Musée des Instruments de Musique. The top-floor restaurant provides magnificent views over downtown Brussels.

2 rue Montagne de la Cour, Le Sablon ☎ 02.545.01.30 Ⓜ Centrale 🎫 free

Place Poelaert
♭F6

Stand in awe at the Palais du Justice then turn around and gawp at the view this square has over the Lower Town. On a clear day you can see right across the city to the Atomium and the Basilique du Sacré-Coeur to the north.

Place Poelaert, Le Sablon Ⓜ Toison d'Or 🎫 free

Le Roy d'Espagne
♭E2

This former bakers' guildhouse-turned-bar, with the best address in town, is spread over a series of floors, each slightly different from the next. Its architecture is amazing, but the real draw is the view over the Gothic Grand' Place, particularly impressive at night. So grab a window seat in one of the upper rooms and drool.

1 Grand' Place, Central ☎ 02.513.08.07 Ⓜ De Brouckère 🎫 cost of a drink

Sheraton
♭A3

The rooftop pool and open-air terrace provide an amazing stance from which to look south over Brussels' inner ring. Catch this vista for Sunday brunch, with access to the pool and organized kids' activities.

3 place Rogier, Central ☎ 02.224.34.56 Ⓜ Rogier 🎫 free

Centre Belge de la Bande Dessinée (Belgisch Centrum van het Beeldverhaal) ♪C3

Epitomising Belgians' fascination with all things *bande dessinée* (comic strip), this centre shows just how seriously they take the eighth art. The museum (which shows some 300 of its 6000 original plates at any one time) is housed in one of the city's Art Nouveau gems, a converted department store designed by the grand master himself, Victor Horta, in 1903. Get yourself re-acquainted with Belgium's two most famous comic exports, the Smurfs and Tintin. The former were, rather disappointingly, born out of a silly conversation about salt between their creater, Peyo, and fellow illustrator Franquin. Tintin, meanwhile, has been the centre of controversy since Hergé's death, due to the illustrator's debatable political views (the quiffed reporter first appeared in 1930 in a strip called *Tintin in the Land of the Soviets*, which made no effort to hide its Bolshevik-bashing intentions; and during WWII Hergé carried on illustrating for the Nazi-controlled *Le Soir*). Although a lot of the museum is a pull for all ages, some is purely for those in long trousers. On the top floor are images to make your grandma blush – bloody babies being pulled from the womb, erotic encounters in bathtubs, and a graphic guide to masturbation. Younger eyes can see how cartoons are made, wander round a life-size animation set, then peek in the world's largest comic library.

👁 Showroom of Imagination.

♻ 1| If comics aren't your bag, but Art Nouveau is, look around the lobby (or grab a bevvy in the café) without paying the entrance fee. 2| The museum shop has a great collection of Belgian comic books, some in English, as well as Tintin paraphernalia.

20 rue des Sables, Central ☎ 02.219.19.80 Ⓜ De Brouckère; Rogier; Botanique ⓑⓕ 250BF 🚭 none ⏰ *10am–6pm Tue–Sun* ♿

Musée D'Art Ancien (Museum voor Oude Kunst) ♪D6/C7

The façade's colossal pillars and the cavernous entry hall proclaim this a serious space, a temple from which to worship the god of fine art. And why not, when you've got one of Europe's best collections of Flemish masters at your disposal?

The museum is split into two main sections, with a sculpture hall (Rodin, Meunier, George Minne) in the basement: the blue route takes in a daunting 35 rooms devoted to 15th- and 16th-century artists, while the brown route covers the 17th and 18th centuries. The blue is the more impressive, with an awesome array of Flemish Primitives. The obvious draw is the Brueghel room, with the magnificent *Fall of Icarus* and the haunting *Massacre of the Innocents*. Alongside Bouts, Memling, Matsys, Pourbus, and Bosch, look out for a strong German collection dominated by Lucas Cranach. If you're overwhelmed by altarpieces and biblical scenes, the brown route offers secular relief, but if you're left cold by banqueting tables and portraits of Dutchmen you've never heard of, you'll be through in a jiffy. Stop, though, in the first of several Rubens rooms, with its intriguing small-format works as well as the signature swirling religious dramas.

👁 The Brueghels; Cranach's *Adam and Eve*; Bouts' *Judgement of the Emperor Otto*; Gerard David's *Madonna with the Porridge Spoon*; Van der Weyden's *Lamentation*; Rubens' *Four Negro Heads & Martyrdom of St Ursula*; Rembrandt's *La Morte*; Jordaens' *The King Drinks*.

🖒 1| The shop has good stock and prices are reasonable. 2| Pleasant sculpture garden just outside.

🖓 You can only buy a combined ticket for the Musées d'Art Ancien et Moderne.

3 rue de la Régence, Le Sablon ☎ 02.508. 32.11 w www.fine-arts-museum.be Ⓜ Parc 🕅 150BF (combined with Musée d'Art Moderne) 🚋 all ◐ 10am–5pm Tue–Sun ♿

Musée D'Art Moderne (Museum voor Moderne Kunst)   ♪D6

A slightly misleading name, given that much of the collection dates from the early 19th century, but think of it as a sample of Belgian art since the country's creation and you won't be disappointed. Like its sister museum, the Musée d'Art Ancien, it is divided in two: the yellow route on the upper floors for the 19th century, and the green route, housed in a subterranean complex, for the 20th.

Upstairs, the tourists go for David's overstylised *Death of Marat*, but the real highlights are the Belgian Impressionists and Pointillists (Monet, Bonnard, Seurat, Signac), Meunier's sculptures and industrial paintings, and the macabre, mask-filled works of James Ensor, usefully shown alongside his accomplished early landscapes. A rough-hewn wooden Zadkine sculpture, *Diana*, ushers you onto the green track, which takes in the world's biggest Magritte collection (on level 6). There are also works by Dalí, Miró, and the even weirder Surrealism of Paul Delvaux, plus an enlightening selection of less famous but equally talented Belgians, notably the intense, proto-noir works of Léon Spilliaert, and Constant Permeke's hulking, gloomy figures. On the international front, the collection opts for quality, not quantity, with top dogs represented by one or two prime-period efforts rather than a slew of artists' studios. Many museums could do with a similar policy.

⊙ Marat, if you must; Meunier's *Old Mine Horse*; Emile Claus' luminist landscapes; Ensor's *Skeletons Fighting Over a Kipper*; Spilliaert's *The Beach*; Permeke's *Potato Eaters*; Delvaux's *Crucifixion*; Bacon's *Pope With Owls*; Magritte's *Empire of Lights*; Broodthaers' *Red Pot of Mussels*.

⊙ There are 12 levels, so pace yourself.

rue de la Régence, Le Sablon ☎ 02.508. 32.11 w www.fine-arts-museum.be Ⓜ Parc 🚇 150BF (combined with Musée D'Art Ancien) 🚃 all ◑ *10am–5pm Tue–Sun.* ♿

Musée Royal de l'Armée & d'Histoire Militaire (Koninklijk Museum van het Leger & de Krijgskunde)
♭B14

You don't have to be a war buff to appreciate this museum. If time's of the essence, head straight to the fourth floor where there's an exhibition of fairly well-preserved military helmets, swords and badges of honour from the Napoleonic era. The 19th-century Belgian section covers the 1830 Revolution (which resulted in Belgium's independence) and features wall displays of swords and guns. Nearby, the section *Air et Espace* (in a hall built to house the *Exposition Universelle de 1910*) holds over 130 flying machines to keep any plane buff in paradise for hours. Or step outside into the courtyard and take the display of WWII tanks head on.

One of the most interesting areas is the Resistance and Deportation display, which charts Nazi occupation in Belgium during WWII – see how and why Léopold III abdicated, and how some Flemish nationalists cooperated with the Germans, lured by false promises of independence. Shop windows from the era (with a 'potatoes sold out' sign outside) and an otherwise cosy kitchen (which has a radio tuned into the news of that era) give a feel for everyday life in wartime. Follow eye-witness accounts of victims of the Nazi occupation on video screens and headphones. Part of the charm of the museum is its haphazardness and lack of explanation for what's on display – it's not unusual to find a statue or an old map hidden in a dark corner.

⊙ 1| The Titeca Collection of weapons and uniforms occupies a room above the Arc de Triomphe – you can step out onto the roof for amazing views over the Quartier Européen. 2| Free admission.

Parc du Cinquantenaire, Quartier Européen ☎ 02.737.78.11 w www.klm-mra. be Ⓜ Mérode 🚇 free ◑ *9am–12pm, 1–4.45pm Tue–Sun.*

Musée Royal d'Art & d'Histoire (Koninklijke Musea voor Kunst & Geschiedenis)
♪B14

From images of kings cavorting with half-human, half-beast crea-tures, to punk wedding dresses with safety-pins, the exhibits in this museum leap from one epoch to another with furious abandon. It houses about a thousand artefacts, the sacred competing with the profane for space. There's no shortage of visual stimulation, yet the lack of obvious logic to the layout, its poor signposting and the fact that much of its cataloguing is exclusively in Flemish may baffle. Trying to catch everything is neither practical nor advisable. Some gems worth hunting for include the limestone relief of Queen Tiy from 1375 BC Egypt, the colossal stone figure of a man from Easter Island, and the immaculately preserved biblical tapestries from 16th-century Belgium. But the most intriguing thing about this museum is that its curators seem to have a Monty Python-like sense of humour. Across from tombs bearing heavy images of death, for example, they have an oddball collection of heart-shaped objects in a room dedicated to the late cardiologist, Dr Boyadjian. They also have a section showing how the costumes of baptism, communion and matrimony have never been based on good taste or sense.

✂ There's an exhibition space for the blind.

❶ The Treasure Room (with medieval jewellery) has limited open-ing hours, so head there first if it's open.

3 parc du Cinquantenaire, Quartier Européen ☎ 02.741.72.11
w www.kmkg-mrah.be Ⓜ Merode 🚇 150BF ◑ 9.30am–5pm Tue–Sun (from 10am Sat–Sun) ♿

Musée Royal de l'Afrique Centrale (Koninklijk Museum voor Midden-Afrika)
♪F3

At its foundation in 1897, this exhibition space was called the Musée du Congo. It was originally built to celebrate, and even brag about, Belgium's imperial expansion into the Congo. Its stance at the time was very much 'see how the savages of Africa live', with Congolese performers regularly brought over for major celebrations. Almost from the moment Léopold II took his place on the throne, he revealed his ambition to create a Belgian empire. By 1884, he had taken personal control of the Congo and, over the next two decades, he made an immense fortune from ivory and rubber, most of it off the work of slaves. Léopold's rule was so harsh that even other impe-rialistic countries, like Britain, expressed concern about conditions; Conrad based *Heart of Darkness* on the notorious brutality of the Belgian Congo.

This museum holds the remnants of decades of colonial rule (the Congo was granted independence in 1960). The museum still bears the hallmarks of its past as an imperial showcase (there's no mention of the millions of Congolese who died under Léopold's rule), but the boastfulness has been replaced by an almost apologetic stance. The museum has a comprehensive collection of insects, masks, and sculpture. But there are other gems worth seeking out: a 22.5m *pirogue* (canoe) that can hold 100 men and was built from the trunk of a single tree; a pickled coelacanth (a living fossil fish believed to have been extinct for 70 million years until its discovery off Africa in 1938); and a wonderful technicolour display of ceremonial African dress.

♧ Tervuren Park, around the museum, offers a peaceful escape.
♕ For information about exhibits in English, buy the guidebook (100 BF).
❶ Temporary exhibitions are usually far more exciting than the permanent ones.

13 chaussée de Louvain, Tervuren ☎ 02.769.52.11 w www.africamuseum.be 🚌 29 BF 200BF 🚊 none ◐ 10am–5pm Tue–Fri; 10am–6pm Sat–Sun ♿

museums

Bijlokemuseum   ♭ off map
Get back to Gent's roots at the Bijlokemuseum, a medieval abbey with a collection exploring local history from the 7th century to the French Revolution.
Godshuizenlaan, Gent ☎ 20.225.11.06 by rail

Ethnografisch Museum   ♭ off map
Houses an impressive array of pottery, jewellery, masks, and musical instruments from around the world.
19 Suikerrui, Antwerpen ☎ 03.232.08.82 by rail

Groeningemuseum   ♭ off map
For more world-class art, the Groeningemuseum (Brugge) houses works by the likes of Van Eyck, Brueghel, Bosch, and Magritte.
12 Dijver, Brugge ☎ 050.44.87.50 by rail

Mayer van den Bergh Museum   ♭ off map
A private collection with one of Breughel's most famous paintings, *Dulle Griet*.
19 Lange Gasthuisstr, Antwerpen ☎ 03.232.42.37 by rail

Museum voor Industriële Archeologie en Textiel ♪*off map*
If you're into industrial heritage, the Museum voor Industriële Archeologie en Textiel gives the lowdown on Gent's 19th-century revival (kick-started by the theft of a spinning jenny from Manchester), and has splendid city views.
9 Minnemeers, Gent ☎ 09.223.59.69 by rail

Museum voor Sierkunst ♪*off map*
On the waterfront, the Museum voor Sierkunst (Gent) is a well-assembled tribute to the applied arts, with a strong collection of Belgian Art Nouveau and Modernist pieces, as well as international-quality shows.
5 Jan Breydelstraat, Gent ☎ 09.225.66.76 by rail

Museum voor Schone Kunsten ♪*off map*
The Museum voor Schone Kunsten, in Citadelpark, has a haunting Bosch, *The Bearing of the Cross*.
5 Jan Breydelstraat, Gent ☎ 09.267.99.99 by rail

Museum voor Fotografie ♪*off map*
An old warehouse devoted to photography and film-making. Besides quality contemporary shows, it has a superb permanent collection featuring work by the likes of Cartier-Bresson and Man Ray.
47 Waalse Kaai, Antwerpen ☎ 03.242.93.10 by rail

Het Steen
A former prison that now houses a maritime museum. ♪*off map*
1 Steenplein, Antwerpen ☎ 03.232.08.50 by rail

famous houses

Gruuthuse ♪*off map*
Built by a noble family in the 1400s and boasting fantastic Gothic halls.
17 Dijver, Brugge ☎ 050.44.87.62 by rail

Hans Memling Museum ♪*off map*
A 13th-century former hospital, is home to six outstanding paintings by the Flemish Primitive.
38 Mariastraat, Brugge ☎ 050.44.87.70 by rail

Maison d'Erasme (Erasmushuis) ♪*off map*
Renaissance philosopher Desiderius Erasmus may only have spent a grand total of five months here, but he might as well have spent his

whole life in this impressive gabled house. Someone must have gone to a lot of trouble to get a piece of his coffin, a cast of his skull and numerous portraits all depicting the man in his signature beret-like hat. They all look similar to each other, except for the unflattering watercolour featuring a pale-looking Erasmus shortly before his death. But even those who are not Erasmus groupies will appreciate the old stuff here, and it's easy to get a feel for what life was like back then. Fortunately, the museum provides thick guidebooks describing all the objects on display, but one would be well-advised to read up on the humanist philosopher beforehand so as not to feel intimidated by this shrine to academia.

31 rue du Chapitre, Anderlecht ☎ 02.521.13.83 w www.ciger.be/erasmus Ⓜ St-Guidon 🚊 50BF (combined ticket with Musée du Béguinage) 🚇 none ◑ 10am–12pm; 2–5pm Mon; Wed–Thu; Sat–Sun ♿ limited

Musée Constantin Meunier (Constantin Meunier Museum) ✏ off map

Tucked away on a residential street, this modest 19th-century town house was the home and studio of an unjustly neglected sculptor, Constantin Meunier (1831–1905), described by the British art critic Brian Sewell as 'a Belgian who deserves to be famous'. Originally a painter of religious scenes, Meunier changed tack completely following a trip to Belgium's industrial heartland, the Borinage, where he was shocked by the conditions endured by miners and steel-workers. The resulting sculptures recall Rodin in their muscular power, while the blend of pain, endurance, and dignity on the faces of his working-class heroes sets a benchmark for social realism throughout Europe, an impassioned reaction against stuffy academies and their narrow conception of fine art. In his group pieces, the energy and dynamo of new technologies shines through, but the intolerable strains they imposed upon the human workers were Meunier's real concern. This coherent collection, displayed on the ground floor and in the studio at the back, includes sketches and paintings as well as imposing bronze sculptures of working men.

◉ *The Reaper; Pain; Le Retour des Mineurs*, one of his best-known paintings.

59 rue de l'Abbaye, Ixelles (West) ☎ 02.648.44.99 🚊 93, 94 🚇 free 🚇 none ◑ 10am–12pm & 1–5pm Mon–Fri, plus every 2nd Sat

Musée David et Alice van Buuren (Museum David en Alice van Buuren) ✏ off map

The wealthy Dutch banker and art collector David van Buuren built this delightful 1930s Art Deco villa on an elegant suburban street in Uccle. Don't be alarmed when the curators ask you to schlep about in ragged overshoes: it's a small price to pay for padding on gorgeous Art Deco carpets and the almost voyeuristic sensation of sneaking round someone's home. Mind you, it's hardly your average home: the lounge is adorned with paintings by Belgian artists Rik Wouters and James Ensor, sketches by van Gogh, and a version of *The Fall of Icarus* thought to be one of three on the theme by Pieter Brueghel the Elder, though some experts claim it was painted after his death. Stylish furnishings include Lalique vases and, in the upstairs office, a magnificent desk with a lush *shagreen* (sharkskin) surface. In fine weather you can explore the garden, which features a labyrinth designed by celebrated Belgian landscapist René Péchère.

41 avenue Léo Errera, Uccle ☎ 02.343.48.51 🚊 23, 90 〔BR〕 300BF (house & gardens), 250BF (gardens only) 🚇 none ◑ 2–6pm Mon; 1–6pm Sat ♿

Musée Horta (Hortamuseum) $off map

Few can resist the full-on enjoyment of this house and studio which Victor Horta, the pioneer of Art Nouveau architecture, built for himself between 1898 and 1901. The façade is far from the movement's most flamboyant, but there's a glorious glow to the interior, thanks to the warm ochre and amber colours of the furnishings. This is Horta at his purest and most inventive, without the vulgar flourishes some of his clients demanded: no expense has been spared, from the exquisite wood panelling and wrought iron, to the swirling door handles and coat hooks. The centrepiece is the stairwell, topped by a glass canopy from which light streams through the house, while the small, peaceful upstairs balcony offers a fine view of the surrounding private gardens. Horta lived here until 1919, by which time the horrors of war and a new austerity had cast a shadow over the excesses of Art Nouveau.

♿ The shop has great books about Art Nouveau.

❶ There's a limit of 45 people in the house at any one time; and it's less crowded on weekdays.

26 rue Américaine, Ixelles (West) ☎ 02.543.04.90 🚊 81, 82 〔BR〕 150BF (200BF Sat–Sun) 🚇 none ◑ 2–5.30pm Tue–Sun

Musée René Magritte (René Magrittemuseum) $off map

True Surrealist art fans should bypass the city's main art museums – crammed with lots of other stuff – and head straight for the house where Belgium's most famous Surrealist lived for 24 years. The home is rather modest – René Magritte was not a collector of others' art – but it is quite extraordinary to see the fireplace and the black bowler hat immortalized in Magritte's work on the coat rack in the hallway.

There is just a small smattering of his work on display, but a rather impressive assortment of personal effects, like his wife's piano notes and Magritte's own camera collection. The room where a dozen or so Belgian Surrealists used to gather at a time is surprisingly tiny. Beginning with the moment you ring the doorbell, visiting this place, where the artist did about half his work, is a very intimate and rewarding experience.

❶ Sat–Sun can be crowded

135 rue Esseghem, Evre ☎ 02.428.26.26 ▣ 18 🔢 240BF 🍴 none ❶ 10am– 6pm Wed–Sun. ☞ 🛈

Musée Wiertz (Wiertzmuseum) ♀E8

A monument to ludicrous delusions of grandeur, the former home and studio of artist Joseph Wiertz (1806–65) offers welcome light relief from the office-block monotony of the Quartier Européen. It's stuffed with overwrought, oversized canvases by a painter whose ego exceeded his talent: a competent Neoclassical artist, he saw himself as the equal of Rubens and Michelangelo. Inspired by Classical and Biblical themes, his paintings alternate between the macabre and the mildly pornographic, with the moral consistency of a modern slasher flick: lithe nudes rub shoulders with gruesome depictions of hell, hunger and the horrors of contemporary medicine. Think *Enfant Brûlé* (Burnt Child) and *Inhumanation Précipitée* (Premature Burial) and you'll get the idea. They went down a storm with his contemporaries, but his continued fame is principally due to a canny deal with the state: build me a studio, and I'll leave you my work when I die. Perhaps prophetically, Wiertz believed that Brussels would one day eclipse 'provincial Paris'; good foresight as the museum is next door to the Parlement Européen.

62 rue Vautier, Quartier Européen ☎ 02.648.17.18 ▣ 21, 34, 80 🔢 free 🍴 none ❶ 10am–12pm & 1–5pm Tue–Fri & every other weekend

Museum Plantin-Moretus ♀off map

Those of a bookish bent will love the Museum Plantin-Moretus. Located west of the cobbled Vrijdagmarkt, in the former marble-floored printing house and mansion of Renaissance publisher Christopher Plantin, it features a stunning collection of presses, rare books, and sketches by Rubens. Plantin's greatest achievement was the Polyglot Bible, written in four languages, although font fanatics might know him as the originator of the Plantin and Garamond sets, both still in use today.

22 Vrijdagmarkt, Antwerpen ☎ 03.221.14.51 by rail

Rubenshuis
♀off map

A red-brick 17th-century mansion where Rubens lived and worked. You can see some of his minor works inside before taking a break in the formal, but cosy, garden out back.

9–11 Wapper, Antwerpen ☎ 03.201.15.55 by rail

Stedelijk Museum voor Actuele Kunst (SMAK)
♀off map

The ultra-contemporary Stedelijk Museum voor Actuele Kunst (aka SMAK). The brainchild of Belgian curating legend Jan Hoet, it's housed in an old casino and showcases Hoet's cutting-edge personal collection, which includes works by Francis Bacon and Andy Warhol.

Citadelpark, Gent ☎ 09.221.17.03 by rail

one-offs

Centraal Station
♀off map

The stunningly flamboyant, neo-Baroque Centraal Station was completed in 1905 as a celebration of industrial progress.

Koningin Astridplein, Antwerpen by rail

Gravensteen
♀off map

A dark, sober fortress with a horribly graphic torture chamber.

St-Veerleplein, Gent ☎ 09.225.93.06

Hôtel de Ville (Stadhuis)
♀B6/F2

The newly cleaned and blindingly spruce town hall, dominated by a slimline 96m tower, is among the city's most beautiful sights, and arguably the finest Gothic structure in Europe. Started in 1402, the spire was completed 50 years later by Jan van Ruysbroeck, and was one of the few buildings on the Grand' Place to survive the French bombardment of 1695. Its charming asymmetry is the result of regulations that forbade building over the nearby rue Tête d'Or. A more interesting local rule is that civil marriage ceremonies for the commune's citizens take place in the town hall – a great reason to live in downtown Brussels. Join a tour and you can view the function rooms, adorned with 18th- and 19th-century tapestries, 19th-century depictions of bygone Brussels, and full-length portraits of Mary of Burgundy, Charles V and other rulers.

❶ The inner Baroque courtyard, with its fountains, is a cool spot for escaping the Grand' Place scrum; and it hosts concerts in summer.

Grand' Place, Central ☎ 02.279.43.65 Ⓜ De Brouckère ⓑⓕ 100BF
🚋 none ◑ *Guided tours only:* 11.30am & 3.15pm Tue (year round); 3.15pm Wed (year round); 12.15pm Sun (Apr–Sep only)

Manneken Pis & Jeanneke Pis
A6/F2

What can you make of a city that promotes a 30cm widdling youth as one of its greatest assets? If you can bear to be seen there, it's worth checking out Brussels' favourite 'little man', if only to see the bemused faces of onlookers and hear the cries of 'but he's so small'. The legends that surround him are less of a let-down. Is he a homage to a quick-thinking medieval lad who put out a firebomb by pissing on it? Or the boy Godrey, future 12th-century Duke of Brabant, who manfully peed on the enemy when taken to battle? Or perhaps he was the creation of a thankful farmer who lost his son during carnival and found him calmly doing a wee? What we do know is that the Manneken Pis was created in 1619, that there have, incredibly, been several attempts to steal him (one successful, in 1817, meaning this is a copy), and that he has been showered with outfits, now exceeding 600. Examples of his fancy dress, including Mickey Mouse and Elvis suits, are in the Maison du Roi. The Jeanneke Pis, off the tacky rue des Bouchers, was created in 1985 by a restaurateur who hoped the statue of a grimacing, peeing girl with pigtails would attract more trade. For locals, she's a shameless travesty, but the tourists look set to make her a fixture.
Manneken Pis: corner of rue du Chêne & rue de l'Etuve, Central; Jeanneke Pis: Impasse de la Fidélité, Central Ⓜ **Bourse** Ⓑ **free** 🚆 **none** 🕐 *24 hours daily*

Musée Bruxellois de la Gueuze (Brussels Museum van de Geuze)
off map

Founded in 1900 by Paul Cantillon, who left the family brewery in Flanders following a fight with his brother, this is the only surviving Brussels brewery dedicated to the production of *gueuze*, a distinctively sour beer unique to the region, and of the famous fruit beers *kriek* and *framboise*. Family-run, and using age-old techniques that rely on natural, spontaneous fermentation, the museum is equally dedicated to educating a public that is used to the ersatz *krieks* produced by Belle-Vue and others: taste the real thing and you'll never forget it. After a wonderfully impassioned introduction, you're free to wander the building and marvel at its magnificent machinery, including a vast copper vat, before heading back to the foyer for a tasting session. The still-working brewery grinds into life in winter, when cooler weather ensures hygienic fermentation; the brewing season kicks off and ends with open days (late Nov and early Mar). If you'd rather savour your *gueuze* in peace, drop in on working days through the rest of the year.
❶ Best time to visit is Oct–Apr when the beer is being produced.
56 rue Ghuede, Anderlecht ☎ **02.520.28.91** Ⓜ **Gare du Midi** Ⓑ **100BF** 🚆 **none** 🕐 *9am–5pm Mon–Sat (from 10am Sat)*

Musée des Instruments de Musique (Muziekinstrumentenmuseum)

C7

If you don't know your Gambian harp lute from your Tunisian rebab, you're in for a treat. Housed since 2000 in the Art Nouveau Magasin Old England, this is a stunning collection of historical instruments from around the world. Interactive headsets, which respond to infrared signals from some of the displays, allow you to hear what the instruments sound like. The recordings are sometimes a touch out of sync, but the irritant factor is outweighed by the pleasure of watching people jiggling their heads to get the music. An extravagant collection of keyboard instruments includes an 18th-century pyramid piano, one of the earliest upright pianos, and a 17th-century Italian harpsichord coated with bouncing cherubs. Touring the World Instruments collection, where you can pour over ancient African lyres and fantastically long Tibetan trumpets, is like speed-travelling through thousands of years of musical history. The café on the sixth floor has superb views of central Brussels, beautifully framed by crescent-shaped wrought-iron windows.

♪ 1| Stylish café with terrace, mod-Med and Belgian cuisine.
2| Excellent shop with specialist music books.
♪ Beautiful but impractical lift, which gets stuck when people forget to close the double doors, which they invariably do.
2 rue Montagne de la Cour, Le Sablon ☎ 02.545.01.30
w www.mim.fgov.be Ⓜ Centrale ⟦BF⟧ 150BF ◑ 9.30am–5.30pm
Tue–Fri; 10am–5pm Sat–Sun ♿

Théâtre de Toone (Theater Toone VII)

F2

There can't be many places in the world where you can watch papier-mâché puppets lampoon politicians by performing *Macbeth* in an incomprehensible dialect. Brussels' tradition of subversive puppetry goes back to the days of Spanish rule, when theatres were closed to stifle local protest and a less obvious form of satire developed. The Théâtre Royal de Toone, founded by Antoine Toone in the Marolles in 1835, moved to this secluded medieval alley in 1966. Shows take place in an intimate atmosphere on a tiny stage. The dialect, Vloms, a weird mix of French, Dutch, and Spanish, is taken very seriously by current master puppeteer José Geal (Toone VII) and a small group of enthusiasts dedicated to preserving a language that nobody speaks. In the unlikely event that you understand the lingo, you'll be in for a feast of Rabelaisian mischief. Otherwise, hold out for performances in English.

♪ Atmospheric bar, great for tasting local beers.
♪ The museum is only open during performance intervals.
6 petite rue des Bouchers, Central ☎ 02.513.54.86 Ⓜ Bourse
⟦BF⟧ performances from 400BF ⊟ none ◑ varies

religious buildings

Basilique Nationale du Sacré-Coeur (Heilig Hat Basiliek) *♪off map*
This early 20th-century twin-towered building is the duckling among Brussels' churches. Still, it has its charms, like the bold colourful windows – especially in the side chapels – which brighten up the drab interior. One wonders what the place looked like before the huge restoration project. The folk here also run their own tourist office and a Christian comic-book store.
👁 Climb up the dome for a spectacular view.
1 parvis de la Basilique, Koekelberg ☎ 02.425.88.22 Ⓜ Simonis ⒝ 100BF 🖃 none ① 9am–6pm daily ঙ

Belfort (Belfry) *♪off map*
Feeling energetic? Then climb the 366 steps of the Belfort (Belfry) for awesome views of the city.
17 Markt, Brugge ☎ 050.44.87.67 by rail

Belfort (Belfry) *♪off map*
The 14th-century Belfort is crowned with a gilded dragon that symbolizes Gent's jealously guarded freedom.
Emile Braunpl, Gent ☎ 09.233.39.54 by rail

Cathédrale St-Michel & St-Gudule (St-Michiels & St-Goedele Kathedraal) *♪E3*
If you only have time for one church in Brussels, this is the one. A one-stop shop, it has everything a Gothic cathedral (started in 1226) should have – impressive towers, a grand collection of golden chalices and other holy artefacts, paintings by famous artists, and a souvenir store to boot. No wonder Belgian royalty, Prince Philippe and Princess Mathilde, chose to get married here.
parvis St-Gudule, Central ☎ 02.217.83.45 Ⓜ Centrale ⒝ free 🖃 none ① 8am– 7pm daily ঙ

Chapelle de la Madeleine (Magdalenakapel) *♪B6*
This quaint little brick church, part of a convent in the Middle Ages, is oozing cuteness. It is decorated with a modern flair: the unusual stained-glass designs could be something out of a Cubist painting, and the ceramic depictions of the stations of the cross are most unusual.
rue de la Madeleine, Central ☎ 02.511.28.45 Ⓜ Centrale ⒝ free 🖃 none ① 7am–7.30pm Mon–Sat; 7am–12pm & 5–8pm Sun ঙ

Eglise des Brigittines (Brigittinenkapel) ♂C6

You'll be drawn to this building by its elaborate gabled façade, with intricate light-stone carvings set against darker brick. Unfortunately, there's not much else to see except the remainder of an old 17th-century convent. Today, the building, which has undergone numerous facelifts over the years, serves as a theatre and exhibition hall.
1 petite rue des Brigittines, Les Marolles ☎ 02.506.43.00
Ⓜ **Anneessens** 🚇 **free** 🗖 **none** ◑ *8am–7.30pm daily*

Eglise Notre Dame du Sablon (Kerk van Onze-Lieve van de Zavel) ♂D6

The place du Grand Sablon's Gothic showpiece is surprisingly not as dark and musty as other religious buildings of the same period. In fact, it is a rather uplifting place, from the glistening pipes on the huge organ topped by a trumpet-playing cherub, to the brilliant stained-glass windows. At night these windows, if viewed from the outside, give the square a magical ambiance. This is one of few consumer-friendly churches, replete with a nun-run gift shop.
3 rue de la Régence, Le Sablon ☎ 02.511.57.41 Ⓜ **Louise** 🚇 **free**
🗖 **none** ◑ *9am–5pm daily (from 10am Sat; from 1pm Sun)* ♿

Eglise Protestante (Protestante Kerk) ♂B6

This petite church, across the courtyard from the Palais des Beaux-Arts, is as glisteningly white on the inside as it is on the outside. Chandeliers and marble give it an unsurpassed elegance, with black and gold railings adding just the right amount of colour. The acoustics are also amazing, so definitely sneak a peak and whisper a few words.
Chapelle Royale, 2 place du Musée, Le Sablon ☎ 02.513.23.25 Ⓜ
Centrale 🚇 **free** 🗖 **none** ◑ *10.30–11.30am Sunday & by request* ♿

Eglise St-Boniface (St-Bonifaaskerk) ♂F7

Named after a local saint who hailed from a noble Brussels family, this unassuming church has some worthwhile gems, despite the somewhat shabby exterior. The elaborately carved wooden confessionals and stations of the cross might entice anyone to become Catholic. A good place for peace and quiet, far, far removed from the hustle and bustle outside.
rue St-Boniface, Ixelles (East) Ⓜ **Porte de Namur** 🚇 **free** ◑ *varies*

Eglise Ste-Catherine (St-Katelijnekerk) ♂C2

This 19th-century church, with a parking lot for a front yard and a row of gourmet fish restaurants at its rear, is worth a trip if only to see the temporary exhibitions housed there from time to time. The building, which was almost converted into the stock market, is in sore need of a paint job. The Black Virgin statue was fished out of the River Senne by Catholics in 1744 after the Protestants had dumped it there, so they're pretty proud of it.

place Ste-Catherine ☎ 02.513.34.81 Ⓜ Ste-Catherine 🏧 free ⊟ none ◑ *8.30am–6pm daily* ♿

Eglise Royale Ste-Marie (Kon. Ste-Mariaskerk)

⌖off map

From an architectural point of view, this is undoubtedly the most unusual religious building in Brussels. An odd mix somewhere between a mosque, a church and a temple, this cream-coloured beauty, with side chapels and towers jutting every which way, has a very exotic feel to it. The large blue dome, speckled with green and orange stars, has photo opportunity written all over it.

rue Royale, St-Josse & Scharbeek Ⓜ Botanique 🏧 free ◑ *varies*

Eglise St-Jacques-sur-Coudenberg (Kerk van St-Jacob op de Koudenburg)

⌖C7

Only the very dull are able to resist the temptation to enter this building after viewing one of the city's most amazing façades. The blindingly white church, with its ornate gold-plated frieze, seems to be a cross between a Greek-Roman temple and an American colonial courthouse. The interior, painted in a cheerful pale yellow, is not as impressive as one would expect, though it is pleasantly refreshing.

1 impasse Borgendael, Le Sablon ☎ 02.511.78.36 Ⓜ Parc 🏧 free ⊟ none ◑ *10am–6pm Tue–Sun (from 3pm Sun)* ♿

Eglise St-Nicolas (St-Niklaaskerk)

⌖E2

This unpretentious Catholic church, one of the oldest in the city, is dedicated to the patron saint of merchants, though he is more commonly known as Santa Claus. Though clearly not the most beautiful, this cluttered church, with its sea of votive candles, is one of the city's most endearing. It's in amazingly good shape, having undergone one restoration after another since a battle between Catholics and Protestants in the late 16th century.

👁 The unique diorama depicting Christ's birth in Brussels, with the amusing by-line 'times and places have been slightly displaced for our purposes'.

1 rue au Beurre, Central ☎ 02.513.80.22 Ⓜ Bourse 🏧 free ⊟ none ◑ *8am–6.30pm Mon–Sun* ♿

Heïlig-Bloedbasiliek
♭off map

The city's most famous square, the Burg, is home to the 12th-century.
The *pièce de résistance* of this church is a phial said to contain the
blood of Christ.

13 Burg, Brugge ☎ 050.31.65.29

Musée du Béguinage (Begijnhofmuseum)
♭off map

It's difficult to imagine what the women – all single or widowed –
who once lived here did for fun. As members of the *béguines* (a
Christian sisterhood that, despite not taking vows, lived an austere
life with strong religious values), their lives were devoted to prayer,
care of the sick and elderly, and making arts and crafts in the
bollewinkel (sweat shop). This tiny museum is just as exciting,
though it makes a sincere (but feeble) attempt to show the area's
history.

♿ One ticket gets you in both here and the Maison d'Erasme, round
the corner.

**8 rue du Chapelain, Anderlecht ☎ 02.521.13.83 Ⓜ St-Guidon ⓑⓕ 50BF
(combined with Musée d'Erasme) 🚫 none 🕙 10am–12pm & 2–5pm
Mon, Wed–Thu ♿**

Notre-Dame de la Chapelle (Onze-Lievevrouw-ter-Kapelle)
♭C6

Like most Brussels churches, this 13th-century one has had its fair
share of damage and patch-ups – a fire in 1405 and the 1695 French
Bombardment saw to that. But you would hardly know it when inside
this peaceful escape, simple yet elegant with light stone walls and
transparent windows. The travelling exhibitions on modern art sometimes seem out of place next to the old religious paintings, and pale
in comparison to the detailed sculptures of the four Apostles.

**4 rue des Ursulines, Central ☎ 02.512.07.37 Ⓜ Anneessens ⓑⓕ free
🚫 none 🕙 9am–5pm Mon–Fri; 1.30–5pm Sat–Sun (to 3.30pm Sun) ♿**

St-Baafskathedraal
♭off map

The Gothic cathedral also houses the city's greatest treasure, Jan van
Eyck's astonishing *Adoration of the Mystic Lamb*.

St-Baafsplein, Gent ☎ 09.269.20.65 by rail

St-Niklaaskerk
♭off map

Gent's rich mix of medieval and Gothic architecture reflects a heady
past, when the wool and cloth trades made it as prosperous as Paris
and Bologna. The most striking legacy is the three-spired skyline of
the austere, Romanesque St-Niklaaskerk.

Korenmarkt, Gent ☎ no phone by rail

St-Pieterskerk
off map

St-Pieterskerk's treasures include an extravagant baroque pulpit and a rich collection of medieval art.

Grote Markt, Leuven ☎ 016.29.51.33 by rail

Synagogue Communauté Israélite de Bruxelles (Synagoge van de Israëlitische Gemeenschap van Brussel)
F6

Brussels' main synagogue, built in Romano-Byzantine style, will not disappoint. The exterior is dramatic, with a gabled façade topped by a giant star of David. Go through the large wooden door and enter an enchanted world. Climb the stairs to get a full glimpse of the ornate interior (lit by lights on golden lampposts), metal chandeliers, and a dome decorated with religious symbols in bright shades of gold, red, and turquoise.

2 rue Joseph Dupont, Le Sablon ☎ 02.512.43.34 Ⓜ Louise Ⓑ free ⊟ none ◑ 9.30am Sun & by request ♿

art nouveau

Centre Belge de la Bande Dessinée
C3

Housed in a former warehouse, built by Horta for draper Charles Waucquez in 1893. Abandoned in the 1960s, when squatters moved in and used the shop fittings for firewood, it became a museum in 1989. The centrepiece is the airy hallway and double-glass ceiling, but if cartoons aren't your thing, have a swiftie in the brasserie, where the chink of glass and cutlery resounds around the high ceilings.

20 rue des Sables, Central ☎ 02.219.19.80 Ⓜ De Brouckère; Rogier; Botanique Ⓑ 250BF ⊟ none ◑ 10am–6pm Tue–Sun ♿

Hôtel Hannon
off map

The former Hôtel Hannon was built in 1903 by Jules Brunfaut for his amateur photographer friend, Edouard Hannon. The curvaceous exterior is more delightful than the inside, where the *trompe-l'oeil* ceiling verges on bad taste. Appropriately, it's now home to the Contretype photography gallery.

1 ave de la Jonction, St-Gilles ☎ 02.538.42.20 Ⓜ Mérode

Hôtel Van Eetvelde
F4

Built for Baron Edmond, Léopold II's administrator in the Congo (and later Secretary of State). Take an ARAU guided tour (complete with cheeky commentary about the rights and endless wrongs of town planning) if you want to drool over the interior: mosaic floors, green onyx walls, crystal doors, and an octagonal stairwell topped with a Tiffany-glass cupola.

4 avenue Palmerston, Quartier Européen Ⓜ Schuman

Magasin Old England   *♪A7*
Wander down to place Royale and admire Paul Saintenoy's Magasin Old England, a glorious iron-and-glass department store that is now home to the Musée des Instruments de Musique.
2 rue Montagne de la Cour, Le Sablon ☎ 02.545.01.30 Ⓜ Centrale

Maison du St-Cyr   *♪off map*
Gustave Strauven's extraordinarily frilly Maison du St-Cyr shows the *fin-de-siècle* movement at its most elaborate (and ultimately ridiculous).
11 square Ambiorix, Quartier Européen Ⓜ Schuman

Maison de Paul Cauchie   *♪off map*
Sgraffiti can be seen at Maison de Paul Cauchie, the house of this architect, a fan of Rennie Mackintosh. Once earmarked for demolition, it was listed in 1975 and its Symbolist-influenced friezes have since been painstakingly restored.
5 rue des Francs, Etterbeek ☎ 02.673.15.06 Ⓜ Mérode

Musée Horta   *♪off map*
Perhaps the purest illustration of Horta's harmonious style, followed closely by the streets around the Étangs d'Ixelles, examples of more affordable Art Nouveau residences built for the middle classes.
26 rue Américaine, Ixelles (West) ☎ 02.543.04.90 🚃 81, 82 ▣ 150BF (200BF Sat–Sun) 🚇 none ◑ 2–5.30pm Tue– Sun

Rue Belle Vue   *♪off map*
Don't miss Ernest Blérot's town houses on rue Belle Vue (Nos. 42, 44, 46)
Ixelles (East) 🚃 93, 94

Rue de la Vallée   *♪E12*
A mass of dwellings by the Delune brothers, Aimable, Ernest and Léon.
Ixelles (East) 🚃 93, 94

13 rue Royale   *♪E3*
This building is a fine example of the sober architecture of Paul Hankar, who favoured red-brick structures over flamboyant metalwork.
Central Ⓜ Parc

De Ultieme Hallucinatie   *♪B3*
Take a breather in the bar of De Ultieme Hallucinatie, which has a mosaic floor and a tendril-like green-metal conservatory.
316 rue Royale Ste-Marie, St-Josse & Scharbeek ☎ 02.217.06.14 🚃 92, 93, 94 ▣ free 🚇 MC/V ◑ 11–2am Mon–Sat (from 4pm Sat) ♿

Artesia Center for the Arts
F2

Brussels' European Capital of Culture 2000 nerve centre, this renovated department store displays a permanent exhibition of 35 contemporary international artists, including Alicia Framis and Stephen Wilks, the fruits of Artesia bank's expendable cash.
50 rue de l'Ecuyer, Central Ⓜ **De Brouckère**

L' Autre Musée
D2

Without its own collection, this place is literally 'the other museum', as it fills in the blanks of the city's public art scene. It includes sculptures, installations and paintings of lesser-known European contemporaries.
41 rue St-Michel, Central ☎ **02.640.84.37** Ⓜ **De Brouckère** 🆓 **free**
🕐 *2–6.30pm Tue–Sat*

Le Botanique
B3

Ornamental greenhouses offer perfect lighting and calm for these disparate displays. One space shows off-the-wall photography, such as family snaps collected from Communist Hungary. The upper, larger gallery attracts contemporary touring displays.
236 rue Royale, St-Josse & Scharbeek ☎ **02.226.12.11** Ⓜ **Botanique**
🆓 **180BF** 🕐 *11am–6pm Tue– Sun* ♿

Centre d'Art Contemporain
D8

The French-speaking community's gallery is devoted purely to contemporary art. Whatever's bubbling under the surface in the Francophone Belgian art scene will be exhibited or referenced here. Unheard-of artists often get shown.
63 ave des Nerviens, Quartier Européen ☎ **02.735.05.31** Ⓜ **Schuman**
🆓 **free** 🕐 *9am– 1pm & 2–7pm Mon–Fri; 1–6pm Sat*

FNAC
C3

Linger while CD-hungry companions browse in the record shop. The smallish room behind the shop's cash desks displays photography, with a preponderance for modern black and white.
City 2, 16 rue Cendres, Central ☎ **02.275.11.11** Ⓜ **Rogier** 🆓 **free** 🕐
10am– 7pm Mon–Sat (to 8pm Fri) ♿

Fondation pour l'Architecture ⚲D11
This impressive building rotates its art and architecture exhibits every few months. Sound, sculpture, installations, and models make up hybrids featuring themes as varied as urban movement or use of plastics.
55 rue de l'Ermitage, Ixelles (East) ☎ 02.644.91.52 🚌 71 🚇 250BF
◑ 10.30am–6.30pm Tue–Sun ♿

Halles St-Géry (St-Gorikshallen) ⚲E2
By day, this ex-meat market houses exhibitions. Belgian art, given a wide definition, links shows of diverse subjects. At night, it's a bar and concert hall.
1 place St-Géry, Ste-Catherine ☎ 02.502.44.24 Ⓜ Bourse 🚇 100BF
◑ 10.30am–6pm Tue–Fri; 2–5pm Sat–Sun

Hôtel de Ville (Stadhuis) ⚲B6/F2
This superb gallery makes the Grand' Place more than just a pretty face. It attracts quality international artists such as the Chilean, Matta, as well as some late 19th- and early 20th-century work.
Grand' Place, Central ☎ 02. 279.64.71 Ⓜ De Brouckère 🚇 100BF
◑ Guided tours only: 11.30am & 3.15pm Tue (year round); 3.15pm Wed (year round); 12.15pm Sun (Apr–Sep only) ♿

Kanaal and Kanaal II ⚲D1
The run-down area by the canals is art central – whether for cheap space or the hope that a docklands recovery is around the corner, two buildings now jam in over a dozen galleries. Kanaal and Kanaal II rent both poky and spacious areas to galleries.
20 blvd Barthélémy, Ste-Catherine ☎ 02.735.52.12 🚌 18

Musée d'Ixelles (Museum van Elsene) ⚲A12
This one-time slaughterhouse is now used to display mainly 20th-century European art – it's big on retrospectives and lesser-known movements. A permanent collection keeps original Toulouse-Lautrec posters away from the more central throngs.
71 rue van Volsem, Ixelles (East) ☎ 02.515.64.21 🚌 71 🚇 varies
◑ 1–6pm Tue–Fri; 10am–5pm Sat–Sun ♿

Palais des Beaux-Arts (Palais voor Schone Kunsten) ⚲A7
Diverse exhibitions from embroidery to video installations can be found in the Palais des Beaux-Arts, a purpose-built Art Nouveau exhibition space, theatre, and cinema.
10 rue Royale, Le Sablon ☎ 02.507.84.66
w www.netpoint.be/abc/psk Ⓜ Parc 🚇 250BF–350BF ◑ 10am–6pm Tue–Sun (to 8pm Fri) ♿

Recyclart
C6

Minding the gaps around Chapelle train station is this urban space that rotates installations and sculptures, often as backdrops for musical events. The group (Recyclart is their name, not the space's) aims to breath new life into the rundown surrounds.

25 rue des Ursulines, Les Marolles ☎ 02.502.57.34
w www.go.to/recyclart Ⓜ **Lemonnier** 🄱🄵 *varies* ◑ *varies* ♿

commercial galleries

Aeroplastics
C11

Aeroplastics would win the contest for hosting the most bizarre exhibitions. This space still buzzes with installations from the recesses of strange, usually sick, and debatably genius minds.

32 rue Blanche, Ixelles (West) ☎ 02.537.22.02 🚌 93, 94

Art Kiosk
B9

For Egyptian antiquities and avant-Russian work stop in here.

9 ave Jean Volders, St-Gilles ☎ 02.534.66.11 Ⓜ **Porte de Hal; Parvis St-Gilles**

Artiscope
off map

The original Artiscope gallery tends to show its better-quality work here: mixed media from names like Warhol and Shapiro have adorned its walls.

35 boulevard St-Michel, Etterbeek ☎ 02.735.52.12 Ⓜ **Montgomery**

Atelier 340
off map

Less central than other galleries, this building is run by a Polish collector well known for giving space and opportunities to up-and-coming artists. Having bought stock through the years, permanent and motley collections are on view in this non-profit-making house.

340 drève de Rivieren, Jette ☎ 02.424.24.12 🚋 **Jette**

CCNOA
F1

Promotes non-objective art, one of the most radical 20th/21st-century art movements.

2 rue Notre Dame du Sommeil, Ste-Catherine ☎ 02.502.69.12 🚌 18

Damasquine
off map

Less far-out than some of the new galleries – but just as contemporary.

62 rue de L'Aurore, Ixelles (East) ☎ 02.646.31.53 🚌 93, 94

Dorothée de Pauw $D11
Into photos, with some paintings too. The contemporary works are judiciously selected.
70 rue de Hennin, Ixelles (East) ☎ 02.649.43.80 🚌 93, 94

Espace Photographique Contretype $off map
Specializes in photography. Good, varied exhibitions vye for attention with the gallery building itself – the Art Nouveau Hotel Hannon.
1 ave de la Jonction, St-Gilles ☎ 02.538.42.20 Ⓜ Albert

Gallery Ronny van de Velde $off map
This is the best-known commercial art gallery, a four-floored house that shows retrospectives of modern masters like Marcel Duchamp, plus the latest in contemporary art.
3 Ijzerenpoortkaai, Antwerpen ☎ 03.216.30.47 by rail

J Bastien Art $B6
Sculpture and paintings fill a small space. Nothing too cutting-edge, but usually good-quality and interesting.
61 rue de la Madeleine, Central ☎ 02.513.25.63 Ⓜ Centrale

Koninklijk Museum voor Schone Kunsten $off map
The neighbourhood's oldest temple to the arts. Located within an overblown, neoclassical building, the collection includes lesser-known, but worth-seeing, works by Van Eyck, Van der Weyden, James Ensor, and René Magritte.
Leopold De Waelplaats, Antwerpen ☎ 03.238.78.09 by rail

Meert Rihoux $A2
The minimalist gallery of Meert Rihoux's conceptual works show a preference for the 1970s and America.
13 rue du Canal, Ste-Catherine ☎ 02.219.14.22 Ⓜ Ste-Catherine

MUHKA $off map
At the northern edge of this once grim area, MUHKA (Antwerpen) (Museum voor Hedendaagse Kunst van Antwerpen), hosts international contemporary art shows.
Leuvenstraat, Antwerpen ☎ 03.238.59.60 by rail

Orion Art Gallery $F6
New, and still establishing its reputation, this European sculpture and painting exhibits rotate every four months,
19 rue aux Laines, Les Marolles ☎ 02.512.63.55 Ⓜ Hôtel des Monnaies

Pascal Polar *♭D10*
A classic gallery, whose paintings and photography are French and Belgian.
108 chaussée de Charleroi, St-Gilles ☎ 02.37.81.61 ▤ 91, 92

Rodolphe Janssen *♭C11*
Painting is the niche of Rodolphe Janssen, where glass ceilings provide fantastic natural light.
35 rue de Livourne, Ixelles (West) ☎ 02.538.08.18 ▤ 93, 94

Sabine Wachters Fine Art *♭D5*
This gallery trades on a reputation for quality, and is as good for installations and photography as it is for paintings.
26 ave de Stalingrad, Les Marolles ☎ 02.502.39.93 Ⓜ Lemonnier

Salon d'Art et de Coiffure *♭A9*
Another for-love collection, as the name suggests, hairdressing is the bread-winning venture, coupled with the gallery, which has mainly Belgian paintings, drawings, and photography.
81 rue de l'Hôtel des Monnaies, St-Gilles ☎ 02.537.65.40 ▤ Hôtel des Monnaies

Taché-Lévy Gallery *♭off map*
This had a real coup showing Tracey Emin's works.
74 rue Tenbosch, Ixelles (West) ☎ 02.344.23.68 ▤ 93, 94

Xavier Hufkens *♭off map*
Showcases the likes of Louise Bourgeois.
6–8 rue St-Georges, Ixelles (West) ☎ 02.646. 63.30 ▤ 93, 94

the green scene

Bois de la Cambre (Ter Kamerenbos) *♭off map*
The manicured northern edge of the Forêt de Soignes is one of Brussels' most pleasant surprises, with hilly wooded sections, an artificial lake and acres of sweeping lawns. There's no better place to rollerblade, especially on weekends when the roads are closed to traffic. The Pélouse des Anglais, a picnicker's paradise, hosts free open-air jazz and classical concerts in summer. It's named after British troops who allegedly played cricket here before the Battle of Waterloo.
♫ **Théâtre de la Poche; outdoor Sunday summer concerts; water towers.**
♫ **Drivers treat the roads through the park as a Formula One track.**
Entrance: ave Louise (Ixelles (West) ☎ 02.775.75.75 ▤ 23, 90, 93▤38 🆓 free
❶ 24 hours daily

Château de la Hulpe (Kasteel van Ter Hulpe)   *♬off map*

This sprawling estate south of Brussels was landscaped by the sun-worshipping Marquis de Béthune in 1842; he put in a Loire-style château, a gamut of exotic trees, and a gigantic stone obelisk. Its proximity to the lake, into which an incredibly steep flight of stone steps disappears, has led many to speculate that the whole thing is a hymn to fertility; a cosy hilltop summer house, with splendid views, may tempt you to get natural.

♧ Café in 19th-century farmhouse.

Entrances: chaussée de Bruxelles (La Hulpe) ☎ 02.653.64.04 Ⅲ La Hulpe ⒝ℝ free ◑ *summer: 8am–9pm daily; winter: 9am–6pm daily*

Forêt de Soignes (Zoniënwoud)   *♬off map*

An explosion of amber in autumn, Europe's largest beech forest stretches 43km/sq south and east into Flemish Brabant, an unbroken expanse of greenery that the locals call Brussels' 'green lungs'. Snaking paths take you through elegant, slender trunks, their uniformity the result of the 18th-century Austrian occupation, when fast-growing beeches were planted as an antidote to pillaging. Some *Bruxellois* want the forest restored to its original oak character, but the joggers, riders, walkers, cyclists, and lovers who flock here at weekends don't seem to mind. Take a break from the beeches at the Rouge-Cloître, a delightful site developed around a 14th-century abbey; the south wing is now a restaurant that offers hungry walkers a barbecue in good weather. The forest is also home to wild boar, deer, pheasants, and sparrow hawks.

♧ 1| In summer, trams from the Musée du Transport run through the wood. 2| Jean Massart Experimental Garden, with 5600 species.

Entrance: chaussée de la Hulpe (Boondael) ☎ 02.775.75.75 Ⓜ Hermann-Debroux ⒝ℝ free ◑ *24 hours daily*

Jardin d'Egmont (Egmonttuinen)   *♬F6/E7*

An oasis of calm, this secluded secret garden is a welcome antidote to this bustling area. There's a fine view of the Palais d'Egmont, named after the 16th-century count whose opposition to Spanish rule cost him his head, and now home to the Foreign Affairs Ministry. And ponder the merits of EU membership, for this is where Britain pledged to join in 1972.

♧ The Peter Pan statue is a hit with kids.

Entrance: blvd de Waterloo (Le Sablon) ☎ 02.775.75.75 🚌 92, 93, 94 ⒝ℝ free ◑ *24 hours daily*

Parc de Bruxelles (Warandepark) ♟A/B7

Once the game reserve of medieval Dukes of Brabant, this central park was redesigned in ultra-neat French Classical style in the 19th century. Formal, and a touch arid, it comes to life during holidays and festivals, especially the Belgian National Day. Alongside the unthrilling statuary is a memorial to paedophile victims Julie and Mélissa, whose deaths in 1996 provoked a national crisis.

Entrances: rue Royale, rue Ducale & place des Palais (Central) ☎ 02.775.75.75 Ⓜ Parc, Arts-Loi, Luxembourg ⓑⓡ **free** ◑ *6am–9pm daily*

Étangs d'Ixelles ♟E12

Surrounded by some of the city's most desirable Art Nouveau and Art Deco houses, the willow-swept Étangs d'Ixelles (Vijvers van Elsene) municipal ponds are a must for architecture enthusiasts.

Entrances: ave des Eperons; ave du Général de Gaulle

Parc de Laeken (Park van Laken) ♟off map

Léopold II's exotic pretensions are perfectly illustrated by this rolling park, where he commissioned a Chinese pavilion and a six-storey Japanese tower, with parts shipped over from the Far East – pop in if you're a fan of Samurai armour or Chinese porcelain. If, and only if, you can stand the queues, the colossal royal greenhouses, filled with exotic flora, open for a fortnight Apr–May.

Entrances: ave du Parc (Laeken) ☎ 02.775.75.75 🚌 19, 23, 81 ⓑⓡ **free** ◑ *8am–8.30pm daily*

Parc Léopold ♟D/F8

Take a stroll through Parc Léopold (Leopoldpark) and you might bump into MEPs taking a break from the European Parliament which overshadows this landscaped park with its little lake and natural history museum.

Entrance: chaussée de Wavre

Parc du Cinquantenaire (Jubelpark) ♟A/B14

Overshadowed by the Arc de Triomphe and its museums, this severe symmetrical garden is another monument to Léopold II's ego. Look out though, for the Mosque and the Pavilion of Human Passions, a Neoclassical temple built by a young Victor Horta. Inside is an erotic relief that outraged public decency on its opening in 1889 and has been off-limits ever since. On summer weekends, the Esplanade is transformed into a faux-50s drive-in cinema.

Entrance: ave JF Kennedy (Quartier Européen) ☎ 02.775.75.75 Ⓜ Mérode; Schuman ⓑⓡ **free** ◑ *24 hours daily*

Parc Duden
♫off map

Hilly Parc Duden (Dudenpark) has a pleasingly untamed atmosphere.
Entrances: ave du Parc, ave des Villas & Mont Kemmel

Parc Tenbosch
♫off map

Local hideaway Parc Tenbosch (Park van Tenbosch) has a *boules* pitch
and a neat children's playground.
Entrances: chaussée de Vleurgat; place Tenbosch

Parc Tournay-Solvay (Park van Tournay-Solvay)
♫off map

It's worth a detour to leafy Boitsfort to stroll through this little-known
gem, an eclectic mix of wilderness and landscaped sophistication. The
peaceful park is also home to the European Sculpture Foundation, with a
perilously balanced permanent piece near the entrance and temporary
outdoor shows by top artists from across the EU. Eco-tourists should check
out activities organized by the park's Ecology Initiation Centre Tournesol.
♿ **The rose garden.**
Entrance: chaussée de la Hulpe (Watermael-Boitsfort)
☎ **02.775.75.75 (Ecology Centre ☎ 02.675.37.30)** ⊟ **94** ⓑⓡ **free**
◐ *summer: 8am–8.30pm daily; winter: 8am–5.30pm daily*

Parc de Woluwe
♫off map

For a surprisingly natural feel, wander along the artificial ponds and
sloped lawns of the English-style Parc Woluwe (Park van Woluwe).
Entrance: ave de Tervuren

Parc de Wolvendael (Wolvendaalpark)
♫off map

One of the beauties of this wooded park is its steep hill, transformed
in snowy weather into a chaotic whirl of sledges and toboggans.
Another, despite the excruciatingly slow service, is the open-air summer café, an extension of the Louis XV restaurant, housed in a splendid 17th-century pavilion. This relaxed locals' hangout is great for
observing Belgian family life, especially in the children's playground.
♿ **Dieweg Cemetery, the city's oldest.**
Entrances: ave Paul Stroobant, ave Wolvendael (Uccle)
☎ **02.348.65.47** ⊟ **92** ⓑⓡ **free** ◐ *8am–4pm daily*

tours

Arcadia
♫C10

Explores art history and architecture on walking tours around Brussels.
38 rue du Métal, St-Gilles ☎ **02.534.38.19** Ⓜ **Parvis St-Gilles**
ⓑⓡ **250BF–750BF** ◐ *times vary (call for details)*

ARAU
D2

Organizes Art Nouveau and Art Deco architecture tours.
55 boulevard Adolphe Max, Central ☎ 02.219.33.45 Ⓜ Rogier
BF varies ⏰ 9am–5pm daily (tours in French: daily; tours in English: Sat mornings only)

Chatterbus
F2

Walking and public-transport tours, plus once- or twice-weekly themed excursions.
Start at: Galeries St-Hubert, Central ☎ 02.673.18.35 Ⓜ Centrale BF 300BF ⏰ times vary

De Boeck's Sightseeing Tours
F2

City-wide bus tours.
8 rue de la Colline, Central ☎ 02.513.77.44 Ⓜ De Brouckère BF 800BF ⏰ 8am–5.30pm daily (to 2pm Sat–Sun)

La Fonderie
C1

15 city tours, most of which are concerned with industrial history.
27a rue Ransfort, Molenbeek ☎ 02.410.99.50 Ⓜ Comte de Flandre BF varies ⏰ times vary (call for details)

Pro Velo
F7

Cycling tours with 18 different themes, like forest and fauna.
15 rue de Londres, Ixelles (East) ☎ 02.502.73.55 Ⓜ Trône BF 500BF (bike hire and guide) ⏰ Apr–Oct: times vary

TIB
B6/F2

Dozens of walking and car day tours of the 19 communes of Brussels. The focus is largely on art and architecture. They also publish a comic-strip map.
TIB, Hôtel de Ville, 1 Grand' Place, Central ☎ 02.513.89.40 Ⓜ De Brouckère BF varies ⏰ times vary

kicks for kids

L'Abbaye Rouge Cloître
off map

On the edge of the Forêt de Soignes is L'Abbaye de Rouge Cloître – spot the carp in the lakes and run riot in the playground.
Forêt de Soigne ☎ 02.775. 75.75 Ⓜ Hermann-Debroux BF free ⏰ 24 hours daily ♿

Antwerp Zoo   *♀off map*
The vast, 150-year old Antwerpen Zoo (Antwerpen), home to some 4000
animals, is worth a visit if you've a soft spot for 19th-century exoticism,
best illustrated by the elephant house that resembles an Egyptian temple.
26 Koningin Astridpl, Antwerpen ☎ 03.202.45.40 by rail

Beersel Castle (Kasteel van Beersel)   *♀off map*
This 14th-century ruined fortress comes complete with a moat, towers, dungeons, and torture chambers. Children are encouraged to
play and explore. There's a picnic area and a small playground for
younger kids.
65 Lotstraat, Beersel ☎ 02.331.00.24 Ⅲ Beersel ▣ 100BF adults;
50BF kids ◑ Mar–Nov: 10am–12pm, 2–6pm Tue–Sun; Nov–Dec & Feb:
weekends only

Bois de la Cambre   *♀off map*
Check out the Bois de la Cambre's lakeside area on Sundays, when the
road is closed to traffic and it becomes Belgium's answer to Central Park.
Entrances: ave Louise, ave Franklin, Uccle ☎ 02.775.75.75 ⬒ 23, 90, 93,
94 ▣ free ◑ 24 hours daily

Bruparck Village   *♀off map*
A purpose-built pleasure park that includes Océade (a swimming
complex with slides, pools, saunas, and Turkish baths), Kinepolis (a
29-screen multiplex cinema), and Mini-Europe (notable buildings
from EU countries, like the Acropolis, at a scale of 1:25). It's tacky,
commercial, but a great place for the kids.
1 avenue du Football, Heysel ☎ Mini-Europe: 02.478.05.50; Océade:
02.478.43.20; Kinepolis: 02.474.26.04 Ⓜ Heysel ▣ Combined tickets
for 3 attractions: 750BF ◑ Mini-Europe: Mar–Jan: 9.30am–6pm daily
(Jul–Aug: to 8pm). Océade: Apr–Aug: 10am–6pm Tue–Thu;
10am–10pm Fri–Sun; Sep–Mar: 10am–6pm Tue–Fri; 10am–10pm
Sat–Sun ♿

Institut Royal des Sciences Naturelles (Kon. Belgisch Instituut voor
Natuurwetenschappen)   *♀E8*
If you can't tell your Diplodocus from your Tyrannosaurus Rex, the
Natural Sciences Museum will set you straight with its impressive
dinosaur displays. Check out the Neanderthal and the stuffed animal
sections. Mollusc fans will find one of the world's largest collections.
29 rue Vautier, Quartier Européen ☎ 02.627.42.11 Ⓜ Maelbeek ▣
150BF adults; 100BF 6–16 yrs; free under 6 yrs ◑ 9.30am–4.45pm
Tue–Fri (10am–6pm Sat–Sun ♿

Musée de l'Enfant (Kindermuseum)   *♪off map*

This kids' museum is filled with all sorts of goodies: giant interactive puzzles, a theatre and dressing-up area, painting and cooking workshops, a nature section, as well as indoor and outdoor play areas.

5 rue du Bourgmestre, Ixelles (East) ☎ 02.640.01.07 🚊 23, 90 🚌 220BF ◑ 2.30–5pm Wed, Sat, Sun, school holidays (closed Aug)

Musée du Jouet (Speelgoedmuseum)   *♪D3*

This toy museum is chocka with antique toys and interactive games. Don't miss the free demo of vintage clockwork toys and the string-puppet show.

24 rue de l'Association, Central ☎ 02.219.61.68 Ⓜ Madou; Botanique 🚌 100BF adults; 60BF 6–16 yrs; free under 6 yrs ◑ 10am–12.30pm & 2–6pm daily ♿

Nautisports   *♪off map*

Nautisports has four pools, from one of fairly large proportions if you want to notch up laps to a baby bath with mini slides. It's set on the edge of Chateau d' Enghien's land, with its Chinese pavilion, ornamental gardens, and duck ponds.

6 chaussée de Soignies, Enghien ☎ 02.397.01.80 Ⅲ Enghien 🚉 80BF adults; 120BF children; free under 12 yrs ◑ 9am– 12.30pm Mon–Fri; 1.30–9pm Sat; 9am–7pm Sun

Parc de la Sauvagère   *♪off map*

Keeps young kids happy with a playground, mini wildlife zoo, duck pond, and woods – a best-kept secret.

Ave de la Chênaie, Uccle 🚊 43 🚉 free ◑ 9am–dusk daily ♿

Parc Régional Tenbosch   *♪off map*

Parc Régional Tenbosch is another find: it's got a pond with terrapins, a sandpit, a well-kept tots' playground, and a basketball court.

Entrances: rue Américaine, Mélèzes, chaussée de Vleurgat ☎ 02.775.75.75 🚊 93, 94 🚉 free ◑ summer: 8am–9pm; winter: 8am–6pm ♿

Parc de Wolvendael   *♪off map*

Kids zip about at Parc de Wolvendael, with its two playgrounds, pony rides, and a grassy slope for ball games.

Ave Paul Stroobant, Uccle ☎ 02.348.65.47 🚊 92 🚉 free ◑ 7.30am–6 or 7pm daily ♿

Planckendael Zoo   *off map*
This breeding ground for Antwerp Zoo has acres of parkland, including a stork colony, ape house, beaver dam, and rhino enclosure. There's an adventure playground, African-style mud-hut village, and farmyard.
582 Leuvensesteenweg, Muizen, Mechelen ☎ 015.41.49.21
🚇 Mechelen, then 🚌 284, 285 📠 460BF adults; 295BF 3–11 yrs; free under 3 yrs ◑ *9am–6pm daily* ♿

Scientastic Museum   *E2*
Discover the fun in physics and puzzle over illusions at this small interactive science museum. For would-be Einsteins, there are 80 experiments to try, either individually or as a guided group (English spoken).
Bourse Metro, blvd Anspach, Central ☎ 02.732.13.36 Ⓜ Bourse 📠
160BF adults; free children under 4 yrs ◑ *school holidays: 2–5.30pm Sat–Sun; term: by appointment*

Théâtre du Peruchet   *off map*
Wooden marionettes act out fairy tales and fables.
50 avenue de la Forêt, Ixelles (East) ☎ 02.673.87.30 🚌 94

Théâtre du Ratinet   *off map*
Presents trad children's tales in an old farm building.
44 avenue de Fré, Uccle ☎ 02.375.15.63 🚌 91, 92

Walibi & Aqualibi   *off map*
Theme park Walibi has 50 attractions, from a Vampire rollercoaster that travels at 81km/hr and with a 30m-plunge, to traditional carousels. Take it easier at Aqualibi next door, which boasts a 29°C heated tropical wave pool, rapids and a 140m-long Boa slide.
9 rue Joseph Dachamps, Wavre ☎ 010.42.17.17 🚇 Bierges 📠 Walibi & Aqualibi: 995BF adults; 445BF 1–1.4m tall; free under 1m.
◑ *Apr–Jun: 10am–6pm daily; Jul–Aug: 10am–9.30pm daily; Sep–Oct: 10am–6pm Sat & Sun* ♿

body & soul

Although the term 'spa' comes from the Belgian town of the same name, the Bruxellois don't go in for high pampering. But there are some gems...

beauty treatments

Espace Beauté *♪B10*
Serious pampering is the deal here, with treats like full-body sea-weed wraps (1750BF) or Finnish sauna (500BF). Indulge in their menu of eight combinations from two hours (2900BF) to a half day (4900BF).
11 chaussée du Charleroi, St-Gilles ☎ 02.537.42.63 Ⓜ Louise

Make-up Forever *♪A6*
This (expensive) staple for pro make-up artists and beauty addicts offers heaps of extraordinary selections. Many treatments (facials, waxing, make-overs, etc) are by appointment only.
62 rue du Midi, Central ☎ 02.512.10.80 🚌 34, 48, 95, 96

health clubs

Champney's *♪B10*
This luxurious centre offers a gym, dance studio, gorgeous pool, and sauna as well as Swedish massage, reflexology, Shiatsu, and Reiki. Choose between two one-day packages: entry with two treatments (1500BF +1000BF per option) or with three treatments, and lunch (8500BF).
Conrad Hotel, 71 ave Louise, Ixelles (West) ☎ 02.542.46.66 Ⓜ Louise

Sauna & Beauty Farm Thermae Grimbergen *♪off map*
A full day of luxury includes services such as rebirthing and chroma-therapy (3200BF–5950BF). For the 490BF entry fee you get jacuzzis and a Japanese sauna. Treatments cost 250BF–2800BF.
74 Wolvertemsesteenweg, Grimbergen ☎ 02.270.81.93 🚌 231

Thermen Dilbeek *♪off map*
Get-togethers in the buff are *de rigueur* here. The entrance fee (690BF) gives access to Turkish baths, saunas, herb baths, and heated indoor and outdoor pools. Pay for extras like a massage with essential oils (1450BF).
290 Kattebroekstraat, Dilbeek ☎ 02.466.00.88 🚌 to St-Antoon, then 🚌

body & soul

fitness

Centre Energetique Humaine   *♀off map*
Individual or collective classes (500BF) such as contemporary dance and Qi Gong soothe your soul in this bright, calm studio. They also do shiatsu and massotherapy.
6 rue du Prévôt, Ixelles (West) ☎ 02.513.85.01 🚍 54, 71

Piscine Victor Boin   *♀D9*
The pool in this *fin-de-siècle* gem is surrounded by tiers of elegant *cabines* (changing rooms). The Turkish baths look as they did in 1905, with mosaic tiles and marble benches. It alternates between ladies' and gents' days (790BF–990BF). Entry to the pool alone is 70BF.
38 rue de la Perche, St-Gilles ☎ 02.539.06.15 Ⓜ Horta

Yogashram-Centre de Bien Être   *♀E6*
This 18th-century town house is a peaceful downtown sanctuary. Hatha, Egyptian yoga, breathing, and anti-stress classes (private and group, 350BF) are provided by 80-year-old Christiane Brandt and her team.
27 rue des Minimes, Le Sablon ☎ 02.512.64.92 🚍 93, 94

hair care

Guillaume Sénéchal   *♀A11*
Clubby comfort for guys only at this branch of Parisian barber Defossé. The range of care includes a facial massage and shave combo (700BF). Cuts from 1000BF.
85 ave Louise, Ixelles (West) ☎ 02.534.33.36 Ⓜ Louise

Herminio   *♀B8*
Herminio's multilingual staff specialize in precision cutting (from 1700BF) and subtle colour techniques (1300BF–3000BF) in this sleek, chic salon.
119 rue Stévin, Quartier Européen ☎ 02.230.48.88 Ⓜ Maelbeek

Santi's   *♀F9*
Frédéric Blondel's flamboyant salon reflects St-Gilles' faded Art Nouveau splendour. The loyal crowd is all ages, genders, and sexual orientations. Cuts: 1300BF for women, 750BF for men.
22 ave Paul Dejaer, St-Gilles ☎ 02.534.64.22 Ⓜ Horta

Hannya Tattoo $E2$

Thumb through the hundreds of designs available, or bring your own. For 3000BF per hour free-hand specialist PsychoPat creates tribal and Polynesian tattoos.

9 passage St-Honoré, Central ☎ 02.219.22.76 Ⓜ Bourse

Ritual Piercing & Tattoo $E2$

This kinky boutique provides a huge selection of excellent-quality jewellery, and they'll pierce almost any part of your body (500BF–2000BF). Henna tattoos are done on request (500BF).

3 passage St-Honoré, Central ☎ 02.223.49.58 Ⓜ Bourse

games & activities

Let yourself go with any or many of these fun-filled activities.

ballooning

Enjoy gliding, sightseeing, navigation tricks, and balloon hide-and-seek as the pilot steers across forests and through quiet valleys.

Aerovlare ♪*off map*
Office: 82 ave van Crombrugghe, Woluwe St-Pierre ☎ 02.762.45.73
🚇 39 📧 5950BF per person ◑ *May–Sep: by appt.*

bowling

The Bowl Factory calls itself the 'most beautiful alley in the world', while Bowling Crosley has 20 lanes in the tradition of pin-smashing.

Bowl Factory ♪*off map*
29 chaussée de Nivelles, Waterloo ☎ 02. 387. 54.31 🚌 365 📧 95BF–145BF ◑ *12pm–midnight daily (to 2am Fri–Sat).*

Bowling Crosley ♪*A2*
43 quai au Foin, Ste-Catherine ☎ 02.217.28.01 🅼 Ste-Catherine
📧 120BF ◑ *12pm–midnight daily.*

breakfast cinema

Join the breakfast club at Petit Déjeuners du Cinéma, where new releases and a few oldies are shown on Sundays.

UGC Toison d'Or ♪*E7*
8 ave de la Toison d'Or, Ixelles (West) ☎ 02.223.20.20 🅼 Louise; Porte de Namur 📧 280BF ◑ *9.30am Sun.*

climbing walls

New Roc and Stadium Centre are suitable for all skill levels, with heights of up to 16m. Walls are regularly re-designed by professional climbers.

New Roc ♪*off map*
136 chaussée de Watermael, Auderghem ☎ 02.675.17.60 🅼 Demey
📧 300BF ◑ *12pm–midnight daily.*

Stadium Centre *♭off map*
1 ave Sippelberg, Koekelberg ☎ 02.414. 40.41 Ⓜ Osseghem 🇧 300BF
◑ *9am–midnight daily.*

dance

Tango, flamenco, even Hungarian dance lessons are on offer at La
Tentation. Those with two left feet can practise castanets, bagpipes,
and accordion, or enjoy the art gallery and concerts.

La Tentation *♭C2*
28 rue de Laeken, Ste-Catherine ☎ 02.537.45.47 Ⓜ De Brouckère
🇧 200BF–450BF ◑ *11am–11pm Mon–Sat.*

go-karting

City Kart offers plenty of practice to perfect your racing skills on a
1000-m track. For more lengthy rides, Brussels Kart has the biggest
indoor track.

City Kart *♭off map*
5a squ E des Grées du Lou, Forest ☎ 02.332.36.96 🚍 15, 50, 98 🇧
350BF–500BF per 15 mins ◑ *12pm–midnight (from 9.30am Sat–Sun).*

Brussels Kart *♭off map*
11 Gossetlaan, Groot-Bijgaarden ☎ 02.467. 28.00 🚍 19 🇧
350BF–500BF per 15 mins ◑ *12pm–midnight daily (from 9.30am
Sat–Sun).*

horseback riding

In Bois de la Cambre, the Royal Étrier Belge provides horseback treks,
lessons, and workouts. The best option is to take a riding tour of the
majestic Forêt de Soignes.

Royal Étrier Belge *♭off map*
19 champ du Vert Chasseur, Uccle ☎ 02.374.28.60 🚍 41, 375 🇧 750BF
per hour ◑ *9am–sunset Tue–Sun.*

paintball

Games with rules are organized to lend some form of order to an otherwise mad firing of paint.

❶ Wear old clothes!

Paintball Sport ASBL *off map*
13 rue Zwartebeek, Uccle ☎ 02.376. 36.67 ⛽ 55 ⚿ 950BF–1200BF
◐ *10am–8pm daily (daylight permitting).*

rollerblading & skateboarding

Brussels' cobblestones don't make for good blading and boarding, so head to Bois de la Cambre (with its free rink) or pay to play at Rollerpark.

Rollerpark *off map*
300 quai de Biestbroeck, Anderlecht ☎ 02.522. 59.15 Ⓜ Veeweyde
⚿ 180BF– 200BF ◐ *10am–10pm daily.*

skating

Olympic-sized and semi-covered Poseidon has a rink a stone's throw from the pool, sauna, and hammam of this sports centre.

Patinoire Poseidon *off map*
4 ave des Vaillants, Woluwe-St-Lambert ☎ 02.762.16.33 Ⓜ Tomberg
⚿ 12BF–160BF ◐ *Sep–Apr: 12–10pm daily (from 10am Wed–Sun).*

hotels

As Brussels has seized the seat of Euro power, its hotel sector has grown almost exponentially. Prices are lower than in many capitals and the quality of accommodation is excellent, if sometimes short on charm. But competition is fierce – prices at top places are often slashed at weekends and holiday periods to attract those not on expense accounts.

ⒷⒻ (Under 2500BF for a double room per night)

À la Grande Cloche
A6

A white façade and green awning fronts this family-run hotel. It's just across the square from the best restaurant in town, Comme Chez Soi, but a meal there is a week's stay here. The bright rooms have green carpets that reach halfway up the walls in true Continental style. Some have bathrooms, some toilets, some neither. There's a 1am curfew.

10 place Rouppe, Central ☎ 02.512.61.40 F 02.512.65.91 w www.hotelgrande-cloche.com Ⓜ Anneessens ♣ 37 ☐ Ⓟ ♿ ⊟ AE/MC/V ⓦ doubles: from 1750BF

Bed & Brussels
off map

Fancy staying with real *Bruxellois*? This not-for-profit organization can sort it out, fixing up rooms in private homes, the majority in the more affluent suburbs south and east of the centre. Breakfast is included, and there are three categories of accommodation, depending on facilities. The longer you stay, the better the deal. Call in advance with what you're after, and they'll send a list of options. Language immersion courses can also be arranged.

Office: 9 rue Kindermans, Ixelles (West) ☎ 02.646.07.37 F 02.644.01.14 w www.bnb-brussels.be Ⓜ Louise ♣ 255 beds in 105 homes ☐ ⊟ all ⓦ doubles: from 1695BF

Les Bluets
A10

Window boxes and a pretty façade welcome you to this highly individual family-run hotel, crammed with charming antiques and other rarities the owners have picked up on their travels. An English grandfather clock chimes in the hall, while a tropical bird twitters in the dining room. The rooms vary in style, most have antique beds, some of which seem a little cramped. The house has strict rules about silence (no noise after 10pm) and is non-smoking throughout.

124 rue Berckmans, St-Gilles ☎ 02.534.39.83 F 02.543.09.70 Ⓜ Hôtel des Monnaies ♣ 10 ☐ ♨ ⊟ AE/MC/V ⓦ doubles: from 2000BF

Les Ecrins
C2

Following a change of ownership, this small, gay-friendly hotel was entirely re-fitted in 2000 in sunny colours. The well-lit green and yellow rooms are very comfortable, with white duvet covers, double-glazing, and gleaming white bathrooms. The jolly, globe-trotting owner is charming and loquacious. Breakfast is served in an equally green and yellow room that looks out onto a tiny garden. Highly recommended for its warm welcome and good value.

15 rue du Rouleau, Ste-Catherine ☎ 02.219.36.57 F 02.223.57.40 w www.lesecrins.com Ⓜ Ste-Catherine ⬧ 11 ☐ 🗎 ◐ 🅿 D 🗖 MC/V ⓑ doubles: from 1900BF

Les Éperonniers
B6

A backpacking clientele stop at this friendly, family-run hotel – economic for groups. All rooms have toilet or shower (some both), plus TVs. The best have varnished floorboards and bright decor. Try breakfast in the café (300BF).

1 rue des Éperonniers, Central ☎ 02.513.53.66 F 02.511.32.30 Ⓜ Centrale ⬧ 30 🗖 AE/MC/V ⓑ beds: from 2095BF (in a room of six)

Galia
E6

On the sunny side of a cobbled square, and close to an Art Deco swimming pool, this place is ideal for early risers and bargain-hunters, as the excellent daily flea market on place du Jeu de Balles is right outside. The sturdy doors and double-glazing in the simply furnished, parquet-floored rooms help dampen the 6am sounds of the market set-up.

15–16 place du Jeu de Balle, Les Marolles ☎ 02.502.42.43 F 02.502.76.19 w www.hotelgalia.com Ⓜ Porte de Hal; Gare du Midi ⬧ 24 ☐ ◐ 🅿 🗖 all ⓑ doubles: from 2200BF

Pacific Sleeping
E2

Old professors and hard-up students gather in this institution. A zebra skin in the breakfast room looks like it's been here since the days of Léopold's Congo, and the elderly Monsieur Pauwels is a mine of information on all things Brussels. Works of art, lino-covered floors, wallpapered ceilings, hospital beds, and enormous china sinks give the place true character. Facilities are minimal: no rooms have en suite bathrooms and you have to pay to use the shower. Also, disappointingly, there's a midnight curfew. Such individualism at such a great price is a very rare thing in Brussels.

27 rue Antoine Dansaert, Ste-Catherine ☎ 02.511.84.59 Ⓜ Bourse; Ste-Catherine ⬧ 15 ☐ 🗖 none ⓑ doubles: from 1800BF

Sleep Well
D2

t calls itself a 'youth hotel' and rightly so. With comic strip murals and
a games room, this place is fab for the budget-conscious. Rooms are
right and clean; all have sinks, some showers. There's a 3am curfew.

23 rue du Damier, Central ☎ 02.218.50.50 F 02.218.13.13
📶 www.sleepwell.be Ⓜ Rogier ♦ 172 (beds) ♋ ♿ ⌀ 🗄 🛗 MC/V
ⓦ beds: from 350BF (in a room of eight); twins: 570BF per person
+ sheet hire)

Ⓑ🄵Ⓑ🄵 (2500–5000BF for a double room per night)

Agenda Louise
C11

This discreet hotel offers a friendly reception with a less corporate
feel. Rooms decorated in jade, russet, and gold tones have little
kitchenettes. A buffet breakfast is served in an attractive navy and
yellow room.

5 rue de Florence, Ixelles (West) ☎ 02.539.00.31 F 02.539.00.63
📶 www.hotel-agenda.com Ⓜ Louise ♦ 38 ♋ ♿ Ⓟ 🛗 🗄 all Ⓑ🄵Ⓑ🄵
Doubles: from 4500BF (w/e rates available)

Arlequin
F2

Tucked between two cobbled streets, this bright, modern hotel is
blessed with two cultural venues practically on its premises: the cool
basement bar with its enticing red-velvet sofas hosts regular live jazz
concerts; the tiny Actor's Studio cinema, in the same arcade, shows
second-run and art-house movies. The restful rooms in pastel shades
are comfortable, while the breakfast room on the top floor has stunning panoramas of the city centre.

17–19 rue de la Fourche, Central ☎ 02.514.16.15 F 02.514.22.02
Ⓜ Bourse; Centrale ♦ 92 ♋ ♿ ⌀ 🗄 all Ⓑ🄵Ⓑ🄵 doubles: from 3950BF
w/e rates available)

Hôtel Saint-Michel
B6

This tall, skinny hotel, on one of the world's most picturesque
squares, the Grand' Place, is sure to make for an unforgettable stay.
Remarkably discreet given its location, it's comfortable and unpretentious, with bright, spacious rooms and amazing views onto the
Grand' Place (the best of which is from room 22). Those at the front
are pricier, but don't count on a quiet night's sleep. And those at the
back can be disappointing. Breakfast is served in the rooms.

15 Grand' Place, Central ☎ 02.511.09.56 F 02.511.46.00 Ⓜ Centrale
♦ 15 📺 🗄 🗄 all Ⓑ🄵Ⓑ🄵 doubles: from 3950BF (w/e rates available)

Hôtel Welcome
C1

This tiny tiny hotel, self-proclaimed as the 'smallest hotel in Brussels', is run by the charming couple who manage the fish restaurant in the same building. The six rooms are all quite different in style and price: one is blue with white wicker furniture; another warm pinks with a comfy sofa. Guests get a special deal at the restaurant and can be served informal meals in the retro-tiled breakfast room. An airport limousine service is available.

quai au Bois à Brûler, Ste-Catherine ☎ 02.219.95.46 F 02.217.18.87 w www.hotelwelcome.com Ⓜ Ste-Catherine ♣ 6 ▤ ◑ ✆ ⧠ Ⓟ 🖃 all ⑧⑧ doubles: from 2600BF

La Madeleine
F2

Very good value for money, this simple hotel, behind a listed façade, is deservedly popular. All the rooms are different in size and style, but all freshly decorated in green and yellow, with white bathrooms. Rooms at the front overlook bustling place de l'Albertine with craft stalls and buskers; those at the back have no view but are quieter. An absolutely fantastic location.

20–22 rue de la Montagne, Central ☎ 02.513.29.73 F 02.502.13.50 Ⓜ Centrale ♣ 52 ⌨ 🖃 all ⑧⑧ doubles: from 3295BF

Noga
C2

This charming hotel blends good taste and comfort with crazy objects: enormous bellows, a waist-high statue, and various maritime curios. The result is cosy rather than cluttered, and there's always a friendly welcome. The spacious rooms are individually decorated, but only some have showers. The bright breakfast room/bar is flooded with daylight.

38 rue du Béguinage, Ste-Catherine ☎ 02.218.67.63 F 02.218.16.03 w www.nogahotel.com Ⓜ Ste-Catherine; De Brouckère ♣ 19 ⌨ ✆ ⧠ Ⓟ 🖃 all ⑧⑧ doubles: from 3300BF (w/e rates available)

Les Tourelles
off map

On a leafy, suburban avenue in bourgeois Uccle, this family-run hotel is something of a folly – with its gables and turrets, it looks more like an antique hunting lodge, and the interior is decorated to match. Rooms are of different shapes and sizes, with traditional furnishings and decor. The breakfast is generous; the service courteous. Rooms at the back overlook the interior courtyard and are quieter. Great for some respite from the city crowds.

135 avenue Winston Churchill, Uccle ☎ 02.344.95.73 F 02.346.42.70 ▥ 23, 90 ♣ 22 ⌨ ✆ ◑ Ⓟ 🖃 AE/MC/V ⑧⑧ doubles: from 4627BF (w/e rates available)

⊕⑧⑧ (5000–7500BF for a double room per night)

Comfort Art Hotel Siru   ⚑A3

What could have been a bland hotel (albeit an Art Deco one) has been transformed into an aesthetic curiosity. An original work of art was commissioned from a different Belgian artist for each of the 101 rooms, making the place one big gallery. The results vary from the sexy to the kitsch. Check out the folder with details of each artist and choose your decor, from fake rocks above the bed to brightly coloured nudes lounging on the bedstead. Ask for a room with a No. 8 at the end – these are in the octagonal tower.

place Rogier, St-Josse & Schaerbeek ☎ 02.203.35.80 F 02.203.33.03 Ⓜ Rogier; Gare du Nord ✦ 101 ◻ ⬧ ✆ ◻ ◘ ⊟ all ⊛⊛⊛ doubles: from 6200BF (w/e rates available)

Le Dixseptième   ⚑B6

This elegant house was the residence of the Spanish ambassador in the 17th century. The enormous rooms of the old house – with original oak beams, some with four-poster beds and antiques – look onto an interior courtyard. The modern rooms have been converted from the former stables, many with terraces and kitchenettes. All rooms are named after Belgian painters, copies of whose works adorn the walls; there's an art gallery in the lounge.

25 rue de la Madeleine, Central ☎ 02.502.57.44 F 02.502.64.24 w www.ledixseptieme.be Ⓜ Centrale ✦ 24 ◻ ▤ ⬧ ✆ ✆ ◻ ⊟ all ⊛⊛⊛ doubles: from 7100BF (w/e & business rates available)

⊕⑧⑧⑧ (7500–10,000BF for a double room per night)

Amigo   ⚑A6

Potted palms and black flagstones strewn with rugs give a Spanish colonial tone to the lobby of this glamorous hotel. And though it looks like it's been here for centuries, the Amigo was only built in 1958. Flagstones, tiling, and furniture are as old as the 16th century, and there are 16th-century Flemish paintings by the likes of Courters and Bastien too. Rooms are decorated in classic blue and cream; and the uniformed staff are so polite they seem to come from another age. Bought by Sir Rocco Forte in 2000, word has it that further embellishments are on the way.

1–3 rue d'Amigo, Central ☎ 02.547.47.07 F 02.502.28.05 w www.hotel-amigo.com Ⓜ Centrale ✦ 170 ◻ ▤ ㉔⬧ ✆ ✆ ◻ ◘ ⬧ ⊟ all ⊛⊛⊛⊛ doubles: from 9500BF (w/e & business rates available)

Bedford
♀A6

A family-run luxury hotel with a marble lobby, thick carpeting, and friendly service. The manager, who knows everything there is to know about the history of the city's hotels, tells how the Bedford is on the site of a hotel where WWII pilots came for romantic rendezvous. The rooms, some for families, are pink with red-wood furniture; the bathrooms are smallish but sparkling.

135 rue du Midi, Central ☎ 02.512.78.40 **F** 02.514.17.59
w www.hotelbedford.com Ⓜ Anneessens ♦ 321 ⌨ 🗐 🕘 ∥ ✆ 💻 🅿 ♿
🍴 all 🔞🔞🔞🔞 **doubles: from 9400BF (w/e rates available)**

Cascade
♀A10

Built around an interior courtyard, which doubles as a breakfast patio in the summer, this modern hotel has 70 studios and apartment. The two-bed flats have the added attraction of washing machines.

128 rue Berckmans, St-Gilles ☎ 02.538.88.30 **F** 02.538.92.79 Ⓜ Hôtel des Monnaies ♦ 80 ⌨ 🗐 ↔ ∥ 🕔 💻 🅿 🍴 all 🔞🔞🔞🔞 **doubles: from 20,500BF per week (w/e rates available)**

Manos Stéphanie
♀B10

You can't help but feel decadent amid the Louis XVI splendour of this hotel, with its marble hallway lined with giant gilt plant-stands. Antiques are dotted all over; red and gold upholstery, and tasteful prints make for an opulent stay. The interior courtyard has tasteful wooden loungers to top off the elegance. There's no restaurant, but an in-house chef caters for room service until 11pm.

28 chaussée de Charleroi, St-Gilles ☎ 02.539.02.50 **F** 02.537.57.29
w www.manoshotel.com Ⓜ Louise ♦ 55 ⌨ 🗐 🕘 ↔ ∥ 🕔 💻 🅿 ♿ 🍴 all 🔞🔞🔞🔞 **doubles: from 8250BF (w/e rates available)**

Royal Crown Grand Mercure
♀B3

It doesn't look much from the outside, but this 1970s luxury hotel offers an exceptionally friendly welcome, floors of no-smoking rooms, and a view over the Jardin Botanique for those lucky enough to get a room on that side. All renovated recently, the good-sized rooms are decorated in one of three colour schemes: pink, honey, or green. There's a valet parking service, and a cosy cocktail bar with cream club chairs and wood panelling.

250 rue Royale, St-Josse & Schaerbeek ☎ 02.220.66.11 **F** 02.217.84.44
Ⓜ Botanique ♦ 315 🗐 🕘 ↔ ∥ ✆ 💻 🅿 ♿ 🍴 all 🔞🔞🔞🔞 **doubles: from 8500BF (w/e rates available)**

Stanhope
D7

A veritable jewel, this former convent is the choice residence of diplomats and politicians. The compact rooms are individually decorated in English stately-home style: the adorable two-floored Goodwood suite overlooks the shady garden, whilst the Linley is kitted out with the Viscount's own furniture. Oozing good taste and attentive service, this hotel's charm is irresistible.

9 rue du Commerce, Quartier Européen ☎ 02.506.91.11 F 02.512.17.08 w www.summithotels.com Ⓜ Trône ◆ 50 🈚 ㉔↔ ✎ ☭ ☏ 🖵 🅿 ♿ 🖃 all ⒷⒻⒷⒻⒷⒻⒷⒻ doubles: from 8900BF (business rates available)

ⒷⒻⒷⒻⒷⒻⒷⒻⒷⒻ (over 10,000BF for a double room per night)

Astoria
D3

The Aga Khan's wife once had her bath filled with asses' milk in this historic *belle epoque* hotel. You may not get the same treatment, but it's still like stepping back in time: staff push brass luggage trolleys, the Pullman bar is modelled on an old Orient-Express carriage, and weekly classical concerts are held in the Waldorf Room. The huge bedrooms are awash with antiques, potted palms, and period features; modern touches like air-conditioning have been seamlessly added.

103 rue Royale, Central ☎ 02.227.05.05 F 02.217.11.50 w www.sofitel.com Ⓜ Botanique ◆ 125 🈚 ㉔↔ ✎ ☭ ☏ 🖵 🅿 ♿ 🖃 all ⒷⒻⒷⒻⒷⒻⒷⒻⒷⒻ doubles: from 10,000BF (w/e rates available)

Château du Lac
off map

This luxury, out-of-town hotel is the retreat for the likes of Boyzone on tour and France's victorious Euro 2000 football team. An ivy-clad, turreted hotel, built in 1904 in the style of a Cistercian abbey, it's half an hour from the centre of Brussels and overlooks lush surroundings, a bowling green, and a croquet lawn. Benefits include special deals with 11 nearby golf courses, a business centre, and residential team-building courses. A gastronomic restaurant and superb fitness centre with pool and tennis courts help make it a resort in itself.

avenue du Lac, Genval ☎ 02.655.71.11 F 02.655.74.44 w www.martinshotels.com/Genval ◆ 121 🍴 🈚 ㉔ ≋ ↔ ✎ ☭ ☏ 🖵 🅿 ♿ 🖃 all ⒷⒻⒷⒻⒷⒻⒷⒻⒷⒻ doubles: from 12,600BF (w/e & business rates available)

Conrad
♭B10

Lou Reed, Bill Clinton and other big names have stayed at this luxurious hotel, enhanced in 2000 by the addition of Champney's health club (open to hotel guests only), with dance studio, pool, and beauty treatments. Service and accommodation meet the needs of exacting guests: rooms are a good size with sofas; pricier ones have enormous oval bathtubs; and there's even a 'cyber concierge' to help with computer problems. Money can't buy love, but it can sure as hell buy luxury.

71 avenue Louise, Ixelles (West) ☎ 02.542.48.00 F 02.542.42.00 w www.brussels.conradinternational.com Ⓜ Louise ♦ 269 📋 ㉔🏵 ↔ 🖉 ☾ 🕸 🖫 🅿 🕭 🖃 all 🏵🏵🏵🏵🏵 doubles: from 16,000BF (w/e & business rates available)

Crowne Plaza
♭A3

Grace Kelly had an apartment decorated to her liking (for her Brussels visits) at this turn-of-the-century hotel. Now it's a suite, and on a quiet weekend you may be able to stay in it for a song. Like many old hotels in the city, this was occupied by the Germans in WWII – the theories flow about their use of the now-defunct lower-ground floors. Many rooms contain original Art Deco beds and wardrobes with gilt Egyptian motifs. The amenities and service are top class. Drop into the art gallery on the eighth floor.

3 rue Gineste, St-Josse & Schaerbeek ☎ 02.203.62.00 F 02.203.55.55 w www.crowneplaza.com Ⓜ Rogier ♦ 358 🖵 📋 ㉔↔🖉 ☾ 🕸 🖫 🅿 🕭 🖃 all 🏵🏵🏵🏵🏵 doubles: from 12,000BF (w/e & business rates available)

Dorint
♭B8

This area isn't usually known for its style, but the Dorint is an exception – sleek and modern, with lots of black, chrome, and spotlights. The rooms are smart (but not large) and each one is decorated with a different local photographer's work. It's a fave with journalists (as it's next to the International Press Centre, has ISDN lines, translation rooms, and a Reuters terminal). Hit the fitness club (with Turkish bath), or chill out in the palm-tree garden.

11–19 boulevard Charlemagne, Quartier Européen ☎ 02.231.09.09 F 02.231.33.71 w www.dorint.be Ⓜ Schuman ♦ 212 📋 ㉔↔🖉 ☾ 🕸 🖫 🅿 🕭 🖃 all 🏵🏵🏵🏵🏵 doubles: from 12,500BF (w/e & business rates available)

Hôtel Métropole
♭D2

A landmark *belle époque* hotel with an incredible 19th-century-style foyer: all marble columns, glittering chandeliers, wood panelling, and stained glass. It's cherished by French actors, and some guests come back time and again to revel in its opulence. Rooms along the 9km of

orridors are spacious and varied, with fine examples of Art Deco and
Art Nouveau furniture. The interior of the café is magnificent, but the
terrace looks out on a busy intersection, and the Alban Chambon restaurant has an excellent reputation and decor to match. Put relaxation first
at the Bio Etna health suite with a hammam and beauty treatments.

1 place de Brouckère, Central ☎ 02.217.23.00 F 02.218.02.20
w www.metropolehotel.be Ⓜ De Brouckère ✦ 303 ▢ 🗏 ↔ 🖉 🕭 🍴 ▯
🅿 ⛴ ▤ all ⓐⓐⓐⓐⓐⓐ doubles: from 12,500BF (w/e rates available)

Montgomery   🖉*off map*

Choose from an Oriental, Laura Ashley, or Ralph Lauren room in this
classy joint near the Cinquantenaire. None will disappoint: fittings
are top quality and the taste impeccable. Although only built in the
1990s, the Montgomery manages a suave, gentleman's-club feel,
with Chesterfield sofas, wood panelling, and a library in the lounge-
bar area. La Duchesse restaurant's French chef does sunny Med (and
veggie fare) very well.

134 avenue de Tervuren, Woluwe-St-Lambert ☎ 02.741.85.11
F 02.741.85.00 w www.montgomery.be Ⓜ Montgomery ✦ 63 🗏 🅩
↔ 🖉 🍴 ▯ 🅿 ⛴ ▤ all ⓐⓐⓐⓐⓐⓐ doubles: from 12,500BF (w/e &
business rates available)

e Plaza   🖉*D2*

There's nothing dated about this magnificent 1930s hotel that
reopened in 1996 after a 20-year closure. No expense was spared to
preserve the cachet of the original – prized by legends of cinema and
entertainment such as Brigitte Bardot and Joséphine Baker – and to
meet modern needs. Enormous china sinks, framed illustrations, and
comfortable armchairs distinguish the traditional-style rooms. The
domed dining room is equally impressive. But for the real cherry,
sneak a look at the hotel's incredible listed theatre, now used for
fashion and media events.

118–126 boulevard Adolphe Max, Central ☎ 02.227.67.00
F 02.227.67.20 w www.leplaza-brussels.be Ⓜ Rogier ✦ 193 ▢ 🗏 🅩
↔ 🖉 🍴 ▯ 🅿 ⛴ ▤ all ⓐⓐⓐⓐⓐⓐ doubles: from 10,900BF (w/e &
business rates available)

Radisson SAS   🖉*F2*

Zip up in the glass elevator of this sleek Scandinavian hotel and
look down on the central atrium's winter garden, complete with
greenery, burbling brook, and the remains of the 12th-century city
wall. Room decor depends on the theme of the floor – Italian,
Oriental, Scandinavian (with parquet floors for allergy sufferers),

and the swish Royal Club. The top floor has a superbly equipped gym. Check out the renowned Sea Grill restaurant.
47 rue du Fossé aux Loups, Central ☎ 02.219.28.28 F 02.219.62.62 w www.radisson.com/brussels.be Ⓜ De Brouckère ♦ 281 ▤ ㉔↔◢ ◖◗◦☞▯▣♿⊟ all ⓑⓒⓓⓔⓕ doubles: from 13,000BF (w/e & business rates available)

Royal Windsor   ♱B6
An English-style luxury hotel that appeals to visiting rock stars and statesmen alike. Rooms, though not enormous, are superbly equipped, with bright, marble bathrooms, dark-wood parquet, and elegant upholstery. There are floors with no-smoking rooms, and those on the Godiva floor (which are sponsored and decorated by the chocolate company) come with complimentary choccies too. The only hotel in the city to have its own nightclub, Griffin's.
5 rue Duquesnoy, Central ☎ 02.505.55.55 F 02.505.55.00 w www.warwickhotels.com/brussels Ⓜ Centrale ♦ 266 ▤ ㉔↔◢◦☞▯▣♿⊟ all ⓑⓒⓓⓔⓕ doubles: from 14,119BF

Sheraton Brussels Hotel & Towers   ♱B2
Whisk through the revolving doors and exchange a busy intersection for some serious pampering. Exceptionally spacious rooms, huge beds, and Playstations to boot: this is where the big boys kick back and chill out. Six floors are dedicated to business travellers (with receptionists and video conference facilities), whilst some rooms keep the offspring happy with toys. The fitness centre has a good-sized indoor pool, with loungers on the outside terrace.
3 place Rogier, St-Josse & Schaerbeek ☎ 02.224.31.11 F 02.224.34.56 w www.sheraton.com/Brussels Ⓜ Rogier ♦ 533 ▤ ㉔≋↔◢◖◗▯ ▣♿⊟ all ⓑⓒⓓⓔⓕ doubles: from 13,000BF (w/e rates available)

Swissôtel   ♱E8
The choice pad of lobbyists, politicians, and consultants with business at the nearby European Parliament. Swish and modern, it caters for the business traveller, with espresso machines and large desks in the navy and yellow executive rooms. There's an apartment block for long-stay guests. The gym and indoor pool are fab, and the Nico Central restaurant pulls a smart crowd.
19 rue du Parnasse, Quartier Européen ☎ 02.505.29.29 F 02.505.25.55 w www.swissotel.com Ⓜ Trône ♦ 257 ▭ ▤ ㉔≋↔◢ ◦▯▣♿⊟ all ⓑⓒⓓⓔⓕ doubles: from 12,800BF (w/e & business rates available)

admission charges

Charges for museums and sights vary but expect to pay 50BF–150BF. Most are closed on Mondays. Some, including the Musée d'Art Ancien and the Musée d'Art Moderne, are free on the first Wednesday afternoon (1pm–5pm) of each month.

banks

Banks are usually open 9am–4pm Mon–Fri. Various branches close for lunch and some stay open late one day a week. A few banks in the suburbs are open Saturday mornings – but none in the centre. Main banks are the Banque Bruxelles Lambert (BBL), Fortis, and KBC. All major branches have 24-hour cash dispensers. Eurocheques of up to 7000BF can be cashed at any bank showing the Eurocheque sign and cash withdrawals can be made at cash dispensers bearing the Eurocheque logo (Eurocheques can also be used in restaurants and shops). For international money transfers:
Western Union ☎ 0800.990.90
Goffin, 88 rue du Marché aux Herbes, ☎ 02.502.23.82
◐ 9am–10pm Mon–Sat
Camrail Cash Services at Gare Centrale, ☎ 02.511.43.14
◐ 7am–9pm Mon–Sat
The most central banks are:
BBL, 90 rue du Marché aux Herbes ☎ 02.506.42.90

◐ 9am–4pm Mon–Fri
Fortis Bank, 3 boulevard Anspach ☎ 02.212.94.11
◐ 9am–4pm Mon–Fri
KBC, 5 pl de Brouckère ☎ 02.250.09.70 ◐ 9am–4pm Mon–Fri.

bars & cafés

Bars and cafés are usually open throughout the day and since there's no official closing time, some stay open until the early hours, depending on the number of customers. As well as alcohol, bars sell tea and coffee, and, usually, light snacks. Cafés serve full menus. Officially, larger cafés are supposed to have a non-smoking area. In reality, only a few bother. Children and pets are usually welcome.

bureaux de change

Expect to pay 250BF on traveller's cheques' exchanges. Beware of good rates but high commission. Thomas Cook doesn't charge a commission if you change their own cheques (now issued in euros) at one of their offices. Banks offer a fixed rate of exchange whereas bureaux de change can vary, so do shop around.
Basle, 23 rue au Beurre ☎ 02.511.56.30 ◐ 9am–6pm daily.
Thomas Cook, 4 Grand' Place ☎ 02.513.28.45 ◐ 9am–7pm daily.
Camrail Cash Services, Gare Centrale ☎ 02.511.43.14
◐ 7am–9pm daily.

Camrail Cash Services, Gare du Midi ☎ 02.556.36.00 ◑ *6.30am–10pm daily.*

children
Activities: check the What's On section of *The Bulletin*, in newsagents every Thursday.
Babysitters: contact Baby Kid Sitting ☎ 02.646.46.11.
Hotels: many hotels allow children to share their parents' room at no extra charge or at a reduced rate per child.
Restaurants, cafés & bars: children are welcomed with open arms in most restaurants, cafés, and bars. Kids' menus are also common. There aren't many high-chairs or play areas, however, and the only downtown public facility for changing nappies is at the M&S store on rue Neuve.
Transport: children under 6 travel free on STIB buses, trams, and metro – a maximum of four kids is allowed per paying adult. Children under 12 travel free on trains within Belgium.

clubs
Admission: clubs are often free 11pm–midnight, but expect to pay 150BF–400BF thereafter (the price usually includes a drink).
Dress code/door policy: dress codes vary so it's best to check ahead. At most clubs, doormen expect a tip of at least 50BF as you leave.
Opening times: generally 11pm until 5–6am.

conversion chart

Clothing	Women's			Men's			
European	36	40	44	46	46	50	54 56
British	8	12	16	18	36	40	44 46
US	6	10	14	16	36	40	44 46

Shoes	Women's			Men's			
European	37	38	39	40	40	42	43 44
British	4	5	6	7	6	7	8 9
US	5	6	7	8	7	8	9 10

courier services
National services within Belgium:
EMS Transport ☎ 078.15.33.43
Taxi verts ☎ 02.349.46.46
BCC ☎ 02.463.44.99
International services:
DHL ☎ 02.715.50.50
FedEx ☎ 0800.135.55
UPS ☎ 0800.128.28

credit & debit cards
The most widely accepted cards are American Express, MasterCard/EuroCard, and Visa. All major credit cards can be used in restaurants, hotels, and some taxis. As long as you have a PIN, you can withdraw cash with your debit or credit card at one of the many ATMs in the city displaying the Eurocheque or Visa logos. Remember there's an extra charge for credit card withdrawals. Cards carrying the Cirrus logo can only be used at ATMs displaying the same logo. For lost or stolen cards call:
American Express ☎ 02.676.26.26
MasterCard/EuroCard
☎ 070.34.43.44
Visa ☎ 070.344.344

currency

Belgium's currency is the Belgian franc, usually referred to as FB or BF. Coins are 0.5BF, 1BF, 5BF, 20BF, and 50BF. Notes come in denominations of 100BF, 500BF, 1000BF, 5000BF, and 10,000BF. On 1st January 2002 the euro will become the official currency of Belgium and on 1st July 2002, the Belgian franc will disappear altogether. Until then prices are given in both Belgian francs and euros (1 euro = 39.2501BF).

customs & quarantine

Brussels customs (*douane*) has 'a goods to declare' exit and a 'no goods to declare' exit. There are no quarantine laws in existence but certain endangered species are prohibited. Meat, flowers, and plants are also prohibited.
Customs ☎ 02.753.48.30

dentists

For urgent dental care:
Service de Garde Dentaire, 107 avenue Jacques Sermon ☎ 02.426.10.26 or 02.428.58.88
St-Pierre hospital:
☎ 02.535.40.55 (for emergency treatment at weekends).

disabled visitors

The Grand' Place and the surrounding streets have cobbled stones making life difficult for wheelchair users. Furthermore, the city's trams, buses, and the metro are not easily accessible for disabled visitors – the exceptions are the T2000 trams which have wide doors and low floors. Contact the **TIB** ☎ 02.513.89.40 for information on disabled access to hotels, museums, and restaurants in Brussels.

driving

Driving in the capital is difficult as the *Bruxellois* tend to drive fast and aggressively. The public transport system, however, is efficient and distances are short, so it's only worth driving for days out of the city.

duty free

Duty-free goods are still available to non-EU nationals and usual restrictions apply. Visitors are allowed a maximum of 200 cigarettes, 1 litre of spirits or 2 litres of wine. EU nationals can still benefit from reductions on clothes, cosmetics, and perfumes.
Customs ☎ 02.753.48.30

electricity

Electrical supply is 220 volts and sockets are the standard European two-pronged type. British appliances need an adaptor; US ones need a transformer and an adaptor. These can be purchased at main airports.

email & internet

You can surf the net in:
Cyberb@r 185 chaussée d'Ixelles ☎ 02.502.51.25 ⊞ 250BF/hour ◑ 12pm–midnight Mon–Sat

Internet Center 182 chaussée de Charleroi ☎ 02.534.61.41 BF 3000BF/hour ◑ *9am–7pm daily*
Pointnet Surf Center 16 Petite rue des Bouchers ☎ 02.513.14.15 BF 200BF/hour (unlimited access over one week for 2000BF) ◑ *10am–10pm Mon–Sat (to 6pm Sat)*
Sport Avenue 4–5 avenue de la Toison d'Or ☎ 02.500.78.78 BF 250BF/hour (50-hour pass costs 5000BF) ◑ *10am–11pm Mon–Sat*
To locate other cyber cafés go to http://cyber café.potaulait.be or www.netcafes.com

embassies & consulates
American Embassy: 27 boulevard du Régent ☎ 02.508.21.11
Australian Embassy: 6–8 rue Guimard ☎ 02.286.05.00
British Embassy: 85 rue d'Arlon ☎ 02.287.62.11
Canadian Embassy: 2 avenue de Tervuren ☎ 02.741.06.11
Irish Embassy: 98 rue Froissart ☎ 02.230.53.37
New Zealand Embassy: 47–48 boulevard du Régent ☎ 02.512.10.40

emergencies
For emergency ambulance, fire brigade, or medical service call 100 or go to one of the following major hospitals:
Hôpital St-Pierre, 322 rue Haute ☎ 02.535.40.51 (emergencies)
Clinique St-Luc, 10 avenue Hippocrate ☎ 02.764.16.02 (emergencies)

Centre Hospitalier Brugmann, 4 place Van Gehuchten ☎ 02.477.20.01 (emergencies).

help & advice lines
Alcoholics Anonymous ☎ 02.513.23.36
Aids ☎ 02.511.45.29 ☎ 078.15.15.15
Community Help Service (CHS) ☎ 02.648.40.14 (24-hr telephone helpline in English)
Télé Accueil ☎ 107 (24-hr Samaritan-type line).

hotels
Charges: surprisingly, low season in Brussels is Jul–Aug and during the end-of-year festivities. This is because Brussels attracts such a large number of business people on weekdays during the rest of the year. Cheap hotel rates are available during these periods and you can book a five-star hotel at a reasonable price. Low rates operate during weekends all year round and there are reductions for children who share their parents' room. Some hotels will charge a cancellation fee if you cancel after 6pm. Check-out time is usually 11am.
Useful contacts: a free hotel reservation service is operated by **Belgium Tourist Reservations** ☎ 02.513.74.84 ◑ *9am–5pm Mon–Fri*
For home-swaps and a bed and breakfast guide, call **Taxistop** ☎ 02.223.23.10

immigration

If you're planning to stay more than 3 months, you have to report to the town hall of the commune where you plan to live (there are 19 communes or districts in Brussels). Telephone in advance for opening hours and the documents you may need as they vary between communes. Most communes will require a passport, 2 passport photos, and either your lease on accommodation or a letter from your employer stating that you are in full-time employment. A fee will be charged to cover administrative costs. For the number of your local town hall look under 'Administrations communales' in the white pages telephone directory (Les Pages Blanches/De Witte Gids). Central Brussels (1000),
☎ 02.279.22.11

insurance

Comprehensive travel and medical insurance is recommended, particularly for non-EU citizens. EU nationals should be in possession of an E111, which covers basic medical treatment. Keep all receipts as you have to pay on the spot and be reimbursed on your return.

left luggage

24-hour access lockers are available at Gare du Midi and Gare Centrale. Manual lockers cost 10BF for 24 hours. Electronic lockers cost between 60BF–100BF (depending on the volume) for 24 hours.

lost property

Report all lost property to the police (☎ 02.279.79.79 for central Brussels) to substantiate insurance claims. If you lose your passport you will also need to report it to your embassy. For lost property on public transport contact the public transport authority (STIB)
☎ 02.515.23.94; at Brussels Zaventem airport
☎ 02.753.68.20.

maps

De Rouck maps (www.derouck.be) are readily available at newsagents, bookshops, and supermarkets. The Tourist Information Brussels (TIB) on the Grand' Place also has city maps for sale.

measurements

As a rule, metric measures are used.

metric : imperial	imperial : metric
1 mm = 0.04 inch	1 inch = 2.5 cm
1 cm = 0.4 inch	1 foot = 30 cm
1 m = 3.3 ft	1 mile = 1.6 km
1 km = 0.6 mile	1 ounce = 28 g
1 g = 0.04 oz	1 pound = 454 g
1 l = 0.6 (US) gallon	1 pint = 0.6 l
	1 (US) gallon = 3.8 l

medical matters

Go to the outpatients department of one of the hospitals listed or call the CHS helpline ☎ 02.648.40.14 for advice if you need an English-speaking doctor. For abortion and contraception advice call **La Famille Heureuse,** 4 place Quetelet ☎ 02.217.44.50 or 02.217.46.02

medicine & chemists

A *pharmacie* (in French) or *apotheek* (in Flemish) sells everything from over-the-counter medicines to prescription drugs, as well as everyday toiletries. An extra charge of 158BF is added to the price of your prescription if you go to chemists outside normal hours. A list of the *pharmaciens de garde* (chemists open at night and at weekends) is posted on chemists' windows. You can also check the *Le Soir* newspaper or call ☎ 0900.105.00 for a list of them. ❶ *generally 9am–6pm. Some open until 7pm and a few open on Saturday mornings.*

office & business services

Faxing, colour copying and binding services are available at:
Business Copy 6a rue Volta ☎ 02.649.76.97
Chasse Copy & Multimedia 16 avenue Pirmez ☎ 02.644.06.34 (also offers use of its computer terminals).
Mister Copy 117–123 boulevard Général Jacques ☎ 02.640.94.21
The **NCI Business Center** offers fully equipped offices, multilingual secretarial and translation services, and personalized answering services: 149 avenue Louise ☎ 02.535.75.11; 50 rue

Wiertz ☎ 02.401.68.11
For stationery, call into the **Inno** department store, 111 rue Neuve ☎ 02.211.21.11

opticians

The following branches of Optic City offer free eye-tests on condition you buy a pair of glasses from them:
Optic City City 2 Shopping Centre, 123 rue Neuve ☎ 02.218.11.55; 30 boulevard Anspach ☎ 02.218.71.97

parking

[→transport]

photography

For a one-hour developing service try:
Flash One City 2, 123 rue Neuve ☎ 02.217.05.15 ❶ *9am–7pm daily.*
For cheaper, three-day options try:
Di stores City 2, 123 rue Neuve ☎ 02.218.01.90 ❶ *10am–7pm daily.* (other branches)
FNAC City 2, 123 rue Neuve ☎ 02.275.11.11 ❶ *10am–7pm (to 8pm Fri).* This is the largest FNAC store and also offers a one-hour development service.
For camera repairs try:
Campion 13 rue St-Boniface ☎ 02.512.13.31 ❶ *10am–7pm Mon–Sat*
Lontie 1528 chaussée de Wavre ☎ 02.672.30.80 ❶ *10am–7pm Mon–Sat.*

police

Only use ☎ 101 in emergencies. Otherwise call the police station in central Brussels, 30 rue du Marché au Charbon ☎ 02.279.79.79 to find out the nearest station.

postal services

Post offices ◑ 9am–5pm Mon–Fri. Most post offices are closed at weekends and on public holidays. The central post office is in the Centre Monnaie, place de Brouckère ☎ 02.226.21.11 ◑ 8am–7pm Mon–Fri (9.30am–3pm Sat). There's also a post office at 48 avenue Fonsny ☎ 02.538.33.98 ◑ 24 hours daily.

Stamps: to send letters and cards within Belgium costs 17BF and 21BF for other EU countries. The post office on rue Cortenberg (near Schuman) has a stamp machine if you want to avoid the queues.

Poste restante: the post office at the Centre Monnaie in central Brussels accepts mail for collection. You will need your passport to claim your poste restante.

Info poste ☎ 02.226.23.10

public holidays

New Year's Day – 1st January
Easter Monday – March/April (variable)
Labour Day – 1st May
Ascension – 6th Thursday after Easter
Whit Monday – 7th Monday after Easter
National Day – 21st July
Assumption – 15th August
All Saints' Day – 1st November
Armistice – 11th November
Christmas Day – 25th December

religion

For information on religious services and places of worship contact:
Catholic ☎ 02.511.81.78
Jewish ☎ 02.512.43.34
Muslim ☎ 02.735.21.73
For further information call:
Bruxelles-Accueil 6 rue de Tabora ☎ 02.511.81.78 ◑ 10am–6pm Mon–Sat

restaurants

Reservations: it's advisable to make a reservation for the more up-market restaurants, particularly at weekends.
Opening times: restaurants usually serve lunch 12–2.30pm and dinner 6–10.30pm. Many close for either the whole of July or August so call in advance if you're going around this time.
Prices: vary enormously but on the whole, eating out is cheaper than in other major cities.
Tipping: is usually left to the discretion of the customer as service is included in the bill. Smoking: non-smoking sections are rare and Belgians don't mind nearby patrons lighting up.
Moules: watch out for moules, which can be unsafe if eaten out of season. Most restaurants will only serve them August–April.

safety

Take the usual precautions that you would in any major city. Avoid walking alone late at night in poorly lit, isolated areas. In particular, be wary of the areas around the Gare du Nord and the Gare du Midi. Public transport is pretty safe, but women travelling alone should be cautious in underground stations off the beaten track late at night. As ID is compulsory, it's preferable to have a photocopy of your passport in your possession.

shopping

Export: some shops offer VAT discounts to non-EU nationals [→VAT]
Opening times: generally from 9/9.30am–6/6.30pm. Supermarkets are open longer.
Payment: can be made by cash or credit card.
Returns: should be made as soon as possible. You will need your receipt in order to exchange goods or get a refund. Note that sales goods are non-refundable.
Guarantees: are available on larger goods and equipment. Keep your receipt and ensure the guarantee is stamped before leaving the shop.
Sales: the winter sale starts in January and lasts the whole month. The summer sale takes place during the whole month of July.

smoking

Belgians tend to smoke in restaurants, bars, and cafés, but public buildings such as banks and post offices are no-smoking areas, as is public transport.

students

USIT Connections ☎ 02.550. 01.00 and **Acotra World** ☎ 02.289.78.00 offer discounts for students under 26 who carry an International Student Identity Card (ISIC). ISIC cards are available at USIT Connections – you will need proof you are still a student plus 350BF.

telephoning

Phone sounds: repeated short beeps = engaged; long beeps = ringing.
Local codes: numbers within Brussels use the prefix ☎ 02.
International codes: to call Belgium from the UK and Ireland dial ☎ 0032; from the US ☎ 01132; from Australia ☎ 001132. To call from Belgium dial ☎ 00 plus the country code: UK ☎ 44; US ☎ 1; Australia ☎ 61; Ireland ☎ 353. Complete international numbers to Belgium by removing the first 0 from the regional code.
Directory enquiries & operator: for numbers within Belgium dial ☎ 1405 (English), ☎ 1307 (French), ☎ 1207 (Dutch), and ☎ 1407 (German).
International directory enquiries: dial ☎ 1304 (French), ☎ 1204 (Dutch), and ☎ 1404 (German).

international prefix information: dial ☎ 1324 (French), ☎ 1224 (Dutch), and ☎ 1424 (German).

Phone directories: the official directory is *Les Pages Blanches/De Witte Gids*. There are two volumes of *Les Pages d'Or/De Gouden Gids* (yellow pages).

Phone rates: standard local rate 8am–7pm weekdays is 2BF/min; evening local rate 7pm–8am weekdays, and all day on weekends and public holidays is 1BF/min. There is a basic connection charge of 2BF per local call within Belgium and 4BF for an international call. 0900 numbers cost 18BF/min while calls to GSMs (mobile phones) cost 3BF/min during peak hours. The same rates apply throughout Belgium.

Freephone numbers: numbers preceded with ☎ 0800 are free of charge.

Phone boxes: most public phone boxes are phone card- or credit card-operated.

Phone cards: Télécards come in units of 200BF or 1000BF and are available from newsagents, supermarkets, and post offices. Scratch the surface of the télécard to reveal a PIN, dial the local number given on the card, then dial your PIN.
A pre-recorded voice tells you how much credit you have on the card before you dial.

Mobile phone hire: try Locaphone at Zaventem airport

☎ 02.652.14.14 who rent mobiles at 365BF per day (for the first 5 days). Insurance costs 430BF and calls are paid by credit card.

time
Belgium is on Central European Time which is one hour ahead of GMT. Clocks go forward one hour in spring (end of March) and back one hour in autumn (end of October). Dial ☎ 1300 for the 24-hour speaking clock.

tipping
Tipping isn't expected in cafés, restaurants, and hotels, as service is included in the bill – it is left entirely to the discretion of the customer. If you do wish to leave a tip in a restaurant, it's usual to give about 10% of the total bill. In hotels you can choose to tip the chambermaid or porter. Hairdressers expect a tip of at least 100BF.

toilets
There are few public toilets so pop into a railway station or a fast-food chain where you'll pay a 10BF fee. Some bars charge a fee even if you are a customer.

tourist information
Tourist Information Brussels (TIB) offers information on restaurants, museums, car hire, and events, and stocks maps and brochures.
TIB Hôtel de Ville, Grand' Place ☎ 02.513.89.40 ◑ *9am–6pm daily*.

Belgium tourist centre, 63 rue du Marché aux Herbes
☎ 02.504.03.90 ◑ 9am–6pm daily (to 1pm Sun).

travel agents
Travel agents offering cheap flights include:
Acotra World ☎ 02.289.78.00
USIT Connections
☎ 02.550.01.00
Last-minute cheap flights are on offer at
Nouvelles Frontières
☎ 02.547.44.44 w www.nouvelles-frontieres.

travellers' cheques
This is still the safest way to carry money. The most widely accepted currencies are pounds sterling and US dollars. The best places to change travellers' cheques are bank-operated bureaux de change or Thomas Cook [→bureaux de change].

VAT (Value Added Tax)
Goods in shops are taxed at 21% and non-EU citizens are entitled to a VAT refund on purchases. Take the relevant forms (a receipt and certified VAT form from the shop where you bought the goods), ID proof of non-EU citizenship, and your unopened goods to the VAT/Customs desk at the airport for refunds.

visas & entry requirements
All nationalities must carry a valid passport (or ID for EU citizens). For most non-EU citizens, a visa is not required but check with the Belgium Embassy or Consulate before leaving.

weather
Brussels' weather is very changeable. You can experience all four seasons in one day. Check the local press for the weather forecast or see www.weather.com for daily reports.

transport

arriving and departing

Brussels' central role in Europe has made it a hub for continent-wide transport networks. Trains from around Europe converge in the central Gare du Midi (Zuidstation), and two airports provide international entry points.

by air

Brussels National Airport (Zaventem)

Located 15km northeast of Brussels, Zaventem Airport is the city's main airport, handling international flights operated by Sabena, the Belgian airline, and other major carriers like Virgin Express.

transport options

Airport City Express
10 mins to/from Gare Centrale also stops at Gare du Nord & Gare du Midi).
⊙ four times an hour from 5am–midnight daily.
90BF (tickets from the desk before boarding)
♺ 1| It's quick, cheap and efficient. 2| The train station is underground in the airport, easily accessible by lift.
SNCB ☎ 02.555.25.25

bus
35 mins to/from Gare du Nord.
⊙ hourly from 6.20am–11.05pm daily.
70BF (tickets on board from the driver)
♺ The cheapest way of getting into central Brussels.
De Lijn ☎ 02.526.28.28

taxis
15–20 mins to/from city centre.
⊙ 24 hours daily
800BF–1000BF
♺ 1| Wheelchair access for foldable chairs. 2| Lots available outside arrivals hall.
♻ Watch out for unlicensed taxi drivers in the arrivals hall.

limos & cars
20–30 mins to/from city centre.
⊙ 24 hours daily.
2000BF–2385BF
♺ Wheelchair access for foldable chairs.
♻ Most expensive option.
Europcar Limo: ☎ 02.348.92.12
Avis Limo: ☎ 02.504.10.30
Modern Car Limousine:
☎ 02.420.10.00
Belgian Limo: ☎ 02.753.63.73

Airportstop
Internet service where a driver offers a lift to/from the airport or a passenger looks for a lift

to/from Zaventem.
⊞ 10BF/km (divided between number of people in the car).
♿ Very quick and cheap.
BIAC ☎ 02.753.42.28
Taxistop ☎ 09.223.23.10
w www.airportstop.org

☎ **useful numbers**
General enquiries:
0900.70000/02.753.21.11
Arrivals/departures: 02.753.39.13
Lost property: 02.753.68.20
First aid: 02.753.69.69
Airport security: 02.753.70.00
Customs: 02.753.48.30
w www.brusselsairport.be
⌖ **Sheraton:** 02.725.10.00
⌖ **Holiday Inn:** 02.720.58.65
⌖ **Mercure:** 02.726.73.35

Brussels South-Charleroi Airport

Brussels South-Charleroi is a small, privately owned airport 55km from the centre of Brussels. It deals mostly with holiday charter traffic, but also scheduled flights from Ryanair.

transport options

🚌 **bus, then** 🚆 **train**
Catch a bus to Charleroi train station (takes 10 mins), then connect onto a Belgian Railways (SNCB/NMBS) train (45 mins to/from Gare du Midi).
🕐 **Shuttle bus:** timed to connect with flight arrivals and depar-

tures; 6.50am–8.30pm Mon–Sat (to 2pm Sat); 2.45–7.55pm Sun.
Train: approx. 7 and 34 mins past every hour 4.31am–11.07pm Mon–Fri; approx. 27 mins past every hour 5.27am–11.27pm Sat–Sun.
⊞ 300BF to/from anywhere in Brussels
⚠ The lack of regularity in this service can make it a slow journey.
☎ 07.160.22.94

🚌 **shuttle bus**
45 mins to/from the Wild Geese pub on avenue Livingstone, Brussels, for Ryanair passengers only.
🕐 **Wild Geese–Charleroi:**
7.50am, 2.30pm, 6.20pm Mon–Fri; 7.50am, 11.40am Sat; 1.50pm, 5.40pm Sun.
Charleroi–Wild Geese: 9.50am, 4.40pm, 8.30pm Mon–Fri; 9.50am, 1.45pm Sat; 7.40pm Sun.
⊞ 250BF
Ryanair ☎ UK: 08701.569.569; Belgium: 07.123.41.15

☎ **useful numbers**
Enquiries: 07.125.12.11 (all enquiries, including flight info, lost property, customs and lost luggage)
w www.charleroi-airport.com
⌖ **Holiday Inn Garden Court:**
07.130.24.24

by train

High-speed services on Eurostar, Thalys and other European rail services have opened up a world of inter-Europe travel. Gare du Midi lies at the heart of the network, creating easy access to and from Brussels.

⫴ Eurostar

Eurostar is the high-speed train linking London Waterloo and Ashford International to the Gare du Midi in Brussels. The journey from London takes 2 hrs 10 mins.

🕙 6.14am–7.27pm daily (approx. 14 times a day Mon–Sat; 8 times a day Sun).

🎫 from 6500BF (from £70) return.

Tickets can be bought on the internet, over the phone, at train stations in Brussels, and in travel agencies. Booked tickets can be picked up at the Railtour desk at Gare du Midi up until 30 mins before departure.

♿ 1| Children under 4 travel free. 2| Eurostar trains are well set up for disabled travellers, with toilets designed for wheelchair-users and low-level flooring at train doors.

⚑ While the interior of Gare du Midi is safe, care should be taken if walking around the surrounding area.

❶ 1| Check in 20 mins before departure. 2| You need your passport even if you are an EU citizen travelling from within the EU.

☎ UK: 0870.160.66.00; Belgium: 0900.101.77

w www.eurostar.com

⫴ Thalys

Thalys is a network of high-speed trains connecting Brussels (Gare du Midi) with Amsterdam, Cologne, Paris, Lyons and Geneva. It takes 1 hr 25 mins to Paris and 2 hrs 38 mins to Amsterdam (with a stop-off at Schiphol Airport, Amsterdam).

🕙 There are 22 trains each way per day between Brussels and Paris; and five trains each way per day between Brussels and Amsterdam.

🎫 Brussels–Paris: 3060BF return; Brussels–Amsterdam: 1860BF return.

Tickets can be bought on the internet, over the phone, at train stations, and in travel agencies. Booked tickets can be picked up at the Railtour desk at Gare du Midi up until 30 mins pre-departure.

♿ 1| Children under 4 travel free. 2| Thalys trains are well set up for disabled travellers, with toilets designed for wheelchair-users.

☎ **Bookings:**
0900.101.77/07.066.77.88

w www.thalys.com

le shuttle

Instead of taking the car over sea, take it underground. Cars go through the Channel Tunnel on Le Shuttle from Folkestone to Calais. There are approx. 70 crossings per day (four per hour during the day, hourly through the night). The journey takes 35 mins and the drive from Calais to Brussels approx. 2 hrs.

UK: 0870.535.35.35 **w** www.euro-tunnel.co.uk

£169.50 return

by sea

Competition from Eurostar and Le Shuttle has made crossing the Channel by sea cheaper than ever, with offers on almost year-round.

P&O North Sea Ferries

P&O North Sea Ferries travel to/from Zeebrugge and Hull every night, taking just over 13 hours.

☼ 6.15pm daily from Hull (arrives Zeebrugge 8.30am); 6.15pm daily from Zeebrugge (arrives Hull 8am).

Foot passenger: from 3832BF (£38) return; car (including 4 passengers): from 6212BF (£161) return.

❶ Train to Brussels takes between 1 hr 15 mins and 1 hr 30 mins (approx. once an hour from 6.03am–9.35 pm Mon–Fri;

approx. every 2 hours 6am–10.02pm Sat–Sun).

445BF.

☎ **UK:** 01482.377.177; **Belgium:** 050.54.34.30 **w** www.ponsf.com

Hoverspeed

Hoverspeed's Seacat operates to/from Ostend and Dover and takes just less than two hours.

☼ Five crossings per day in high season; two or three a day in low season.

Foot passenger: from 3000BF (£56) return; car (including 2 passengers): from 12,580BF (£218) return.

⤷ Train connections to Brussels (4 times hourly, 3.57am–10.38pm, 460BF).

☎ **UK:** 0870.524.02.41; **Belgium:** 059.55.99.11 **w** www.hover-speed.co.uk

by coach

Eurolines runs direct routes to and from major European destinations and the Gare du Nord in Brussels.

☼ **London:** 7 times daily each way, 7 hrs 30 mins; **Paris:** 8 times daily each way, 3 hrs 45 mins; **Amsterdam:** 7 times daily each way, 4 hrs; **Berlin:** once a day each way, 10 hrs 15 mins.

Single fares: to/from London: 1690BF; to/from Paris: 550BF; to/from Amsterdam: 600BF; to/from Berlin: 2100BF.

⌂ The cheapest way to travel.
⌂ The journeys are often long and arduous.
☎ **UK:** 0870.514.32.19; **Belgium:** 02.274.13.50/ 02.538.20.49

out and about

STIB/MIVB is Brussels' city transport authority. It operates the entire metro, bus, and tram network in the Brussels Region.

general information

BF tickets & travelcards
The same type of ticket is used on all trams, buses, and on the metro. Tickets can be bought in metro stations and on buses and trams and are valid for one hour once validated in the orange machines. The STIB/ MIVB Anspach Agency (31 rue de l'Evêque) – the transport authority office – gives out information and sells tickets.

⌂ On-the-spot fines of 2200BF are incurred for not having a valid ticket.

♿ disabled travellers
Most trams and buses, as well as the metro, are not accessible to wheelchair users, apart from the newer T2000 trams, which have wide doors and low floors. STIB/MIVB runs a minibus serv-ice for the disabled which operates 6.30am–11pm daily. But it needs to be booked 8 days in advance.

⚇ kids
Children under 6 yrs, accompanied by an adult, travel free (four per paying adult).

maps & leaflets
STIB/MIVB maps are available from Porte de Namur, Rogier and Midi metro stations, as well as the STIB Anspach Agency at 31 rue de l'Evêque.

public transport weekend
Buy a ticket (450BF) and travel as much as you like on the metro, buses, trams, and trains all over Belgium for one weekend in October.
☎ 02.555.25.25

☎ useful numbers
STIB/MIVB: 02.515.20.00
Lost property: 02.515.23.94
Minibus for the disabled: 02.515.23.65
w www.stib.be

types of tickets

Carte d'un voyage
A single journey, for 1 hr after ticket validation. BF 50BF (from drivers on buses and trams, and metro stations)

Carte STIB + Taxi

A single journey, for 1 hr after validation, plus an 80BF reduction on a return taxi journey. ⛽ 60BF (from metro stations) ☎ Taxi Verts: 02.349.49.49

Carte d'un jour

Unlimited travel for one day on all buses, trams, metro, De Lijn, and TEC. ⛽ 140BF (from drivers on buses and trams, and from metro stations)

Carte de 5 voyages

Five single journeys, all for 1 hr after ticket validation. ⛽ 240BF (from metro stations)

Carte de 10 voyages

Ten single journeys, all for 1 hr after ticket validation. ⛽ 350BF (from metro stations)

on wheels

🚕 taxis

Officially registered taxis display a yellow and blue emblem with the words Région de Bruxelles. You can hail a taxi, go to a rank (biggest are at mainline train stations), or order one by phone. ⏰ 24 hours daily.

⛽ The pick-up rate is 95BF, plus 38BF per km within Brussels. The rate doubles when you leave the city. A tip is included in the fare on the meter. A night tax of 75BF is added from 10pm–6am.

❶ 1| Have 100BF notes ready. 2| They take four passengers only, and mean it. 3| A prix forfaitaire (fixed price fare) can be arranged if booked by phone.
Taxis Verts ☎ 02.349.49.49
Autolux ☎ 02.411.12.21
Taxis Bleus ☎ 02.268.00.00
For complaints about services or drivers, call ☎ 0800.147.95

driving & biking

Driving in Brussels is not for the faint-hearted and is only recommended for getting out of the city. Walking the centre is easy, and longer distances are quicker by public transport.

rules of the road

1| Drive on the right. 2| Trams have *absolute* priority. 3| The *priorité à droite* rule means you have to yield to the right – if in doubt, stop. 4| Speed limits are 50km/hr in cities, 90km/hr on other routes, and 120km/hr on motorways.

car rental

Most international companies have branches at Zaventem airport and Gare du Midi. Minimum age is usually 23. It's expensive – expect to pay £60 per day and £200 per week.
Avis: ☎ 02.527.17.05
Budget: ☎ 02.527.59.47
Europcar: ☎ 02.522.95.73
Hertz: ☎ 02.524.31.00
National Car Rental:
☎ 02.524.57.38

motorbike/moped rental

Age requirements vary – some companies will hire mopeds to 18 yr olds, others only to the over 21's. Expect to pay 1000BF–5000BF per day as well as helmet hire.

Dockx Motorrental:
☎ 02.245.75.75
Brussels Motor Renting:
☎ 02.725.34.35
Baele & Schmitz Motos:
☎ 02.762.60.27

parking

Parking meters take 5BF, 20BF and 50BF coins. 24-hr car parks cost 70BF–200BF per hr and 600BF–800BF for 24 hrs.

Agora: 104 rue du Marché aux Herbes ☎ 02.513.33.18
Écuyer: 13 rue de l'Écuyer
☎ 02.219.07.18
Hilton Hotel: 38 boulevard de Waterloo ☎ 02.504.11.11

cycling

Brussels is not a bike-friendly city – bicycle lanes are rare, dodging wet tram lines is like flirting with death, and car drivers are none too helpful. But hiring a bike in the leafy suburbs or outside the city is a joy. You'll pay between 250BF–400BF per day and 1250BF–2000BF per week.

Pro Velo: ☎ 02.502.73.55
Bike Events: ☎ 02.757.94.44
Vélo Cité: ☎ 02.241.36.35

public transport options

Ⓜ metro & pre-metro

Looking at a metro & pre-metro map of Brussels, you'd be forgiven for assuming that there's a large network of underground trains. In actual fact, there are only three routes on the metro; the rest is the underground section of the tram network, known as the pre-metro.

◑	BF	☎	❶
5.30am–12.30am daily	single journey: 50BF [→types of tickets]	STIB/MIVB: 02.515.20.00	▸ Validate tickets in the orange machines on trams and at underground stations. ▸ To open the doors on a pre-metro tram, press the central green strip. ▸ To request a stop on a pre-metro tram, press the black buttons next to the doors. ▸ Metro stations are identified by a white M on a blue background. ▸ There are three main metro routes – line 1A, line 1B and line 2. ▸ It's a fast, safe and efficient system.

🚊 trams

The distinctive blue-and-yellow trams circulate at street level all over Brussels and the suburbs. Route numbers and final destinations are displayed on the front.

◑	BF	☎	❶
5.30am–12.30am daily	single journey: 50BF [→types of tickets 129]	STIB/MIVB: 02.515.20.00	▸ Stops are indicated by red and white signs with the stop name and tram numbers they serve. ▸ Trams don't stop automatically, so raise your hand to attract the driver's attention. ▸ The doors don't automatically open, so press the green strip down the centre. ▸ To request a stop once you're on, press the black button – a light comes on over the door, which opens automatically. ▸ Validate tickets in the orange machines. ▸ Hold on tight as many drivers slam on the brakes at times.

🚌 buses

Buses run in Brussels and the suburbs. To travel out of the city, use De Lijn for Flemish towns (from Gare du Nord) and TEC for places in Walloon (at place Rouppé).

◐	⟨BF⟩	☎	❶
5.30am–12.30am daily	single journey: 50BF [→types of tickets 129]	STIB/MIVB: 02.555.25.25 De Lijn: 02.526.28.28 TEC: 01.361.94.44	▸ Validate tickets for inner-city buses in the orange machines on board. ▸ Hold on tight standing up, as buses brake quite hard for the priority to the right rule of driving. ▸ Both De Lijn and TEC offer a limited, rather irregular service.

🚂 trains

Belgium's railway network, the SNCB/NMBS, is excellent and the distances between destinations never far. There are frequent trains to all towns in Belgium, as well as Brussels' suburbs.

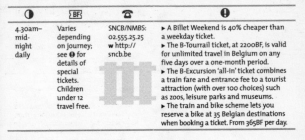

◐	⟨BF⟩	☎	❶
4.30am–midnight daily	Varies depending on journey; see ❶ for details of special tickets. Children under 12 travel free.	SNCB/NMBS: 02.555.25.25 w http://sncb.be	▸ A Billet Weekend is 40% cheaper than a weekday ticket. ▸ The B-Tourrail ticket, at 2200BF, is valid for unlimited travel in Belgium on any five days over a one-month period. ▸ The B-Excursion 'all-in' ticket combines a train fare and entrance fee to a tourist attraction (with over 100 choices) such as zoos, leisure parks and museums. ▸ The train and bike scheme lets you reserve a bike at 35 Belgian destinations when booking a ticket. From 365BF per day.

phrasebook

Brussels is the bilingual capital of a trilingual country with a Flemish, Walloon, and German community. Although Brussels is geographically situated in the Flemish area, you cannot speak of its inhabitants as Flemish or Walloons. The majority speaks French, a minority speaks Flemish, and a bunch of people use both languages miscellaneously. Since a third of Brussels' population consists of immigrants, the safest language to use is French.

Dutch pronunciation

Consonants

ch	as in loch (coming from your throat)
g	as in loch (never pronounce it as the English g, except when words end in ing)
j	as in yes
k	as in cat
p	as in a short English t
sch	a combination of s and ch (as above)

Long vowel sounds

aa	as in flat but longer
ee	as in same or fail
eu	sounds similar to flirt, but with rounded lips
ie	as in eat
oe	as in look
oo	as in goat
uu	sounds similar to good/übermensch

Short vowel sounds

a	as in card
e	as in lazy
i	as in thin
o	as in dot
u	as in hurt

Vowel combinations

au/ou	as in loud
aai	as in bye
eeuw	as in fail (but a much longer vowel sound)
ei/ij	as in fight
ieuw	as in feel
ooi	as in oi, but with a much longer o
uw	as in phew
ui	similar to house (but say with rounded lips)
oei	pronounced oo-ee (as one long sound)

French pronunciation

Consonants

ce/ci/ça	as in centre
ca/co/qu	as in catch
ge/gi/j	as in Zhivago
ga/go/gu	as in game
r	as in lair
t/th	as in table
w	as in vanilla

i	as in tick
oi	as in one
ou	as in book
u/ue	as in übermensch

Combinations

aile/el/elle	as in L
ain/ein/in/un	ahn
on	ohn
an/en	on (with a shortened, nasal n)
ette	as in let
euil(le)/oeil	as in oi-ye (with a shortened oi)
ien	as in yen, but more nasal
ière	as in as in premiere
ill	as in year
oin	as in one, but more nasal

Vowel sounds

a	as in hat
ai/è/ei/er	as in bay
au	as in boat
e	as in bay (if followed by a double consonant); as in fur (in any other case)
eau/o	as in Omagh
é	as in neigh
eu/oeu	as in fur

Essentials

hello/hi	bonjour/salut	bon-zhoor/sa-lü	hallo/dag	hu-llo/**duch**
bye	au revoir	o rev-**wahr**	tot ziens	tot-seens
yes	oui	wi	ja	yaah
no	non	nohn	nee	nay
thank you/thanks	merci	mair-**si**	dank u wel/bedankt	dank i wel/be-dankt
please	s'il vous plaît	seel voo play	alstublieft	als-too-bleeft
sorry	désolé	day-zo-lay	sorry	sorry
excuse me	pardon	par-dohn	párdon	pardon
How are you?	Comment allez-vous?	Co-**mon**-tallay-**voo**?	Hoe gaat hét?	Who chaaht et?
good	bon	bon	goed	chood
bad	mal	mal	slecht	slecht
open	ouvert	oo-**vair**	open	o-pen
closed	fermé	fair-**may**	gesloten	che-sloaw-ten
entrance	entrée	on-**tray**	ingang	in-chang
exit	sortie	sor-**tee**	uitgang	owt-chang
toilet	toilettes	twa-**lett**	wc	vha-say
left	gauche	goash	links	links
right	droite	drwat	rechts	rechts
what?	quoi?	kwa?	wat?	what?
when?	quand?	kahn?	wanneer?	whan-**eer**
where?	où?	oo?	waar?	whaar?
how?	comment?	co-**mon**?	hoe?	hoo?
how much?	combien?	com-**byan**?	hoeveel	**hoo**-vay
Do you speak English?	Parlez-vous anglais?	**Par**-lay-**voo** on-**glay**?	Spréek jij Éngels?	Sprayk yiy Engels?
I don't speak French/Dutch	Je ne parle pas français/néerlandais	Zhe ne **parl** pa fran-**say**/nay-air-lahn**day**	Het spijt me, ik spreek geen Frans/Nederlands	Et **spight** meh, ik **sprayk** chane frans/**Na**-der-lands
Could you repeat that please?	Pouvez-vous répéter s'il vous plaît?	Poo-vay-**voo** ray-pay-**tay** seel voo **play**?	Wilt u dit een keer herhálen?	wilt oo dit an kayr her-ha-len?
Do you take credit cards/traveller's cheques?	Acceptez-vous les cartes de crédit/ traveller's chèques?	Accept-ay-**voo** lay kart de kray-**dee**/traveller's **shek**?	Accepteert u credit cards/traveller's cheques?	Ack-cep-tiert oo cred-it cards/traveller's cheques?
help	à l'aide	a led	help	help
emergency	urgence	ühr-**zhonse**	noodgeval	**nowt**-ge-fall
police	police	po-**leese**	politie	**pow**-leet-see
ambulance	ambulance	ahn-bü-**lahnse**	ambulance	ahm-boo-lans-e
fire brigade	pompiers	pom-**piay**	brandweer	**brahnt**-wir
doctor	docteur	doc-**ter**	dokter	**doc**-tur
hospital	hôpital	o-pi-**tahl**	ziekenhuis	**seek**-en-howse

Numbers

1	un	eun	een	ayn
2	deux	deu	twee	tway
3	trois	twra	drie	dree
4	quatre	**kat**-re	vier	veer
5	cinq	sank	vijf	fayve
6	six	sees	zes	zehs
7	sept	set	zeven	safe-en
8	huit	wheat	acht	ackt
9	neuf	neuf	negen	nay-gen
10	dix	dees	tien	teen
11	onze	ohns	elf	alf
12	douze	doos	twaalf	twahlf
13	treize	trays	dertien	der-teen
14	quatorze	kat-**ohrs**	veertien	veer-teen
15	quinze	kahns	vijftien	fayve-teen
16	seize	sez	zestien	zehs-teen
17	dix-sept	dees-**set**	zeventien	safe-en-teen
18	dix-huit	dees-**wheat**	achttien	acht-teen
19	dix-neuf	dees-**neuf**	negentien	nay-gen-teen
20	vingt	vahn	twintig	twin-tich
21	vingt-et-un	vahn-tay-**eun**	eenentwintig	ayn-en-twin-tich
30	trente	trohnt	dertig	der-tich
40	quarante	karohnt	veertig	veer-tich
50	cinquante	sank-ohnt	vijftig	fayve-tich
60	soixante	swas-ohnt	zestig	zehs-tich
70	septante	set-ohnt	zeventig	safe-en-tich
80	quatre-vingts	kat-re-vahn	tachtig	tach-tich
90	novante	nov-ohnt	negentig	nay-gen-tich
100	cent	sohn	honderd	hohn-derd

Days & months

Monday	lundi	lurn-**dee**	maandag	maahn-darg
Tuesday	mardi	maar-**dee**	dinsdag	**dins**-darg
Wednesday	mercredi	mair-cray-**dee**	woensdag	**woo**-ns-darg
Thursday	jeudi	zheu-**dee**	donderdag	**don**-dehr-darg
Friday	vendredi	vondre-**dee**	vrijdag	frei-darg
Saturday	samedi	sam-**dee**	zaterdag	**sat**-er-darg
Sunday	dimanche	dee-**monsh**	zondag	son-darg
January	janvier	zhon-vee-**ai**	januari	jan-oo-ar-ee
February	février	fev-ree-**ai**	februari	fe-broo-ar-ee
March	mars	mahrs	maart	maahrt
April	avril	avril	april	a-pril
May	mai	mai	mei	my
June	juin	zhü-ahn	juni	ju-nee
July	juillet	zhwee-**yeigh**	juli	ju-lee
August	août	oot	augustus	**ouw**-gus-tus
September	septembre	sept-**om**-br	september	**sep**-tem-ber
October	octobre	octo-br	oktober	**ok**-too-ber
November	novembre	no-**vohm**-br	november	no-vem-behr
December	décembre	day-**som**-br	december	**day**-cem-behr

Hotels

I have a reservation	J'ai une réservation	**Zhay** ühne raysayr-vaziohn	Ik heb gereserveerd	Ik heb chu-ra-zur-**vayrd**
Do you have any vacancies?	Avez-vous des chambres libres?	Avay-**voo** day shambre lee-bre?	Heeft u een kamer?	Hayft oo an **kah**-mer?
single	simple	**sahm**-ple	eenpersoons	ayn-per-soans
double	double	**doo**-bleu	tweepersoons	**tway**-per-sowns
with bath/ shower/toilet	avec baignoir/ douche/toilettes	avec **bay**-nwar/ doosh/twa-**lett**	met bad/douche/ toilet	mit baht/doosh/ **twa**-let
half/full board	demi-pension/ pension complète	deu-**mi** pon-**sion**/ pon-**sion** com-**play**-te	half/vol pension	holf/vol **pen-syon**

Shopping

antiques shop	antiquaire	ahn-tee-**kayr**	antiekwinkel	an-**tick**-winck-el
bakery	boulangerie	boo-lan-zheree	bákker	**back**-er
bookshop	librairie	lee-brai-**ree**	boékwinkel	**book**-en-winck-el
chocolate shop	chocolaterie	sho-ko-la-te-**ree**	chocolatier	shocko-la-**tyay**
chemist	pharmacie	far-ma-**see**	apothéek	a-po-**tayk**
delicatessen	traiteur	tray-**tehr**	delicatessenwinkel	delicatessen vinck-el
newsagent	tabac	ta-**ba**	krántenwinkel	**kran**-tun winck-ul
supermarket	supermarché	su-pair-mar-**shay**	súpermarkt	**soup**-er-markt
price	prix	pri	prijs	priys
sale	solde	sol-de	uitverkoop	**owt**-ver-coup
special offer	offre spéciale	ofre spayciale	aanbieding	**arn**-bee-ding
secondhand	d'occasion	do-ka-**ziohn**	tweedehánds	tway-deh-**honts**

Transport

I want to go to...	Je veux aller à...	Zhe **veu** allez a ...	Ik wil naar ... gaan	Ik wil **naahr** ... daahn
How much is the fare to...?	Combien coûte un billet pour...?	Com-**byan** cooht ahn bee-**yay** por...?	Hoeveel kost het naar...?	Hoo-vayl cost et nahr?
bus	bus	büs	bus	buzz
tram	tram	trahm	tram	trom
train	train	trahn	trein	trayn
metro	métro	may-**tro**	metro	**ma**-tro
bicycle	vélo	vay-**low**	fiets	**feet**-s
platform	quai	kay	perron	**pur**-ron
ticket	billet	bee-**yay**	kaartje	**kaahrt**-ye
airport	aéroport	a-eigh-ro-**por**	vliegveld	**vleeg**-velt
arrivals	arrivées	a-ree-**vay**	aankomst	**aahn**-cumst
departures	départs	day-**par**	vertrek	**vur**-trek
customs	douane	doo-**ane**	douane	**doo**-ahn-e
baggage-claim	consigne	cohn-**seegne**	baggage claim	baggage claim
check-in	enregistrement	on-reg-eestre-**mon**	check-in	check-in
delay	retard	ray-**tard**	vertraging	**vur**-trah-ging
single/return ticket	aller simple/aller retour	allez **sahmple**/ allez re-**toor**	enkele reis/ retour	**ankel**-e reys/ re-toor
first/second class	première/seconde classe	pre-**miayr**/se-**gohnd** clas-se	eerste/tweede klasse	**ar**-ste/tway-deh **clas**-se

Telephoning & posting

telephone	téléphone	tay-**lay**-phone	telefoon	ta-la-**phone**
telephone box	cabine téléphonique	ca-been tay-**lay**-phone-eek	telefooncel	ta-la-**phone** cell
telephone directory	annuaire	an-nü-**air**	telefoonboek	ta-la-**phone**-book
phonecard	télécarte	tay-lay-**kart**	telefoonkaart	ta-la-**phone**-caahrd
out of order	en dérangement	on day-ronzhe-mon	buiten dienst	**bowten** deenst
post office	poste	**poh**ste	postkantoor	**post**-khan-toar
postcard	carte postale	kart post-al	ansichtkaart	**ahn**-sickt-karht
stamp	timbre	**tahm**-bre	postzegel	**post**-za-gel

Eating & drinking

bill/check	l'addition	la-di-**siohn**	rekening	**ray**-ke-ning
menu	menu	me-**nü**	menukaart	menu carht
service included	service compris	sair-vees com-**pree**	bediening inbegrepen	be-**dee**-ning in-bhe-grayp-en
service not included	service non compris	sair-vees **nohn** com-pree	exclusief bediening	**ex**-cloo-ceive be-**dee**-ning
breakfast	petit-déjeuner	pay-**tit** day-zhay-**ner**	ontbijt	**ont**-bite
speciality of the day	plat du jour	pla dü **zhoor**	dagschotel	**dach**-schoa-tul
starter	entrée	on-**tray**	voorgerecht	**fohr**-ge-reckt
main course	plat de résistance	pla de ray-zistohns	hoofdgerecht	**howft**-ge-reckt
dessert	dessert	day-**sayr**	dessert	**da**-surt
wine list	carte des vins	kart day van	wijnkaart	**wine**-cahrt
cheers	santé/tchin	sohn-**tay**/**chin**	proost	prowst
vegetarian	végétarien	ve-zhay-tah-**ryahn**	vegetarisch	vay-ge-**tah**-ris
glass	verre	vair	glas	glas
bottle	bouteille/carafe	boo-**tayeu**/ca-**raff**	fles	fles
bread	pain	pahn	brood	browd
sugar	sucre	sü-kr	suiker	**souw**-ker
tea	thé	teigh	thee	tay
coffee	café	ca-**feigh**	koffie	**cough**-fee
orange juice	jus d'orange	zhü do-ranzh	jus d'orange	shoo-d'orange
red/white wine	vin rouge/blanc	van rouzh/blon	rode/witte wijn	**roa**-der/**wit**-eh wine
beer	bière	bi-**yair**	bier	bee-ehr
blonde/brown	blonde/brune	**blohnd**/**brün**	blond/bruin	blond/brown
draught beer	demi pression	dum-**my** pre-**syohn**	bier van't vat	beer van **tvat**
gin	genièvre	zhun-**yay**-**vruh**	jenever	zhu-**na**-vur
mineral water	eau minérale	o mee-ney-**rahl**	mineraal water	mi-nehr-al **wah**-ter
salt & pepper	sel & poivre	sel ay **pwavre**	peper en zout	**pay**-per en **sowt**
garlic	ail	eye	knoflook	**knof**-lowk
eggs	oeufs	urfs	eieren	**ay**-r-en
cheese	fromage	fro-**mazh**	kaas	kaars
milk	lait	lay	melk	melck
french fries	frites	freet	frieten	**free**-tun
crisps	chips	sheeps	chips	chips
I have a reservation for..	J'ai une réservation pour..	zhay ün ray-sayr-va-**siohn** poor..	Ik heb gereserveerd	ik **eb** ge-**res**-ser-veehrd
Have you got a table for...?	Avez-vous une table pour...?	avay-**voo** ün **tab**-le poor...?	Heeft u een tafel voor...?	**hayft** u ayn **tarf**-el for...?

menu guide

English	French	Pronunciation	Dutch	Pronunciation
mussels with chips	moules-frites	mool-**freet**	mosselen met friet	mos-sel-lun met freet
eel stewed in sorrel, chervil and citronelle	anguille au vert	ahn-**gueeye** o **vare**	paling in 't groen	**paah**-ling int **chroon**
veal stew	blanquette de veau	blahn-**kett** de **vo**	kalfszwezerik	**calfs**-zwa-zurick
venison	chevreuil	she-**vrolye**	wild gebraad	wild chah-**braahd**
rabbit with prunes	lapin aux prunes	lap-**ahn** o **prüne**	konijn met pruimen	co-**nayn** met **proy**-mun
wild boar	marcassin	mar-ca-**sahn**	wild zwijn	wild zweyn
chunks of chicken in pastry with creamy sauce	bouchée à la reine	boo-**shay** ah lah **rahn**	koninginnehapje	koan-**ing**-ginna-hapya
lean chunks of beef simmered in beer	carbonnades	car-bo-**na**-der	carbonnaden	car-bo-**naah**-der
endives wrapped in ham with cheese	chicon au gratin	shick-**ohn** o grat-**ahn**	witloof met kaas en hesp	**wit**-loaf met **kaahs** en hesp
Flemish stew with oxtail, pigs trotters	hochepot	osh-**po**	hutsepot	**hut**-sah-pot
sprouts with bacon and goose fat	choux de Bruxelles	shoe de brü-**sell**	Brusselse spruitjes	**brus**-sels-e **sproyt**-yus
white asparagus dressed with melted butter and crumbled hard-boiled egg	asperges de Malines	as-perzhe de ma-**leen**	Mechelse asperges	**mech**-chals-e as-**per**-zhes
red cabbage cooked with apples, onions, red wine, and vinegar	chou rouge à la fla-mande	shoe **roo**-zhe allah fla-**mond**	Vlaamse rode kool	**Vlaahm**-se **roa**-de koal
white and black sausages	boudin blanc/noir	boo-dan **blon**/**nwar**	witte en zwarte pensen	**wit**-te en **zwar**-te **pen**-zun
mashed potatoes & vegetables	purée	pür-**ay**	stoemp	stoomp
tomatoes stuffed with boiled fish	tomates garnies	to-**matt** gar-**nee**	gevulde tomaten	chu-**vul**-de **tom**-aah-tun
chicken or fish stew with vegetables	waterzooï	**waah**-ter-soy	waterzooï	**waah**-ter-soy
raw minced beef with chopped onions and mayonaise	filet américain préparé	filay ah-ma-ri-**ckahn** pra-pa-**reigh**	filet américain pré-paré	filay ah-ma-rick-ahn pra-pa-reigh
onion soup	soupe à l'oignon	soop a lon-**yon**	ajuinsoep	ah-**yoyn**-soop
open sandwich with soft white cheese and chopped radishes	tartine au fromage blanc	tar-**tin** o fro-mazh **blon**	boterham met plat-tekaas	**boat**-er-ham met **plat**-te kaahs
grilled ham & cheese sandwich	croque-monsieur	crock me-**syur**	croque-monsieur	crock me-**syur**
Brussels waffles	gaufres de Bruxelles	gow-fre de brü-**sell**	Brusselse wafels	**Brüs**-sels-e **waah**-fuls
Luikse waffles (with crumbled sugar)	gaufre de Liège	gow-fre de lee-**ayzh**	Luikse wafels	Loyck-se waah-fuls
pancakes	crêpes	crayp	pannenkoeken	**pah**-ne-cooker
fried doughnuts	beignets	bay-**nyah**	smoutebollen	**smaw**-tu-bowler
brown spicy biscuits	spéculoos	spay-cü-**loas**	speculoos	**spa**-cu-loas

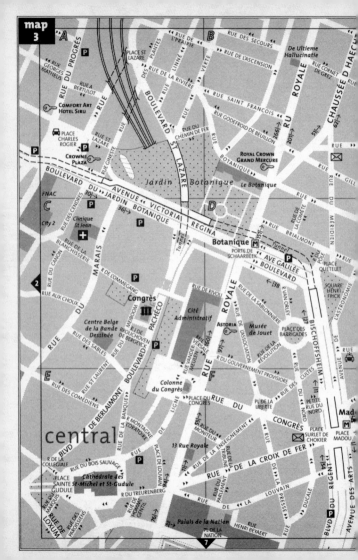

map
4

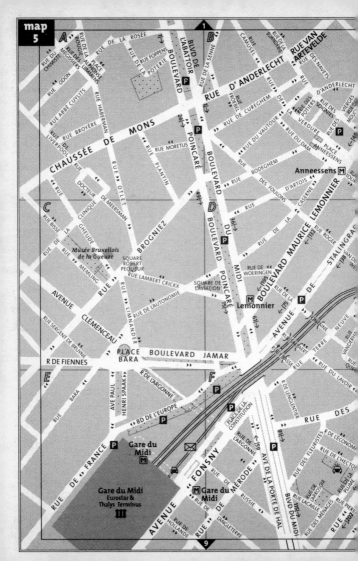

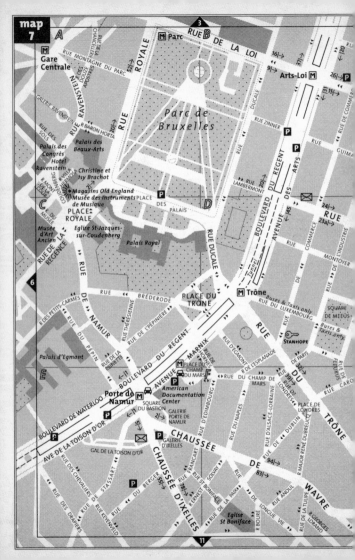

map
8

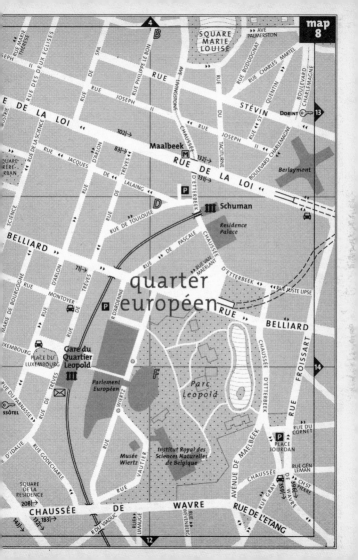

SQUARE
MARIE
LOUISE

AVE PALMERSTON

RUE MARIE THÉRÈSE

SEPH

RUE DES DEUX ÉGLISES

RUE DE SPA

RUE PHILIPPE LE BON

RUE

II

DE

JOSEPH

RUE CHARLES MARTEL

RUE RODUOGNAT

RUE QUENTIN

BOULEVARD CHARLEMAGNE

STÉVIN

DORINT 13

E DE LA LOI

RUE DE LA SCIENCE

102|→

831|→

Maalbeek M 132|→

RUE DE LA LOI

RUE DU

JOSEPH II

RUE TACITURNE

BOULEVARD CHARLEMAGNE

Berlaymont

SQUARE FRÈRE-ORBAN

RUE JACQUES

RUE D'ARLON

DE

TRÈVES

131|→

LALAING

P

D'ETTERBEEK

RUE DE TOULOUSE

Schuman

Residence Palace

SCIENCE

BELLIARD

RUE

DIARLON

DE TRÈVES

71|→

RUE

MARIE DE BOURGOGNE

RUE DE BOURGOGNE

MONTOYER

DE TRÈVES

D'ARDENNE

P

CHAUSSÉE DE PASCALE

RUE VAN MAERLANT

D'ETTERBEEK

RUE JUSTE LIPSE

quarter
européen

RUE

BELLIARD

IXEMBOURG

PLACE DU LUXEMBOURG

Gare du Quartier Leopold

RUE DE TRÈVES

RUE DU PARNASSE

SSOTEL

Parlement Européen

WIERTZ

F

Parc Leopold

CHAUSSÉE D'ETTERBEEK

RUE FROISSART

14

RUE DU CORNET

P

PLACE JOURDAN

D'IDALIE

RUE GODECHARLE

Musée Wiertz

RUE VAUTIER

Institut Royal des Sciences Naturelles de Belgique

AVENUE DE MAELBEEK

RUE GÉN LEMAN

CH ST PIERRE

SQUARE DE LA RESIDENCE

208|→

143|→

121|→

CHAUSSÉE

DE

RUE DU VIADUC

RUB LIMAUGE

181|→

183|→

WAVRE

RUS WEYENBERG

RUE DE L'ETANG

165|→

RUE GRAY

map
11

ixelles
(east)

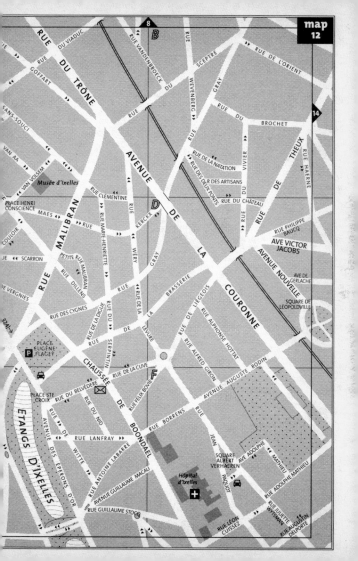

map
12

map
13

Meiser

map
14

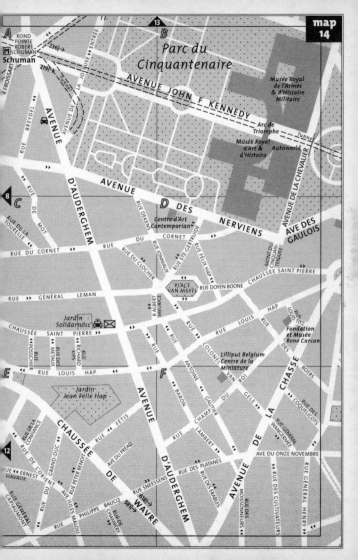

A

ROND
POINTE
ROBERT
SCHUMAN
Schuman

236

219

R FROISSART

*Parc du
Cinquantenaire*

B

AVENUE JOHN F KENNEDY

AVENUE DE LA JOYEUSE ENTRÉE

Musée Royal
de l'Armée
& d'Histoire
Militaire

Arc de
Triomphe

Tunnel

Musée Royal
d'Art & Autoworld
d'Histoire

AVENUE

RUE BREYDEL

AVENUE DE

RUE DE MOT

AVENUE D'AUDERGHEM

AVENUE DES

8

RUE DE LA TOURELLE

C

D

NERVIENS

AVENUE DE LA CHEVALIER

AVE DES GAULOIS

Centre d'Art
Contemporian

RUE DEKEN

CORNET

RUE STE-GERTRUDE

RUE FÉLIX HAP

ARENE DU CINQUAN-TENAIRE

RUE DU CORNET

RUE DU

RUE DU CLOCHER

RUE JONNIAUX

CHAUSSÉE SAINT PIERRE

RUE >> GÉNÉRAL LEMAN

PLACE
VAN MEYEL

RUE DOYEN BOONE

R ALBERT MEURICE

RUE LOUIS

RUE LOUIS HAP

RUE LOUIS TITZ

CHAUSSÉE SAINT PIERRE

Jardin
Solidarnosc

Fondation
et Musée
Rene Carcan

POSSCHIER

RUE DES METAUX

RUE RICHARD KIPS

RUE

RUE

COLONE

Liliput Belgium
Centre de la
Miniature

RUE DE LA CHASSE

RUE DES BOSERS

E

RUE LOUIS HAP

F

AVENUE

ANTOINE

VAN ROI

RUE DES COQUELCOTS

Jardin
Jean Felix Hap

RUE FÉTIS

RUE DE LA CONFIANCE

BARON

GAUTIER

CHAMPIR

DU GELE

RUE GÉNÉRAL WANCERMÉE

AVE DU ONZE NOVEMBRE

12

RUE D'ORIENT

CHAUSSÉE

GRAND-DUC

AVE DU PRÉAU

LAMBERT

RUE DES PLATANES

AVENUE D'AUDERGHEM

RUE DES MOISSONNEURS

RUE DES CULTIVATEURS

RUE GÉNÉRAL HENRY

RUE ERNEST HAVAUX

RUE GÉNÉRAL CAPIAUMONT

RUE DU

AVE JULES MALOU

RUE PIER BENOIT

DE

PHILIPPE BAUCQ

RUE DES ÉRABLES

RUE SNEESSENS

WAVRE

618

RUE DE CHAMBERY

Key to symbols

☎ telephone number
F fax
W worldwide web
👁 things to see
❶ hot tips
🖒 good points

◑ opening times
♿ wheelchair access (phone to check details)
🍴 restaurant/café or food available
🍷 bar
🗝 hotel
💷 price
⚑ map reference

🖃 credit cards

AE = American Express
D = Discovery
DC = Diners Club
MC = MasterCard
V = Visa
all = AE/D/DC/JCB/MC/V are accepted
☆ recommended (featured in listings section)

sights, museums, galleries & parks

BF Main courses under 400BF
BF BF Main courses from 400BF–800 BF
BF BF BF Main courses over 800BF
☞ guided tours

restaurants & cafés, bars & clubs, entertainment

👚 dress code
🕐 frequency/times

hotels

🛏 number of beds
🍽 breakfast included
▤ air conditioning
㉔ 24-hour room service
📺 satellite/cable TV
≋ swimming pool
↔ fitness facilities
✐ business facilities
🅿 parking (on or off site)
BF double room under 2500BF
BF BF double room from 2500BF–5000BF
BF BF BF double room from 5000BF–7500BF
BF BF BF BF double room from 7500BF–10000BF
BF BF BF BF BF double room over 10000BF

transport

🚌 bus/bus station
🚋 tram/tram stop
Ⓜ Metro & pre-metro/metro & pre-metro station
🚉 overground train station
🚕 taxi/car
⛴ ferry/cruise boat